France
in *1938*

France
in 1938

Benjamin F. Martin

Louisiana State University Press
Baton Rouge

DESIGNER: Barbara Neely Bourgoyne
TYPEFACES: Minion, text; Brioso Pro, display

Illustrations are from the Archives of Nicolas Kariouk Pecquet du Bellay de Verton.

ISBN 0-8071-3050-8 (cloth : alk paper)

For

Carol Louise Bird

Jane Catherine Overton Scanlan

John Raymond Walser

Contents

Preface and Acknowledgments

When was it that I decided to write a book about France in 1938? I like to believe the thought came to me in 1965, when I was seventeen years old and learning modern European history at the Episcopal High School in Virginia from James Merlin Seidule. He taught with such brilliance and intensity that we created the word *Seiduleism* to define belief in getting down to work. His description of Europe balanced on the edge of catastrophe in the late 1930s captivated me. Three years later, at Davidson College, Norman McClure Johnson, a professor of history, wise, wry, and cynical, renewed my intention with his dramatic portrayal of the Munich conference. Two more years later, as a graduate student at the University of North Carolina, I read Jean-Paul Sartre's *L'Age de raison* and *Le Sursis,* which hurtled me into 1938 as I turned the pages almost feverishly.

Why France? I have taken refuge in the language since I began to learn it at the age of five, and when I came to Paris in my early twenties I knew I was at home. Why now? In four previous books I have written my way through the Third Republic from its inception to the late 1920s. I avoided the promise I made to myself about the 1930s until I believed that by living, figuratively, through the earlier decades I could understand how French men and women were living in 1938. Five of my graduate students at Louisiana State University—Bettina Mercedes Söhnigen, Katherine Louise Smith Patin, Anne Ashley Ewing Manning, Tracey Leigh Kimbrell, and Tim Kurt Georg Fuchs—encouraged me through their own fine work. Eugen Weber's study of the period, *The Hollow Years: France in the 1930s*, provided the final impetus because his masterful synthesis left just enough room for what I planned to do.

As historians, we are what we are, and we cannot change our spots. Because I write political and social history, I am intimate with certain archival collections but not with those for diplomacy and military affairs. But I do know that they have been exhaustively examined by others, and for that material I have relied upon those others. As my contribution, I have prowled through newspapers and more newspapers, novels, and movies to taste the flavor of what people were reading and seeing in hope of sensing what they were thinking. I have written for general readers because general readers seek out history but too often find it in a form and in prose accessible only to professionals. Why should only professionals have the joy of historical discovery? Why should general readers be left to popularizers?

The librarians at the Bibliothèque Nationale de France and the interlibrary loan office of Louisiana State University's Middleton Library were magicians at locating everything I needed. Maureen G. Hewitt encouraged the project from the outset. Amanda Marie Duhon assisted with the research. Ashley Anne Allen Kirkland applied her considerable skills to editing and to compiling the index. Nicolas Kariouk Pecquet du Bellay de Verton contributed the photographs of his family in France during 1938 from his personal archives. Elizabeth Gratch ably copyedited the manuscript. Julia Alayne Grenier and Tyler Caitlin Lott helped with the final stages of production. At the Louisiana State University Press, my publisher for the fourth time, MaryKatherine Callaway and Lee Campbell Sioles converted the manuscript into a book. For three decades, my entire professional career, Jacqueline and Eugen Weber have been my unfailing friends. Although they had to live through 1938, they were willing to read about it again in these pages. During times bad and good Carol Louise Bird, Jane Catherine Overton Scanlan, and John Raymond Walser have been on my side. At last they get the dedication they have long deserved.

France
in *1938*

Prologue

At the beginning of December 1937 in France, if you closed your eyes and wished hard enough, you could almost believe that everything was all right—or at least not any worse than it had been. There was, of course, the continuing tension, a political civil war of sorts for the last eighteen months, between Left and Right. The 1936 elections had produced a majority for the so-called Popular Front, an uneasy coalition of Communist, Socialist, and Radical parties which ran from the far Left almost to the Center of French politics. There was also the ongoing labor militancy touched off by this victory and then inspired by initial successes to demand a reckoning with the *patronat,* the "bosses" who had for so long lorded it over their workers. But the weather was unusually mild—days in the fifties and clear. French culture had its latest validation in the award of the Nobel Prize for Literature to Roger Martin du Gard. For distraction there was a compelling murder trial, of the serial sex killer Bruno Weidmann—providentially a German. And the *réveillons,* the celebratory dinners for Christmas Eve and New Year's Eve, were close enough to plan.

Yvon Delbos was among those trying to keep his eyes closed and wishing hard enough. This slender, middle-aged, bookish man with a prominent nose, pomaded hair, and carefully brushed mustache had served as France's minister of foreign affairs since the beginning of the Popular Front's accession to power in June 1936. He looked the academic because he had begun as one, earning the *agrégation* in letters at the Ecole Normale Supérieure. Although afterward he rejected teaching for journalism and, from 1919 on, politics, he projected a certain quality that might charitably be called "intellectual" but was more accurately "effete." Inevitably, he was a moderate Radical—meaning that he was as close to the Center as the pivot of a compass inscribing a circle. In 1925 he was briefly minister of public education and from 1932 to 1936 one of the vice presidents for the Chamber of Deputies. Little but friendship with Léon Blum, the leader of the Socialist Party and first premier of the Popular Front majority, prepared Delbos to be foreign minister.

Yet as a member of the Chamber since 1924 and a keen-minded observer, he understood the bases of French foreign policy since the Great War and the Paris Peace Conference. In the best of all possible worlds for France, Germany could be kept in relative weakness, Great Britain would remain a willing ally, and various East European states would combine as a credible barrier to German ambitions. France could then maintain a high degree of diplomatic independence. The 1920s and 1930s had demonstrated that the best of all possible worlds was illusory. The only possible means short of another war for keeping Germany weak was enforcement of the Versailles treaty to the letter, above all requiring full payment of reparations, and so at least complicate severely the German government's determination to infringe the military clauses. Controlling Germany would have required continued cooperation among the wartime alliance, France, Great Britain, and the United States. But the United States Senate never ratified the Versailles treaty, and Great Britain tergiversated over its enforcement. Germany began to recover, and British-French entente suffered.

Aristide Briand, foreign minister from 1921 to 1922 and from 1925 to 1932, recognized the reality of something much less than the best of all possible worlds by negotiating what amounted to revisions of the Versailles treaty. If Germany could not be held down forever, Germany would have to be made a friend. The Locarno Pact, admission to the League of Nations, the dramatic reduction of reparations, and the early withdrawal of occupying troops from the Rhineland were carrots to Germany—and, without the backing of Great Britain and the United States, France was not strong enough alone to use a stick. British leaders applauded the carrots, convinced that their war-damaged economy required Germany's revival for recovery and because they perversely concluded that France's temporary hegemony in Europe threatened the traditional balance of power on the Continent so revered by Britain prior to the war. However distorted their motives, they made up with France, and that was the end Briand sought. He recognized that a bet on Germany's good intentions long-term might be a loser, but if he could hold onto Britain, France might survive.

That left Eastern Europe. In 1914 Germany might have won the war but for the impact of Russian troops allied to France and Great Britain. Imperial Russia was long gone, the victim of defeat and revolution. Between Germany and the Bolshevik Soviet Union lay the so-called successor states, formed from the collapse of Romanov and Habsburg empires: Czechoslovakia, Romania, Yugoslavia, Poland, Hungary, and Austria. The first three were loosely joined in the Little Entente, aimed at preventing the last two from attempting a revival of Austrian-German and Magyar imperialism over the Slavs. France encouraged the Little Entente and Poland to be a collective replacement of Russia as an Eastern counterweight to Germany. There was nothing collective about them except for their near-constant recriminations against each other. Still, French leaders hoped that general apprehension about Germany would draw them together. Failing that, France had alliances with Czechoslovakia, Poland, and the Soviet Union, although the details of military assistance were either vague or nonexistent.[1]

At the end of November 1937 Delbos and French premier Camille Chautemps met their British counterparts, Foreign Secretary Anthony Eden and Prime Minister Neville Chamberlain, for two days of talks in London. Germany's remilitarization of the Rhineland in March 1936, illegal but unopposed other than by formal protests, had seriously undermined the potential of the Western democracies to intervene against Hitler's ambitions in the East. Delbos now predicted that Germany would next seek *Anschluss,* union with Austria and banned by the Versailles treaty, followed by demands on Czechoslovakia to give up the

Sudetenland, its western regions, where ethnic Germans were a majority. Chamberlain replied that Britain was unwilling to risk war to preserve Czechoslovakia even if Germany resorted to aggression. The Czechs, he proposed, should satisfy the legitimate demands of the Sudeten Germans and thereby prove their goodwill. Closing his eyes and wishing hard, Delbos interpreted this response to mean that British reluctance to intervene beyond the Rhine might be overcome and that when he began a long-planned circuit of Eastern European capitals, he could claim to speak for Britain as well as France.[2]

Early in the evening on 2 December Delbos left Paris on the Nord-Express train accompanied by Charles Rochat, chief of the European division of the Quai d'Orsay, the foreign ministry. The following morning, when the train stopped in Berlin, they were met first by the French ambassador, André François-Poncet, and then by Baron Constantin von Neurath, the German foreign minister, who paid a courtesy visit that flattered Delbos in no small measure. Taking the gesture as a mark of respect and of détente toward France, Delbos was happy to pose for photographs on the station platform with Neurath and François-Poncet. When one of the flashbulbs burst, he remarked happily, "In France broken glass is considered lucky." Maybe not, because later in the day, when the train rolled toward Poland, the weather became appreciably colder, and so would be the reception.[3]

The large crowds to greet Delbos at Warsaw were enthusiastically friendly, but not so government leaders, especially the dominant figure, Colonel Jozef Beck, the foreign minister. Although Beck referred to the "vitality, strength, and permanence" of the Franco-Polish alliance, he pointedly insisted, as Delbos and Ambassador Léon Noël squirmed, on Poland's right "to pursue its own aims and interests." Whether with Beck, President Ignacy Moscicki, or military chief General Edward Smigly-Rydz, Delbos had no success over the next four days raising the primary item on his agenda, conciliating relations between Poland and Czechoslovakia. Beck bitterly protested Czech treatment of ethnic Poles, accused Prague of peddling Communist propaganda, and rejected French mediation in favor of bilateral negotiations— which had been fruitless since 1920. Delbos was glad to leave for Romania.[4]

The first signs were encouraging: at the border town of Cernauti a delegation of peasants offered the traditional loaf and salt cellar. Crowds cheered the train's progress to Bucharest, where King Carol, Prime Minister George Tatarescu, and Foreign Minister Victor Antonescu continued the warm greeting with four days of feasting. Behind the smiles and toasts there were admonitions. Delbos urged Romania to mechanize its army, to cement trade relations with France through exchanging oil for armaments, and to promise the right of passage for troops from the Soviet Union if they were fighting with France against Germany. Antonescu was evasive, recalling that France had spent the last eighteen months backing down to Germany and coordinating with Great Britain on a foreign policy that amounted to nonintervention. What, Antonescu implied, would France do if Germany called its bluff in Eastern Europe as Germany had already done in the Rhineland? What exactly did collective security mean? Antonescu's answer was that it could "exist only if the security of Central and Eastern Europe is not detached from the security of Western Europe." The best Delbos could do was offer the ambiguous statement "Romania is faithful to France just as France is faithful to Romania."[5]

Yugoslavia was next, on 12 December. As in Warsaw and Bucharest, the Belgrade crowds were noisily pro-French, this time waving a cascade of French flags and hoisting a large panel portrait of Delbos. The demonstrations were exactly not what the government of Prime Minister Dr. Milan Stoyadinovitch wanted. He had just returned from talks with Benito Mussolini in Rome and was altering his view about which side of Yugoslavia's croissant was pâtéd. In meetings with Delbos, Stoyadinovitch and the regent, Prince Paul, did not conceal their contempt for the policies of France's Popular Front and the alliance with the Soviet Union. To the critical question of Yugoslav allegiance if war came, the unreassuring answer was "We want peace." After three days of this treatment, Delbos was gladder to leave Belgrade than he had been either Warsaw or Bucharest. He was now bound for Czechoslovakia, but first there was the transit through Hungary. Diplomatic courtesy required at least a symbolic meeting, and Delbos got nothing more. The Hungarian foreign minister, Kalman Kanya, declared himself otherwise engaged and sent an underling to meet the train at the border crossing.

Afterward Delbos remarked, hopefully and revealingly, "At last we are going to see some real friends," meaning the Czechs.[6]

That evening, 15 December, the only real friends France had left in Eastern Europe put on a spectacular welcome in Prague. President Eduard Benes, Prime Minister Dr. Milan Hodza, and Foreign Minister Kamil Krofta were waiting at the station backed by a near-delirious crowd of two hundred thousand, waving French and Czech flags. After all, France was the only real friend Czechoslovakia had left, period. And so both spent the three days of talks reminding each other of their solidarity—thus their isolation. For one after-dinner toast Delbos completely abandoned diplomatic parlance to proclaim, emotion choking his voice: "Czechoslovakia is like an extension of France. We are united by so many ties, we feel things in such a similar way, and our regimes are so similar that a Frenchman in Czechoslovakia feels as though he were in France, and a Czechoslovak in France feels as though he were in Czechoslovakia." He and Benes publicly and loudly affirmed their community of interests and their mutual obligations to "make every sacrifice for common defense." What they did not do was discuss seriously the Sudeten question, the one issue Delbos had promised at London to raise forcefully. Benes described the concessions he had made to the German minority and suggested that more might come later. Delbos did not press the point—an error but comprehensible given the progress of his journey.[7]

As the French delegation headed home through western Czechoslovakia on 18 December, every station had a demonstration of Francophilia: more flags, banners in French, schoolchildren in native costume lined up to cheer, bands playing "La Marseillaise." Perhaps that impression was foremost in Delbos's mind when his train arrived in Paris shortly after breakfast on the following day. As he stepped from his compartment, he was welcomed back by a delegation from the foreign ministry and by representatives of the Czech, Romanian, and Polish embassies. A crowd, smaller than any he had seen during the last two weeks, cried out, "Vive Delbos! Vive la paix!" Perhaps the heavy snow that had been falling since the previous night and freezing temperature held down their number. The photographers caught a sad smile on his face, but to all, especially the journalists, he declared, "I had an excellent trip."[8]

Of course, reality was the opposite, as Delbos admitted several days later to the foreign affairs committee for the Chamber of Deputies. Confidence in French leadership, dropping since the remilitarization of the Rhineland, was now in free fall. Outside, the cold turned bitter, with ice slicking the sidewalks. Just after Christmas, there were work stoppages in the transports and food deliveries that culminated in a general strike throughout the Paris region just in time for the New Year's *réveillons*. Maurice Ravel, last of the great Impressionist composers, died on 28 December.[9] At the end of 1937, no matter how you scrunched your eyes or how fervently you wished, you could no longer stay the recognition that things were not all right and that they were much worse than they had been. If you peeked, you suspected that they could get a great deal worse. You would be right.

In the February 1936 *Esquire,* twenty months before Yvon Delbos circled plaintively through the Eastern European capitals, F. Scott Fitzgerald, the shining star of American letters become a has-been drunk, began the account of his crack-up with these desolate words: "Of course all life is a process of breaking down, but the blows that do the dramatic side of the work—the big sudden blows that come, or seem to come, from outside—the ones you remember and blame things on and, in moments of weakness, tell your friends about, don't show their effect all at once. There is another sort of blow that comes from within—that you don't feel until it's too late to do anything about it, until you realize with finality that in some regard you will never be as good a man again. The first sort of breakage seems to happen quick—the second kind happens almost without your knowing it but is realized suddenly indeed."[10] He could have been writing about the French Third Republic, its precipitous decline paralleling his own.[11]

There is a famous cartoon from the 1880s showing a stout society matron at a formal reception. She is Marianne, the youthful, thrilling symbol of French republicanism grown older, of a "certain age" as is said. One of the gentlemen in attendance remarks to another, "How beautiful she was under the Empire." Proclaimed from the balcony of the city hall in Paris on 4 September 1870, when news arrived of Emperor Napoléon III's defeat and capture by the Prussians at Sedan, the

Third Republic was Cinderella without a fairy godmother. Adolphe Thiers, the liberal Monarchist turned conservative Republican, claimed that the regime survived because "it is the form of government that divides us least." Perhaps so eventually, but at first the Republic was a placeholder, while the three varieties of French monarchism—Legitimism, Orleanism, and Bonapartism—struggled for dominance, none too skillfully. The last of the Bourbons, the descendants of Louis XIV, was the Count of Chambord, the would-be Henri V. He made so clear his longing for the pre-1789 "Old Regime"—symbolized by his rejection of the revolutionary tricolor for the family's white flag with gold fleurs-de-lis—that he alienated all but the true "ultras" among the Legitimists and so otherwise misunderstood his responsibilities that he failed even to reproduce. Although Orleanists were prolific, they were as limited in attraction, with the Count of Paris, the would-be Philippe VII, much like his grandfather, King Louis Philippe, in avarice and open preoccupation with the possessing classes of society. Through its evocation of equality, meritocracy, and universal male suffrage, Bonapartism had a considerably broader appeal even after the foreign policy disasters of Napoléon III, but in 1879 the prince imperial, the would-be Napoléon IV, died seeking military glory in Africa. With contempt Thiers explained, "There wasn't enough room on one throne for three fat asses."

But in their stead, a republic—again? The First Republic (1792–1804) was forever associated with Jacobinism: rough justice of the guillotine for kings, aristocrats, priests, and anyone else who opposed it; Terror; inflation; instability; war; and its culmination in Napoléon Bonaparte. The Second Republic (1848–52) reserved its rough justice for the working class during the June Days of 1848 and to avoid any further repetition of Jacobinism, immediately embraced Louis Napoléon Bonaparte. Like his uncle, the nephew understood how to make quick work of republics—"Authority from above, confidence from below." He meant making a fetish of universal male suffrage while depriving it of any significance and then using popular acclaim to justify declaring himself emperor. For advocates of a Third Republic the precedents were so discouraging that their only recourse was to abandon them.

The constitutional laws of 1875 created a bicameral parliamentary republic in waiting for a monarch. To represent popular sovereignty, there was the Chamber of Deputies, elected to four-year terms from single-member constituencies by the now sacrosanct universal male suffrage. To temper popular sovereignty, there was the Senate, elected to nine-year terms by local officeholders. To ensure a certain stability, there was the largely ceremonial president of the Republic, elected to a seven-year term by the Senate and the Chamber of Deputies sitting together as the National Assembly. If an acceptable pretender did appear, and if popular opinion called for a revival of the throne, transforming the regime into a bicameral parliamentary monarchy would require only the substitution of king for president. The constitutional laws were short on detail, and how this regime would govern was left to evolve through practice, which did not make perfect and proved that details always harbor devils.

Because the single-member constituencies for the Chamber of Deputies could not exceed 100,000 people—meaning usually no more than 20,000 adult males—the deputies were many, varying from 533 in 1876 to 612 in 1936, and highly independent. Political parties rely on the award of campaign funds to compel discipline, but with most districts smaller than the maximum and the number of voters fewer than in most American municipal ward elections, not many candidates needed outside financing. Once in Paris, they organized themselves in shifting factions, looking after themselves and their districts, any ideological commitment coming in a distant third. As Robert de Jouvenel claimed cynically, "There is less difference between two deputies one of whom is a revolutionary than between two revolutionaries one of whom is a deputy."[12] Without strong parties, which never developed within the political Right or Center and only slowly within the Left, cabinet government was tempestuous. To construct a majority in the Chamber, the premier (prime minister) parceled out ministries to faction leaders, but their ambitions and the variant quality of the factions meant that sure support was uncertain. From 1876 to 1940 no cabinet lasted longer than three years, and several collapsed within days. There might be a strong majority for a single policy, most often in wake of a crisis, but rarely for the broad range of policies that a British cabinet or an American presidential administration expects to carry out. Although every Third Republic premier listed a number of objectives in his ministerial declaration, he was counted successful if he accomplished the one that drove his cabinet's creation.

With their long terms and many fewer electors, the senators could be even more independent than the deputies, and the Senate itself was resistant to changes in popular opinion because only one-third of the seats came up for vote every three years. Given the potential for conflict between the two houses over support for a cabinet or a set of policies, the president of the Republic had the power, with the consent of the Senate, to dissolve the Chamber of Deputies and hold new elections. The reasoning of the conservatives writing the constitution was to give popular sovereignty a chance to rectify the mistake of voting for men whose opinions were too advanced. They failed to consider the implications of a refusal by popular sovereignty to admit any mistake. In 1877, when President Patrice de MacMahon, a Monarchist, faced a Monarchist majority in the Senate and a Republican majority in the Chamber, he invoked dissolution but was humiliated when the elections renewed Republican control of the Chamber. The precedent was set: no president ever dared try it again, and the Senate was sufficiently chastened that for almost twenty years it did not seriously oppose any cabinet with a working majority in the Chamber. Theoretically, even a vote of no confidence by the Senate did not require the cabinet's resignation because the senators were not directly elected, but the links between senators and deputies meant that no premier or his ministers dared alienate the men whose votes they might need at another time.

As the regime evolved in practice, political power shifted from the Center-Right to the Center-Left and then back again until the Great War in 1914. The Monarchists still had faint hopes when the constitutional laws went into effect, but first the Chamber, next the Senate, and inevitably the presidency fell to the Republicans. Clearly, *enough* Frenchmen decided that the *Third* Republic was better than *any* brand of monarchy. Moderate Republicans then sought to justify their victory. They built roads, railroads, and canals; they made primary schooling mandatory, free, and secular; they made military service universal for all young men; they conquered an empire second only to Great Britain's in Africa, Southeast Asia, and the Pacific—thereby creating the context that bound together the nation economically and culturally. They did it all in the midst of the great deflationary spiral that depressed growth during the last quarter of the nineteenth century. But in doing so, the moderate Republicans did not always keep their hands clean. Scandal after scandal, usually involving deputies and senators but one toppling a president, kept alive the suspicion that the Third Republic, like every other regime in France since the 1789 Revolution, might collapse after only two decades or so.

Collapse, not topple: the threats from enemies of the regime were dangerous only in pointing out its weaknesses. In May 1871 the provisional government elected to make peace with the new German Empire and headed by Thiers brutally suppressed an uprising by leftists of many stripes calling itself the Paris Commune. On the hands of both sides there was enough blood to make its place in French history an abattoir, but in its aftermath the forces of order had a monopoly on vengeance. So many defeated partisans of revolution were executed or exiled that the Left did not revive until the mid-1890s and then as part of the broad European movement for reformist Marxism. The factions could not manage to unite in a single Socialist Party until 1905 and limited their clout by refusing to serve in any "bourgeois" cabinet. Although their legislative proposals were essentially modest reforms sometimes already achieved in other European nations, the idea of "socialism" struck terror in capitalist hearts because the party refused to disavow the Marxist goal of expropriating the expropriators. French capitalists, determined to resist any infringement of their rights, saw themselves in the sights of that rhetorical weapon.

More dangerous than the timid Left was a revived Right, which benefited from the most profound ideological transformation of the late nineteenth century. Born in the fires of the 1789 Revolution, nationalism belonged to the Left until Otto von Bismarck demonstrated through the unification of Germany under Prussian domination that it could serve the Right equally well. In France nationalism had always been closely identified with the army, through the conquests of the Revolution and its ideas—and so both were the pride of the Left. But when the army spilled the blood of the June Days in 1848 and the blood of the Commune in 1871, the Left began to associate nationalism and the army with militarism and reaction, while the Right began to regard them as the ultimate bulwark against revolution. The moment when nationalism shifted decisively to the right side of the political spectrum came in the late 1880s with the Boulanger affair. Bonapartism had not survived the death of the prince imperial, and Legitimists had lost their pretender when the Count of Chambord died in 1883, but the hopes of Orleanism remained. In the trinity of a military figure on a black charger, a scandal forcing the resignation of President Jules Grévy, and an economy in doldrums, the Count of Paris discerned the hand of fate dealing monarchism one last card. He committed his reputation and his money to a political campaign for the popular but unscrupulous General Georges Boulanger, who would seize power and restore the monarchy. In retrospect the scheme appears farfetched, but it showed promise until Boulanger lost his nerve and fled into exile.

Not in the sense the Count of Paris had thought, the last card for monarchism had been dealt. Conservatives faced hard choices. Some "rallied" to the Third Republic at the behest of Pope Leo XIII, who hoped to end the long association of throne and altar which had made the Catholic Church and especially its schools the object of attack during the last decade. Although their conversion should have been welcome to a regime that had barely avoided a serious threat, anticlericalism was so ingrained in the Republican mentality that they were regarded with grave mistrust. And almost immediately the Panama Canal scandal besmirched so many deputies and senators that the *Ralliés* had another reason to doubt their new allegiance. For others of the political Right there was a different lesson to be learned from the Boulanger experience. Although the campaign had emphasized nationalism above all, there had also been antiparliamentary rhetoric and some bombast—aimed at the overwhelmingly Republican middle-class—about how an evil capitalism exploited the working class and peasantry. The word *socialism* was used occasionally but in the sense of "national socialistic" in contrast to Marxian. Although "Boulangism" borrowed some aspects from the Bonapartist past, the combination of nationalism, socialism, and mass politics was a radical change from traditional conservative elitism. Had they stumbled upon new tactics that might work?

The answer came when the Dreyfus affair cast the Third Republic into the crisis avoided by Boulanger's cowardice. What began with the army's conviction of a Jewish captain for espionage grew into a moment of truth for the regime. As evidence emerged that Alfred Dreyfus might well be innocent and that army leaders had certainly engaged in actions of dubious legality and then concealed them, the government that divided France least had to govern a France more sharply divided than at any point since the 1789 Revolution. The Third Republic had fulfilled Thiers's promise by governing from the Center, but in a crisis polarization eliminates any center. The Dreyfus affair was a contest of values: Dreyfusards, mostly on the Left, standing for individualism and justice; anti-Dreyfusards, mostly on the Right, countering with authority and tradition. Almost as if the entire nineteenth century had meant nothing, the Revolution took the field against the Counter-Revolution again. And for power, not just for principle: each side bid to take control of the Third Republic through the politics of fear. The Left warned of a military coup d'état that would extinguish democratic freedoms; the Right found a shorthand for its Boulanger issues in the accusation of a "Jewish conspiracy" already taking power. For just a moment France appeared to stand at the brink of civil war, partly because the tactics of the Right were appallingly effective and, more important, because both Left and Right had come to believe their own propaganda. But there was no Jewish conspiracy, and whatever the regime, the French army had never revolted against the state.

The Third Republic survived because by 1900 the Center revived, although it moved to the left. Now, the Radical Republicans, whose "radicalism" meant a progressive income tax and stringent anticlericalism, with the support of the Socialists, whose "socialism" meant social reforms for the working class, joined with some more traditionally moderate Republicans. The "Affair" and its losing elements were dealt with: Dreyfus pardoned and eventually cleared, the army purged of its most reactionary officers, many Catholic schools closed, virtually all orders of monks and nuns banned, and Napoléon's 1801 Concordat linking church and state abrogated. By then it was 1906, and the domestic agenda of the Center-Left was still to be accomplished. If it were, the toll of new taxes would fall on the stalwarts of the Third Republic, the middle class and the peasantry. Just in time to prevent that result, the political Center moved rightward, with the increasing menace of foreign affairs leading up to 1914. As German bullying in Morocco and the Balkans aroused fears of war, nationalism regained respectability and became less the property of the Right, while the internationalism and antimilitarism of the Socialists appeared idealistic and perhaps foolish.

This evolution of the Third Republic was associated with five political leaders whose names, then and until the republic fell in 1940, would stand as symbols of certain policies. Jean Jaurès, unifier of the Socialists and their impassioned orator, represented reformist Marxism and a conviction that the working classes of all nations could band together to prevent war. Joseph Caillaux, plutocrat turned Radical, stood for the progressive income tax and for economic arrangements with Germany even if France were reduced to a junior partner. Georges Clemenceau, Radical of the old school, was a Jacobin redux: in his hatreds—for his ruthlessness he was called the "Tiger," for his anticlericalism the "Priest-Eater"—and in his leftist nationalism. Aristide Briand, the ultimate centrist, conciliated through his confidence that differences can always be negotiated. Raymond Poincaré, pragmatic conservative, defined the moderate Right through his fiscal prudence and his Lorrainer's antipathy toward Germany. The process began during Clemenceau's cabinet (1906–9), his first, at age sixty-four, and destined to be the republic's longest lasting. Although Caillaux was his minister of finance, Clemenceau refused to press for a tax on income. Although the Socialists were Dreyfusard allies, Clemenceau broke with them and Jaurès over new working-class militancy, calling himself France's *premier flic* (top cop) as he repressed their strikes. Although Clemenceau always warned that a good priest was more dangerous than a bad one, he permitted Briand to negotiate a détente with the Catholic Church.

This shifting toward the Center continued under a Briand cabinet (1909–11), reversed abruptly under a Caillaux cabinet (1911–12), then revived so strongly under a Poincaré cabinet (1912–13) that he was elected president in January 1913. Fear among the middle class and the peasantry drove the Third Republic rightward, fear that "socialist" reforms might mean expropriation or toppling the social structure or even revolution, and fear that Germany was plotting a new war and would take advantage of leftist naïveté. During Poincaré's first year as president the army, its sins during the Dreyfus affair forgiven, was strengthened, but to cover the heavy new expenses there was no alternative to enacting an income tax. For the legislative elections in 1914 Caillaux and Jaurès combined forces. To combat them Poincaré, Briand, and their close associate Louis Barthou mounted a campaign of personal vituperation against Caillaux through the powerful conservative newspaper *Le Figaro.* When Caillaux's wife shot its editor dead in retaliation, Caillaux himself became damaged goods. Even so, the outcome of the elections was ambiguous, implying that France was evenly divided over how the Third Republic was to evolve. The summer of 1914 then canceled whatever the preceding months had appointed for the future. A jury acquitted Mme Caillaux of murder, Germany took advantage of another Balkan crisis to provoke the war that had loomed for nearly a decade, and a nationalist fanatic assassinated Jaurès on 31 July for fear that he would convince the French working class to resist mobilization.

The death of Jaurès had the unexpected result of sending France into the Great War more united than at any time since the 1789 Revolution. Jaurès was dead, and so was his inconvenient idealism when the German Socialist Party proved more German than Socialist. In August, to create a government of *union sacrée* (sacred union) stretching from end to end of the political spectrum, the French cabinet added an urbane Royalist and a stern Marxist, both of whom laid aside ideology for nationalism. This sense of political solidarity was absolutely vital because the war went badly from the beginning. Germany blunted French efforts to attack into Alsace and Lorraine while sweeping through Belgium and northern France heading for Paris. A masterful counterattack in early September finally stopped the Germans at the battle of the Marne River, the sound of the artillery audible in the capital. This victory saved France from defeat and made its author, General Joseph Joffre, the de facto ruler of the nation. Ironic it was that Republicans turned so willingly to another man on horseback when they had defined Bonapartists, Boulangists, and anti-Dreyfusard generals as the enemy incarnate of *Liberté, Egalité, Fraternité.* Poincaré as president and Briand as premier were able to restore civilian authority only because Joffre could find no solution to the stalemate of trench warfare that developed on the Western Front and thus to driving the Germans from France.

Solutions, in fact, were not to be found anywhere. France began the war allied to Great Britain and Russia. The British were holding the Flanders sector and imposing a naval blockade on Germany. Since attempting an ill-planned offensive in late August 1914, Russia had been largely in retreat. When Franco-British diplomacy added Italy to their side, the result was that Germany's ally, Austria-Hungary, finally had an opponent it could defeat with regularity. German submarine attacks risked drawing the United States into the war, but the Americans were an ocean away and an unproved military power. As the fighting continued on the Western Front, the power of modern industrialized war produced casualty lists that were literally so inconceivable as to be mind-numbing. The French diplomat Philippe Berthelot famously remarked of them, "One man's death affects me; fifteen thousand deaths are only a statistic." And fifteen thousand was merely what might be the total for a single bad day, for by the end of 1916 French losses already surpassed a million young men dead in their prime.

Mort pour la patrie—dead they were for the nation, but not from all social classes equally. Marianne called to serve especially the sons who were her stalwarts, the peasantry and the middle class, and they were the ones who died in the largest numbers; needed in the mines and the factories, the working class was relatively spared. What is worth dying for must be the ultimate issue between the government and the governed. By early 1917, after two and a half years of war and no end in sight, the sacred union of August 1914 was breaking apart over the answer to that question. Poincaré and a series of cabinets steadfastly demanded "victory" over Germany. Caillaux sought political revival by leading the doubters who questioned what victory would cost and whether it was even possible. Although reviled as *défaitistes* (defeatists) by the government and most of the press, they gained support from news of the revolution in March which overthrew czardom in Russia and even more from the disastrous failure in April and May of new French offensives. Although the United States had entered the war against Germany during that time, no one could gauge how soon or how effectively American forces might give support.

By late fall 1917 the options for the Third Republic and its leaders were stark: either make peace with Germany on whatever terms were possible or make war as if it were the time of the Terror. If the former, Caill-aux should be premier and preside over the permanent diminution of France as a world and European power. If the latter, Clemenceau should be premier as a latter-day Maximilien Robespierre. And Clemenceau, at age seventy-six, it was. In the best Jacobin tradition he arrested leading defeatists and cashiered losing generals "to encourage the others." He pulled on high boots, greatcoat, and steel helmet to visit the French sol-diers in the front line trenches and promise that he would wage *guerre à outrance* (war without limit) on the home front if they did on the battle-front—and *jusqu'au bout* (to the end). The *poilus* (dirty, hairy ones) who had borne so much recognized in Clemenceau the authentic and essential revolutionary tradition symbolized by the tricolor and "La Marseillaise," and they believed him. The cabinet as a revived Commit-tee of Public Safety stiffened patriotic resolve. The soldiers withstood a final German offensive in the spring and summer of 1918 and in July, with fresh American troops, finally took control of the war in a second battle of the Marne.

When the Germans asked for an armistice in November 1918, Clemenceau had been in power—"in office" is much too tame—for less than a year. Rarely have a man and a moment so rightly converged. But at what price? A victory so costly as to be effectively a defeat is called Pyrrhic, from the king of Epirus who warred against Rome and won, thereby ensuring his loss. Given the history of the 1920s, 1930s, and 1940s, *French* should be considered the synonym of *Pyrrhic.* For despite the celebrations of victory in 1918 and the satisfactions realized in the Treaty of Versailles, the triumph turned to ashes, and the hope of an enduring peace crumbled and moldered.

France was not and could not be the same nation after the Great War as before it. Of its blood 1.3 million soldiers were dead, 4.3 million had been wounded, 1.1 million were left with permanent disabilities, and 56,000 were amputees: thus, one-eighth of all adult males were killed, one-quarter of them men in their twenties. They left behind not only 600,000 widows and 750,000 orphans but also a quarter of the young women who would never find marriages and a generation to come which would be short all the children never conceived during the war and afterward. Of its treasure ten northern departments lay in such ruin that comparison to the lunar landscape was appropriate. The "devastated region" had accounted for two-thirds of national mining, metallurgical, and textile output. During its restoration the lost production meant the necessity of imports and the loss of exports and so would create a balance of payments calamity. The franc was already under enormous pressure in foreign currency markets because of lost public and private investments in Russia when the Bolshevik government renounced czarist debts and because of wartime borrowing from Great Britain and the United States. At home there were the domestic war bonds to service and repay while rebuilding the devastated region as rapidly as possible. Prewar France was owed a net 40 billion francs in foreign obligations; postwar France owed 15 billion. Prewar France had a domestic national debt of 33 billion francs; postwar it was 175 billion.[13]

The French psyche was not and could not be the same either. Dominating the social ethos of the prewar Third Republic had been the spirit of the rentier. A private income permitted an anti-necessitarian life—freedom from financial worry and therefore freedom to experiment. Almost every political and cultural figure and many government officials and professionals were rentiers. For them the cost of independence, of outpacing public taste, of mediocre salaries, of neglecting their practices for belles lettres, was low. They had a certain ease and stood above grubbing for money. The impact of the war destroyed rentier wealth beyond recovery: foreign investments became worthless, inflation eroded the value of fixed income from bonds and dividends, and the death rate among rentiers was especially high because many of them were officers and few had a valid reason for avoiding service. The destruction of rentier wealth meant the destruction of the rentier mentality and great confusion for survivors. There was a new emphasis on making money and on displaying its spending as proof that it had been made. Women, who had taken up men's jobs during the war, now more openly demanded equality and emancipation from traditional roles and morals and mores. The lower orders, having fought side by side with their presumed betters, were less deferential and unwilling to serve in menial capacities. Whether from despair or from a sense that the old rules were superseded, murders and suicides increased and cocaine dealing spread. The Dada movement attacked the very essence of French cultural tradition by celebrating the cult of the irrational. A sense of anomie was inevitable.

Legislative elections at the end of 1919 produced a majority for the Center-Right, a coalition calling itself the Bloc National (National Bloc). Its members convinced themselves that they represented the true temper of the nation when in fact their victory had more to do with the disarray of the Left. In the wake of the war Jaurèsian internationalism was as dead as its symbol: German Socialists supported the invasion of France; Russian Bolsheviks made a separate peace with Germany and stiffed French bondholders. Although the centrist Radicals could tell which way the political wind was blowing and prudently drew a line between themselves and their sometime allies, they wore the albatross of Caillaux's defeatism. So, as the members of the National Bloc took their seats, two of the five pivotal figures from the prewar years had been eliminated, and they quickly added a third. Clemenceau was loath to admit the ambition, but he had come to covet the presidency. If the vote had been in January 1919, the adulation for *Père-la-victoire* (Old Man Victory) would have brought him an overwhelming triumph. A year later he had against him a long career of making enemies, the grudge held by the many Catholics among the National Bloc for his anticlericalism, the authoritarian manner of governing he had maintained long after the armistice, and, most of all, the fear that he had won the war but lost the peace negotiations. The Treaty of Versailles did indeed regain for France Alsace and Lorraine, which Germany had taken in 1871, did require reparations for the physical and financial damage to France's devastated region, did disarm Germany, and did demilitarize and occupy Germany's Rhineland. But the imposition of this treaty upon what had been the most powerful economic and military nation in Europe required that the three Atlantic democracies—the United States, Great Britain, and France—maintain their wartime alliance and act in concert. By January 1920 the United States Senate had made clear its refusal to ratify the treaty, and relations between Great Britain and France were already deteriorating.

In a retreat to the president as figurehead, the deputies and senators rejected Clemenceau in favor of the ineffectual Paul Deschanel, the important fact being not the latter but the former. Clemenceau understood the insult and abruptly quit public life, although he would live another ten years. With him departed an important French political tradition, a nationalism of the Left. Henceforth, nationalism would belong to the Right, and the Left would regard it as a reversion to the dangers of the Dreyfus affair. Eight months later Deschanel was gone, his resignation compelled by the appearance of mental instability. Given the need to restore confidence, the legislators replaced him with Alexandre Millerand, the premier and leader of the National Bloc. His elevation opened the way for the return of the two remaining dominant figures, Briand and Poincaré.

As premier in 1921 and early 1922, Briand, true to his nature, sought solutions through finesse. He proceeded from the evidence of the war that France could not control Germany alone and therefore set as his highest priority arranging a permanent defensive pact with Great Britain. On that basis he could secure the peace and enforce the treaty, above all the payment of reparations. But in Britain there was little fear of Germany as a military power and much fear that a failure of the German economy to recover quickly would depress all European economies and especially their own, for which Germany had been the primary trading partner. British leaders such as Prime Minister David Lloyd George were backing away from heavy reparations as an excessive burden that would slow or even prevent Germany's economic revival— and thought the French only too happy at that prospect. So far was postwar Britain from the wartime ally that German delays in fulfilling coal deliveries to France, to make up for the destruction of French mines in the devastated region, were greeted as an opportunity to sell British coal to France at exorbitant prices. Briand was willing to cede some ground on reparations in return for a defensive alliance, but here, too, he found British and French comprehension of its structure fundamentally at odds. France wanted a comprehensive and mutual guarantee; Great Britain wanted a limitation to Western Europe. The source of the discord was France's new defensive treaties with Poland and Czechoslovakia as a (weaker) replacement for Imperial Russia. If France went to war against Germany in support of an Eastern European ally, would Britain be at France's side?

Because Lloyd George considered that he had the stronger hand, all of Briand's efforts at negotiation were bound to fail: no alliance and a

Germany ever more recalcitrant about paying reparations. What Lloyd George failed to reckon was that the National Bloc was willing to jettison Briand for a premier whose attitude was less conciliatory. The moment came in January 1922, at the Cannes conference, the latest in a seemingly interminable series. Briand had conceded all he could, but Lloyd George wanted more, and when the National Bloc majority in the Chamber of Deputies recalled Briand to Paris, he resigned. His successor was Poincaré, who had hated and mistrusted Germans since losing his home in Lorraine to them as a child, who had overseen the war from the Elysée (presidential) Palace, who had urged an even more punitive peace, and who was determined that France—at least for the present with the whip hand—get its due. Here was an audacious policy: if successful, France would be more powerful than at any time since Napoléon Bonaparte; if a failure, France's weakness would be clear to all.

For a year, from January 1922 to January 1923, Poincaré tried a stiffer version of Briand's policy while implying that France might go it alone. When the British refused to take the hint and the Germans called his bluff by finding ever more reasons not to make reparations payments, Poincaré sent French troops to occupy Germany's industrial heartland, the Ruhr Valley—what the National Bloc had been demanding almost from the beginning. He had the support of Belgian and Italian contingents but nothing from the British, although they acknowledged that Germany's default gave France the legal basis for action. Among Germans there was first shock that Poincaré had carried out his threats and then fear that he had a knife to their jugular. French occupation meant that the output of the Ruhr industries would be lost to Germany and perhaps even exploited for France. If so, even acquiescence in the payment of reparations might be preferable, but German leaders were willing to risk catastrophe rather than accept that. Their call for passive resistance in the Ruhr forced the French to take over the entire cost of administering the region and operating the factories and so increased enormously the cost of the occupation. Their promise to pay industrialists for lost profits and workers for lost wages and then printing enough marks to do so generated hyperinflation. By November the mark had declined one *trillion* percent, and uprisings by the elements of both the extreme Left and the extreme Right threatened national disintegration.

Yet, though Germany capitulated, the French gamble failed. The German collapse was destabilizing the world economy, and the United States, with British support, devised a rescue scheme called the "Dawes Plan." American banks would make loans to Germany, which would use the money to stimulate its economy and make (reduced) reparations payments, which would in turn be used by France and Great Britain to stimulate their economies and make war debt payments to the United States. From the outset it should have been obvious that reparations would last only as long as the American loans, but the occupation expenses had accelerated the decline of the franc and left France vulnerable to Anglo-American pressure.

By the inauguration of the Dawes Plan in the summer of 1924, the Cartel des Gauches (Coalition of the Left) controlled the Chamber of Deputies, Poincaré was no longer premier, and Millerand was no longer president. The National Bloc had gone so far wrong by making three critical mistakes. First, it had assumed that its victory in 1919 meant France had embraced government by the Center-Right when the history of the Third Republic was of small shifts left and right with a strong tendency toward government of the center. Second, it failed to recognize—if not immediately, then at least quickly—that the enormous sacrifices for the war had to be followed by enormous sacrifices for the peace: that, however painful, the only means of paying for the war and its destruction was through heavy new taxes and not through the mirage of German reparations. Third, it believed that France could pursue an independent policy against Germany even though victory in 1918 was barely won even with the support of many allies. By 1924 and new legislative elections the air was thick with chickens coming home to roost. Public opinion was turning leftward. New taxes had to be voted to defend the franc. Poincaré's occupation of the Ruhr, heroic in a sense, had failed. Defying the intention and tradition of the presidency as a nonpartisan head of state, Millerand had tried to strengthen its powers and had acted more as the head of the National Bloc. When the Coalition of the Left won the elections, it refused to form a cabinet unless Millerand resigned and forced him from office.

This Coalition of the Left was not much to the left. Its spokesman, Edouard Herriot, corpulent, good-hearted, bumbling as only a former academic can be, had no real ideas beyond a sentimental evocation of Dreyfusard ideals. For most of the Radicals, whom he led and who made up the great majority of the Coalition, that meant above all regaining their prewar dominance. Allied to them were the much-reduced Socialists. In late 1920 the party split over allegiance to Moscow and the one variety of Marxism to have seized power successfully. A large majority— 70 percent—sided with the Bolsheviks, called themselves Communists, and declared unceasing war against the capitalist society of the Third Republic. The remainder, led by Léon Blum, more an intellectual than a politician, energetically defended the Jaurèsian tradition of democratic socialism. When Poincaré said, once the ballots had been counted, "Clearly, the French are too tired to follow me," he defined the essence of why the Coalition of the Left won the 1924 election: the combination of the Radicals and the Socialists was a comforting reminder of better times. Including anything farther to the left, the Syndicalist Confédération Générale du Travail (CGT, General Labor Confederation), which had led massive but unsuccessful strikes in 1919 and 1920 and called for the nationalization of key industries, and more so the Communists, would have brought electoral doom. Proof of how comforting came after the new majority politically executed Millerand and elected as the new president of the Republic Gaston Doumergue, a moderate, even conservative, Radical.

The problem with coming to power because the opposition has failed to solve major problems is then having to solve them. As premier and foreign minister, Herriot agreed to the Dawes Plan and then was disillusioned that all was not sweetness and light, not to mention peace and brotherhood, among France, Great Britain, and Germany. There was concurrently the pressing matter of the budget, ballooned out of any accounting regularity by the need to spend francs that thus far had not been reimbursed by reparations to restore the devastated region and thereby restore the economy. With spending surpassing revenues to such a degree—what the 1930s learned to call "deficit financing"—the result was inflation domestically (the cost of living index at 378, compared to 100 in 1914) and the precipitous decline of the franc internationally (down 317 percent against the dollar, 441 percent against the pound). The National Bloc had finally faced up to the issue by passing a package of taxes called the "double décime"—a 20 percent surcharge across the board. The Coalition of the Left had declaimed before the elections about reversing some of the increase but discovered that much more was needed. The Socialists favored a tax on wealth—which smacked of bolshevism to the middle-class Radical voters and was ruled out of bounds immediately. But the best the Radicals could do was propose a forced conversion of state bonds, lowering rates and extending maturities. Here was a fine reward for the patriotism of purchasing them during the war and would be the final destruction of rentier income.

What reason did investors have for confidence faced with this threat and the proof, in the Dawes Plan, that much of the anticipated German reparations, which presumably backed the government's obligations, was imaginary? And so investors went on strike, refusing to renew the shorter-term bonds as they came due. With the budget dependent on these loans, a series of Coalition cabinets, marching steadily away from the Left and into the Center under Herriot, Paul Painlevé, and finally Briand, either had to declare national bankruptcy or have the Bank of France issue sufficient francs to cover the deficit. The former was an impossible capitulation, the latter, given the precedent of Germany in 1923, a horrifying glimpse into the abyss. The Coalition of the Left played its last card by rehabilitating Caillaux, the only Radical with credible financial expertise. When Caillaux's presence did not restore calm, when the cost of living index reached 532 and the franc's decline against the dollar and the pound surpassed 600 percent, the time had come for savior seeking, and the only savior left was Poincaré.[14]

Thoroughly frightened, the Chamber of Deputies agreed on 23 July 1926 to support a "Government of National Union" under the former president, former premier, former occupier of the Ruhr, and former target of the Coalition in elections only two years earlier. Poincaré made accepting this turn of affairs easier by constructing a cabinet that stretched broadly across the Center, by including Herriot and several other Radicals, and by turning foreign policy over to Briand. But there was no mistaking who was in charge, and the moment required exactly that. Poincaré demanded and got whatever he wanted in economic and fiscal policy from the cowed and docile deputies. As for international relations, French weakness demanded not heroics but cooperation, and no one was better with soothing conciliation than Briand, who, after all, had long been Poincaré's friend and ally. Together for three more years, they performed a very miracle, the revival of a panicked, isolated, almost moribund France.

Poincaré was the symbol of fiscal rectitude: *honnête* (honorable)—the only president of the Republic to leave the office poorer than upon entering—and above all *sérieux* (reliable). The steps he took, obvious and uncomplicated, had previously been evaded because they were also unpopular and painful. But as elements in a Poincaré program, they inspired confidence. He sharply raised all taxes and made their evasion difficult. He cut spending, not uniformly but with sedulous attention to details that were bloated. He imposed efficiencies and set the example with his own diligence and energy. He ended the fiction-become-chicanery of a budget balanced by receipts and a budget to be balanced by reparations. And investors returned to buying bonds. That much stanched the hemorrhage. A certain recovery came with German payments under the Dawes Plan, which at least covered the last rebuilding in the devastated region and some of the pension expenses. After nearly two years of this therapy, the cost of living index had risen slightly to 549, but the franc's decline against the dollar and pound was reduced to just under 500 percent.[15] On 24 June 1928 the government officially stabilized the franc at a new rate, one-fifth of its prewar value. Better could not be done, even by Poincaré, but he had saved *something:* 20 percent was better than anything less or nothing at all. Without irony, his achievement was called the "Poincaré franc."

That Germany was actually paying reparations, no matter how much less than required under the Treaty of Versailles, owed much to Briand's foreign policy. Like Poincaré with the franc, he had a hand of mediocre cards and a large pot at stake. His guiding philosophy was to restore as much as possible the position France held in the summer of 1919 upon the signing of the treaty: Germany weakened economically and militarily, France strengthened by the pledge of the United States and Great Britain to sign an alliance for mutual defense. That position had eroded rapidly. Within a year Germany was resisting the treaty strictures, and France had no pact of guarantee. Briand's experience negotiating with Lloyd George and Poincaré's occupying the Ruhr were the proof that France was not strong enough to carry out an independent policy. Although the Dawes Plan confirmed that assessment, each had the wisdom to recognize its possibilities: the Western democracies were acting in concert, and Germany would pay. Briand saw the next steps as gaining Germany's willing acceptance to the outcome of the war and Britain's to defending it. The Locarno Pact, signed in October 1925, took both, as France, Great Britain, Germany, Italy, and Belgium agreed to guarantee the existing boundaries in Western Europe. Although there was celebration in this undeniable recovery of French interests, a disquieting portent could not be ignored. For France's Eastern European allies and their boundaries, Germany had ambitions and Britain disregard. Instead of a five-power guarantee, Poland and Czechoslovakia got only meaningless arbitration treaties with Germany. Much talk about a "Spirit of Locarno," about a new sense of optimism, hope, and security, made the rounds as Briand, British Foreign Secretary Austen Chamberlain, and German Foreign Minister Gustav Stresemann seemed to have established a rapport. But Briand knew the difference between the French position in 1919 and the French position in 1925: he hastened to sign a new treaty of mutual assistance with Czechoslovakia.

Soon the various trammels of the Versailles treaty fell away. When the League of Nations welcomed Germany as a member in September 1926, the apposite analogy was the return of the prodigal son. In the parable there followed the killing of the fatted calf to provide for joyous feasting. Long starved for support, the treaty was anything but fatted, but it was now as helpless as a calf and quickly sacrificed to assuage German sovereignty. From the beginning Germany had flouted the disarmament provisions, but at least the interallied military control commission with the responsibility of monitoring compliance complained and sometimes applied sanctions. In January 1927 the League took over the enforcement, in practice meaning its abandonment. The Dawes Plan had reduced Germany's reparations payments but imposed certain controls on its finances and the provisions for monetary transfers. In June 1929 the Young Plan modified the Dawes provisions by eliminating these restrictions and further reducing the payments. To seal this reconciliation of Western Europe, the occupation of the Rhineland, symbolic of protecting France against a renewed German attack and projected under the treaty to last until 1934, was terminated four years early. Already there was a new symbol for a new devotion by men and nations, the Pact of Peace drawn up by Briand and the American secretary of state, Frank B. Kellogg, which renounced war as an instrument of national policy and was solemnly signed by twenty-three nations in Paris on 27 August 1928. Briand had not so much restored the French position, impossible without the strength to act independently, as maneuvered to a different position, based less on power and paragraphs and more on compromise and consideration. Everything, he had always insisted, was a question of personalities, but what would happen when the cast changed? At the end of July 1929 Poincaré retired from politics seriously ill. Stresemann died two months later, at the beginning of October. Briand lived another thirty months, until March 1932, long enough to question how firmly seated his policies had left France.

Charles de Gaulle once remarked that treaties are like flowers and young girls—they last while they last. He could have added illusions. At the end of the 1920s Poincaré was the "savior of the franc" and Briand the "apostle of peace." No matter that the miracles they achieved were considerably short of what were mere ambitions in 1918. For the moment France had recovered its nerve. There was proof in the statistics. Reconstruction of the devastated region was essentially complete: nearly 600,000 houses, 20,500 public buildings, 7,800 factories, and 250,000 barns had been rebuilt in a decade. Industrial production finally attained the prewar 1913 level in January 1924 and by the end of 1929 was 35 percent higher. For the first time since the war exports exceeded imports in 1924, 1925, and 1927, and although afterward exports slipped slightly, in 1929 they were still 87 percent of imports. The cost of living index had continued to rise slowly since 1928, to 582, but wages were now going up faster.[16] The illusion of prosperity lasted through the beginning of the Great Depression. The crash of the American stock market which began in October 1929 was followed quickly by bank failures, a general business collapse, and unprecedented levels of unemployment that spread to Great Britain, Germany, and Eastern Europe. France alone seemed an island of reprieve.

Much was the relief on this island of reprieve and almost as much smugness. The French believed that they had suffered long enough and that it was the turn of others, especially others who, like the "Anglo-Saxons," a collective disparagement for the British and the Americans, had been profligate in their economic and strategic advice. There was a certain rejoicing that the crisis of the franc having been surmounted, the traditional verities of politics could resume. In an axiom as hackneyed as a La Fontaine fable and as deadly accurate, the Radicals were said to vote with their hearts on the left and their pocketbooks on the right. Anxious to share the prestige of Poincaré's economic policies, they had hugged the Center during the 1928 legislative elections. Once the savior of the franc retired, and especially as it became clear that his chosen successor was André Tardieu, more to the right and scornful of sometime supporters, the Radical Party longed to return to its policy of "no enemies to the Left"—of course leaving aside the Communists. Moving the Radicals in this direction was their young man of great promise, Edouard Daladier, who used the issue to challenge for leadership of the party. His target was Herriot, who three decades before had been Daladier's schoolmaster and who by serving throughout Poincaré's national union government was made the symbol of a Radical Party divorced from the Left.

The battlefield turned out to be Tardieu's grand proposal for a massive public works program of "national equipment." With the devastated region restored and its factories all of the latest design, the rest of the nation was to have its turn, the expense covered by a treasury flush with budgetary surpluses. Such a program of patriotic investment had enormous appeal—to those who would be able to claim the credit. Under Tardieu that meant a cabinet with its axis in the Center-Right. Unlike Poincaré, whose preference was always to govern from a broad Center and therefore welcomed any Radicals who would follow him, Tardieu wanted to rely on a smaller, tightly disciplined majority. A man of haughty brilliance and clear principle, he had only contempt for the slack allegiance of individual Radicals and the plastic ideals of the party as a whole. So, of course, the Radicals did not support Tardieu's proposal for national equipment because they recognized that he would use its passage in the 1932 elections for the benefit of his majority. And, of course, they offered their own competing proposal instead. Finally, of course, the legislative maneuvering and infighting ultimately undermined the narrow but insufficiently disciplined Center-Right majority, and no bill of national equipment won passage. An important opportunity was lost. By the middle of 1931, six months after Tardieu's defeat, the depression was beginning to bite in France. A program of massive public works might well have been a Keynesian stimulus to forestall what became economic disaster.[17]

That assertion begs the question of whether anyone in French politics was sufficiently acquainted with the theories of John Maynard Keynes to consider them. Certainly, the keenest economic mind, Poincaré's, was gone. Although he was an old-fashioned fiscal conservative, he had grasped absolutely the fundamental requirement for French recovery, officially stabilizing the franc slightly below its market value and thus making French exports a bargain. As long as the pound and the dollar remained at their fixed rates of gold, France could be an island of reprieve from the world depression. But fixed the pound and the dollar did not remain. Great Britain abandoned the gold standard on 21 September 1931, the United States on 19 April 1933. By the end of 1933 the franc had risen 33 percent against the pound and 36 percent against the dollar. For France a second devaluation was the proper response, but the Poincaré franc was the symbol of French recovery, and bondholders were vehemently opposed. The consequences of then defending the franc at its 1928 level were utterly predictable. From 1931 to 1932 exports declined from 30.9 million francs to 20 million, down 35 percent. In 1931 alone the level of industrial production fell from 102 in January to 84 in December, a nearly 18 percent drop, and reached 76 by mid-1932, down a further 9 percent. From almost invisible unemployment at the beginning of 1931, 28,500, the total exploded to 248,100 in only a year, an increase of 771 percent. The cost of living index did decline, from 587 at the end of 1930 to 523 at the end of 1932, but that was from a reduction in spending.[18] The respite was over.

What could be done? If a new devaluation was ruled out, the economic alternatives were limited. But because crisis produces polarization, the political possibilities were magnified, and all the more so because in a year and a half there would be legislative elections to fight. Throughout 1931 and into 1932, under Pierre Laval for twelve months and then under Tardieu again for three more, the Center-Right tried to blame all of France's current problems on the Left, especially the Communists, and for good measure all of France's problems since the armistice. Driven leftward, the Radicals made up with the Socialists and responded that the Center-Right had been in charge for six years and that the mess had to be all of its making. In the midst of this calumny Doumergue's presidential term expired. Briand deserved the honor of election, but his talent for conciliation was hardly the preference of the day. He was, more important, nearly a great man, and no one of stature had ever sat in the Elysée Palace—with Poincaré the exception that proves the rule. Instead, the deputies and senators chose Paul Doumer, who had been governor-general of Indochina and minister of finance in a Briand cabinet. Almost exactly a year later, May 1932, a deranged White Russian exile hoping to focus attention on Soviet atrocities in the Ukraine assassinated him. Briand had died in March, but even if he had been available, he would have lost to Albert Lebrun, once colonial minister and now president of the Senate, who fit the pattern of mediocre achievement so excellently that he became the last president of the Third Republic. There was also a new majority, elected as Doumer lay dying. Eight years after their triumph as the Coalition of the Left in 1924, the Radicals and the Socialists regained control of the Chamber as French voters punished conservatives and their allies among the moderates for having been in power when the storm of depression struck.

Despite the challenge of Daladier, Herriot was the grand old man of the Radicals and became premier. He had certain strengths, perhaps just enough to disqualify him as a future president of the Republic, but comprehension of economic theory was not among them. Tardieu and even Laval were said to have some grasp, but during the preceding year and a half they had never seriously confronted the growing crisis. Although aware that French exports were increasingly undersold and that other countries were dumping their products on the French market, they dared not propose a new devaluation. To protect against the flood of imports, a traditional tariff was not sufficient—nations in depression were willing to sell at any price. Instead, a rickety structure of import quotas emerged which in theory permitted the entrance and sale only of products that could not be made in France—in theory, because the practicalities of such a system encouraged fraud and smuggling. Herriot adopted the idea as his own because he did not know what else to do. As in 1924, the Radicals and the Socialists who made up his majority had utterly different economic proposals. Radicals argued for deflation: decreasing state expenditures and imposing higher taxes. Socialists argued for inflation: increasing state expenditures and promoting consumption. And so nothing much was done as the situation worsened. The budget surplus happily touted by Tardieu in 1930 had all but disappeared. Germany had ceased to pay reparations in 1931, and Germans were increasingly giving their votes to the National Socialist Party of Adolf Hitler. Herriot was relieved to use a dispute over whether to make one last war debt payment to the United States as a reason to resign at the end of 1932.

The decisive shift of power within the Radical Party had occurred: Daladier became premier for the first time on 31 January 1933; Herriot would never be premier again. Hitler became chancellor of Germany one day earlier. Daladier had made his reputation by cajoling the Socialists about elections, and now he did so about economic policy. Blum and his party continued to refuse participation in any cabinet they did not head, but they had made up a crucial component of the Center-Left majority since May 1932. Would they support Radical-sponsored deflation through a 6 percent cut of civil service salaries in return for a promise to consider Socialist-sponsored nationalization of the armaments factories and reduction of the workweek from forty-eight to forty hours? After much vacillation, the Socialists declined. And so nothing much continued to be done as the Daladier experiment ended in October, followed by a brief interlude under Albert Sarraut, and then in late November by a cabinet under longtime Radical stalwart Camille Chautemps. All the while, the economy steadily eroded. By the end of 1933 unemployment reached 312,900. Consumers hoarded cash and drove the cost of living index down to 500. Although the production level climbed to 87, exports fell further, to 18.8 million francs.[19] What was the point of a government that would not, perhaps could not, govern? That question, posed only rhetorically even in bad times, may be posed severely in worse times. And Christmas brought them, with the news of a scandal that laid bare corruption at the highest levels.

Financial peculation, rumors and fact, hung about the history of the Third Republic like a fetid scent only occasionally acknowledged. Most recently, at the end of 1930 the inquiry into Albert Oustric's illicit speculations revealed involvement by the Bank of France, perhaps innocently but, if so, proof of an appalling gullibility, and something more by Senator Raoul Péret, then minister of justice in the Tardieu cabinet. Three years later Oustric's connections were made to seem innocuous when compared to the reach of one Serge Alexandre Stavisky. Russian, Ukrainian, Bessarabian—his exact origin unknown: what would matter was that he was a foreigner taking advantage. From small-time confidence schemes he had advanced to larger deceptions, wound up briefly in prison, and upon release was no less larcenous but more prudent. Using the currency of the demimonde, he made friends among journalists, politicians, magistrates, and the police to provide cover. Ambitious, shrewd, daring, he parlayed a pyramid scheme involving fraudulent bonds into the appearance of a fortune. The last version, which collapsed in late December 1933, had been endorsed by politicians ranging from a mayor to deputies to the current minister of the colonies, all of them Radicals, and was a swindle of no less than 239 million francs. Fraud at that level was sufficient to make Stavisky front-page news and, with that, the revelation that his trial for an old offense had been postponed by the Paris prosecutor's office nineteen times since 1927. The Paris public prosecutor was Georges Pressard, and he was the brother-in-law of Premier Chautemps.

Stavisky went into hiding, knowing well that he was wanted more for what and whom he knew than for his crimes. Their orders from on high imperative, his friends among the police were now a liability. Detectives from the Sûreté Générale (State Security Police) tracked him to Chamonix, where he hoped to cross the border into Switzerland, and brought him back dead. He had, they claimed, committed suicide. Journalists, some of whom had lately lived high at his table, wrote "suicide" or even "suicided" (*suicidé*), and they were right. As the agents forced the door of Stavisky's chalet, he shot himself, but the wound would not have been fatal had he not been left to bleed on the floor for more than an hour. During three weeks, until almost the end of January, Chautemps brazenly denied any improprieties by anyone despite the withering abuse from all sides. When he did resign, what had begun as a mere scandal was becoming a crisis for the regime.

Between the end of 1930, when Tardieu's grand scheme for national equipment foundered, and early 1934, France and the French had undergone a profound transformation. Then France was that island of reprieve in a sea of economic depression, confident—even arrogant—that persevering through lean years had earned fat ones for the present and future. Now, after so brief a respite, the lean years were back with a vengeance. Had all the struggle been for nothing? Like Sisyphus of Greek myth, the French had pushed the great stone up the hill over and over only to have it roll back upon them. Taking on the heavy task again, this Sisyphus could not be imagined happy. Misery does not always build character, but it always creates characters. Their plight could not be explained by the relentless wrath of Zeus: somebody had to take the blame. In 1930 it was politics as usual. In 1934 it was politics for blood—literally. Polarization had encouraged the political extremes to recruit shock troops for street battles, and economic resentment filled the ranks. On the far Left the Communists were declared revolutionaries with a disciplined party structure that could turn out demonstrators quickly and reliably. The far Right had multiple formations, with names like Solidarité Française (French Solidarity), Jeunesses Patriotes (Young Patriots), and Camelots du Roi (Hawkers of the King)—none of them much disciplined but all entranced by the example of Benito Mussolini's Fascists. By far the largest pool of potential demonstrators was the determinedly not extremist Croix de Feu (Cross of Fire, from the medal for heroism, the Croix de Guerre), a veterans association founded and led by Colonel François de La Rocque de Sévérac, Center-Right in politics but as Republican as Tardieu. If members of the extreme Left or the extreme Right took to the streets, they could easily be accused of ideological posturing. If the Cross of Fire marched, it would be a moral indictment of the republic by the men who had sacrificed their youth in its defense.

Perceiving real danger, the Radicals, who still controlled the Chamber of Deputies, led with their brightest hope, Daladier. A veteran himself of the trenches, headstrong pursuing power, and as brooding as most of his fellow deputies were genial, he was reputed a man of

strength—and quickly gave that reputation the lie. He could not as-
semble something approaching a cabinet of national union because no
one wanted to share the taint of what was now called the "Stavisky affair." He could not rapidly purge that taint because it attached most to
his own party and its allies. He thought to sanction the compromised
high administrators by promotion: the public prosecutor and brother-
in-law to France's highest court, the Cour de Cassation, the Paris prefect
of police to governor-general of Morocco, and—absurdly—the head of
the State Security Police to director of the Comédie Française (National
Comedy Theater). Jean Chiappe, who had been the most powerful prefect of police in decades and had more friends among the Right than the
Left, rejected the kick upstairs and vowed revenge. On 6 February the
Chamber formally invested Daladier and his cabinet, but outside in the
streets there was a public vote of no confidence. The smell had simply
become too pervasive, the failures too absolute, the politics as usual too
usual. Various small groups of demonstrators had clashed with one
other and the police over the preceding weeks, but on this night there
were thousands because the Cross of Fire was out in force. Waving banners, proudly wearing their wartime decorations, veterans and the fed-
to-the-teeth gathered in the Place de la Concorde, only a bridge across
the Seine from the Palais Bourbon, where the Chamber of Deputies was
in session. They sang "La Marseillaise," literally the French battle hymn
of the Republic, and drowned out the smaller Communist detachments
howling "The Internationale." What they wanted was not clear, but
the police barely held the Concorde bridge against their assault. Before
order was restored, fifteen were dead and fifteen hundred wounded.

In fear for their lives or at least their careers, some of the deputies,
especially on the Left, thought that 6 February 1934 had almost been a
French 28 October 1922—referring to the Fascist "March on Rome."
They were misreading history, underestimating themselves, and over-
estimating the demonstrators: France in 1934 was nowhere near the
depths of Italy in 1922; the deputies were not so craven and do-nothing;
and La Rocque's Cross of Fire was not revolutionary. With a majority
in the Chamber, nothing prevented Daladier from seeking to resolve
the crisis, but with something less than valor he and his cabinet resigned the following morning. Although the necessity now to construct

a government of national union behind a great man was obvious to all, no great men were left. The closest semblance was former president Gaston Doumergue, but his recall on 9 February was not a new 23 July 1926, the return of Poincaré, much less a new 28 August 1914, the sacred union of the Great War. Doumergue had nothing approaching Poincaré's personal authority, and his definition of a national union cabinet was narrow, leaving out the far Right, the Socialists, and of course the Communists. But sensing that, besides the rot of the Stavisky affair and the intractable economy, France faced a growing security threat from Nazi Germany, he picked two men who, like himself, recalled the past, Louis Barthou, boon friend of Poincaré and Briand for the foreign ministry, and Marshall Philippe Pétain, the hero of Verdun for the ministry of war.

The Doumergue experiment lasted exactly nine months, a period when brought to term engendered no birth of recovery. How deeply the decay of the Stavisky affair penetrated could be assessed when the body of Albert Prince was discovered on 21 February near Dijon. He was an assistant prosecutor in the Paris office and said to be responsible for the now notorious nineteen postponements. He was also said to have documents proving the complicity of superiors. Before he could talk, he was drugged, tied to the railroad tracks, and dismembered by a passing train. Without irony, the police declared his death a suicide. Various legislative inquiries did not improve on this verdict or even seriously implicate any political figures or their bureaucratic allies in the scandal. The measure of the Doumergue government's futility was its reluctance to do anything more than change the name of the State Security Police from Sûreté Générale to Sûreté Nationale. Likewise on the economy, the cabinet could propose nothing better than cutting war pensions and further cutting civil service salaries. The statistics gave proof of continuing dismal decline. With the franc now having risen 39 percent against the pound and 40 percent against the dollar, exports continued to fall and were 59 percent lower than in 1931. The policy of deflation, regarded by its victims as progressive impoverishment, so reduced French purchasing power that the domestic economy stalled badly, industrial production dropping back to 79, unemployment rising more than 24,000 to 375,200, and the cost of living index falling from 500 to 482.[20]

The only shining light of the Doumergue cabinet was the energy, at age seventy-two, of Louis Barthou at the Quai d'Orsay. Brittle, sarcastic, at times brilliant, he had become embittered by the death in battle of his only son during the Great War. His animus against his fellow deputies who refused to recognize the danger of a revived Germany was exceeded only by his hatred of Germany. He regarded his appointment as the opportunity to put right a French foreign policy adrift since Briand's death. Hitler's consolidation of power in Germany, his avowed ambition to reverse the verdict of 1918, and his unpredictable tactics altered the stakes of diplomacy. Barthou believed that Germany could be controlled only through the construction of an "iron ring" and so began to tighten relations with Poland and the Little Entente nations of Czechoslovakia, Romania, and Yugoslavia. He had never forgiven the Bolsheviks for renouncing the czarist debt, but to the outrage of his fellow moderates he proposed an alliance with the Soviet Union using the rationale that the enemy of France's enemy ought to be France's friend. What Barthou might have accomplished is history in the subjunctive because on 9 October he and King Alexander I of Yugoslavia were shot dead in Marseilles by Croat terrorists. His closest friend, Poincaré, died a week later. The old order was gone, and Doumergue joined it shortly. What was the point of a national union government that had so little union and that used the specter of national emergency to such little effect? Doumergue had also demonstrated, at least to the deputies and senators, an unseemly taste for authority. He asked and was given decree powers to deal with the economy—although he did not do much. He went over their heads to address the nation in a series of radio speeches he called "family chats." He proposed strengthening the premier and the president and weakening the Chamber and the Senate. Because even a little reform was more than enough, Doumergue was sent back to retirement.

Such discredit attached to the leading Radicals—Herriot for even greater economic illiteracy than usual, Chautemps for Stavisky, and Daladier for 6 February—that successors had to come from the Center-Right, and that meant more so-called orthodox economics. From November 1934 to January 1936 first Pierre-Etienne Flandin and then Laval adamantly rejected devaluation despite increasing calls even from among moderates like Paul Reynaud. Arguing that France suffered from "overproduction," they persevered with deflation and pushed the cost of living index down to 446, a 22 percent decrease since 1931. Industrial production did recover to 86, but exports continued to decline, now down to 15.7 million francs. And there were another 102,000 unemployed, making the total 477,200.[21] January and February 1934 had revived the taste for confrontational politics even among the middle class, and in August 1935, when Laval imposed drastic new cuts in the pay of government employees from the highest to the lowest, there were ugly demonstrations, sometimes riots, leaving dead and wounded. More ominously, there was a turn toward extraparliamentary solutions that had the potential to turn antiparliamentary. Henri Dorgères and his "Green Shirts" attracted peasants with his wild threat to raise prices by withholding all crops from the market. La Rocque drew large crowds in the cities and towns with speeches about "public service" and "moral vigor." Membership in the Cross of Fire swelled as it came to symbolize everything the political system was not. The Communists also appeared to be winning new recruits—at least they were able to demonstrate, counterdemonstrate, and fight as often as anyone else.

This new proof of domestic polarization came as France's international position began to disintegrate. Hitler had withdrawn Germany from the symbols of peaceful intention, the general disarmament talks and the League of Nations. He was behind the murder of Chancellor Engelbert Dollfuss and the attempted coup d'état by the Austrian Nazis. He won overwhelmingly the January 1935 plebiscite that returned the Sarre to Germany after fifteen years of French rule. He proclaimed that Germany was rearming in spite of the Versailles treaty provisions. To contain, if no more, the revived German threat, Barthou had sought to encircle Hitler. Laval took over as foreign minister after Barthou bled to death in Marseilles and in his own fashion carried on the policy. He did follow up negotiations with the Soviet Union for a mutual assistance pact, signed it in May 1935, but then put off indefinitely the military staff talks that would have given it effect. And he did sustain French contacts with the Eastern European successor states but with less enthusiasm. His real interest was a pact with Mussolini, who had made a great display of his determination to uphold Austrian independence. In January 1935 Laval announced that France and Italy had resolved colonial differences and would soon coordinate military policies—perhaps there was also a secret understanding that France would not oppose Italian ambitions in Eastern Africa. At least Mussolini appeared to believe so when he invaded Ethiopia in October. British opinion swung heavily for the underdog and against the bully, especially because Mussolini was attacking a fellow League of Nations member. Laval faced a dilemma, absolutely unwilling to separate from France's most important ally but reluctant to lose France's latest. Trying to have both, he favored imposing largely symbolic League sanctions on Italy while dividing Ethiopia to Italy's benefit. To British leaders this diplomacy was the essence of duplicity and cynicism. To the Italians it was betrayal pure and simple.

Laval had run headlong into the double bind constricting French foreign policy when confronting the threat from Germany after 1933. To rely on the alliance with Great Britain meant adopting an essentially passive role because British aid was contingent upon Germany's attacking France and because British leaders consistently opposed fighting in support of France's Eastern European allies and were especially wary of the Soviet Union. Yet France had no basis upon which to construct an alliance system in Eastern Europe other than on mutual assistance. Doubt that France would defend Eastern allies facing German attack would mean no iron ring, but could France risk fighting Germany without Britain? Relying upon a coalition of allies to deter German aggression could mean France's standing shoulder to shoulder with dictators like Mussolini and Stalin—and necessarily assenting to their actions. If doing so was abhorrent, as it was with Mussolini over Ethiopia and would be soon with Stalin over the purge trials, the only alternative—because the United States had withdrawn into isolationism—was the League ideal of collective security. But where was the line of enforcement to be drawn: if not for Ethiopia against Italy, why for France against Germany? Laval is sometimes compared to Briand, whose protégé he had briefly been. Both, so goes the argument, considered everything open to negotiation, but the difference between them was stark. Briand believed in compromise but drew a line beyond which he would not go. Laval believed in the deal and would do whatever he could to close and maintain it. In 1934 Briand would have done just what

Barthou attempted; Laval went through the motions. In 1935 Briand would have sided emphatically with Great Britain to uphold collective security; Laval equivocated. Under a Briand policy Mussolini would likely have been curbed. Under a Laval policy Mussolini first preened at his conquest and then turned toward Hitler.

Certain days are seen, retrospectively, as turning points—Bastille Day 1935 was so apparent immediately. In the wealthy western end of Paris disciplined ranks from the Cross of Fire marched thirty thousand strong as proof that moral order stood firm. In the poorer eastern end of Paris unruly crowds of Radicals, Socialists, and Communists paraded three hundred thousand strong—ten times greater—as proof that change was under way. The disproportion in numbers was important, but the amity of the far Left, Left, and Center-Left was serious. Here was the first demonstration of the Popular Front. For a decade and a half the Communists had reviled the Socialists as "social fascists" more to be scorned than the bourgeoisie. Now that France and the Soviet Union had signed a defensive agreement and now that the rise of right-wing demonstrations inspired (unreasonable) fears that France might be incubating true fascists, the objective situation, as good Bolsheviks were wont to say, had changed. Stalin himself gave the order, and Communists sought an electoral alliance with the Socialists which was extended to the Radicals. The next nine and a half months made their victory in the 1936 legislative elections inevitable. Laval's domestic and foreign policy failures rendered government by the Center-Right so unpopular that in January public opinion welcomed back a largely Radical cabinet, Stavisky-tainted or not. A month later the far Right earned opprobrium and Blum sympathy when the Hawkers of the King beat him nearly to death. Three weeks more, on 7 March, Hitler sent troops into the demilitarized Rhineland, directly violating the last element of the Versailles treaty which provided security for France. Premier Albert Sarraut, who had been decorated for bravery at Verdun, at first sought a decisive reaction. But the chief of the general staff, General Maurice Gamelin, declared that any response required a general mobilization. British leaders insisted that Hitler's actions *within* Germany were no cause for war. A majority of the cabinet, the great bulk of the legislators, most of the press, and public opinion in general urged caution. Elections were only two months away. And so France was content to file a protest with the League of Nations. Or perhaps not so content: for if traditional politics had come to this pass, dramatic change looked better and better.

In the May 1936 legislative elections change was voting for the Popular Front coalition, which won an overwhelming 380 of the 612 seats in the Chamber of Deputies. But the real meaning was in the distribution: the Radicals actually lost seats from 1932, dropping from 158 to 106; the Socialists took their place as the largest single party by gaining from 97 to 147; and the Communists had an astonishing increase from 21 to 72. Everything about the vote indicated that Blum should become premier, the first time for a Socialist and the first time for a Jew. Conservatives were aghast, but with only 232 seats for the Center-Right and the Right, they were, for now, reduced to watching the program of the Left in action. Aloud, they predicted that any Popular Front cabinet would be in thrall to the Communists, and all the more so because the Radicals had been weakened. Not quite as loud yet, they worried that Blum would be influenced in foreign affairs by the increasing number of Jewish refugees from Germany and Eastern Europe. And, immediately, they claimed their apprehensions were justified, at least about the former. In late May and early June a wave of more than twelve thousand strikes involving nearly two million workers swept across France. Many adopted a new tactic, the so-called sit-down strike, occupying factories and businesses until their demands were met because they were confident that the Popular Front would not begin by using force against its electors. Blum fulfilled their expectation by declaring that government had too long emphasized order over the legitimate struggle of the working class. Through the power of his triumphant majority he imposed the Matignon agreements—named after the premier's residence—on French employers. In return for evacuating the factories and businesses they had illegally held and returning to their jobs, French workers won the right to collective bargaining, wage increases ranging from 7 to 15 percent, the forty-hour week, and two-week vacations with pay.

Cynicism teaches that you do not always get what you pay for but that you always pay for what you get. Because the Matignon agreements increased costs while decreasing hours, the inevitable result was a decline in productivity which made French exports even less competitive.

And it came as there was massive new spending to restore the cuts made in wages, salaries, and pensions by Laval. To reassure Radical voters, the Popular Front had promised during the campaign to defend the franc, but by the end of the summer these economic policies drove Blum and his minister of finance, Vincent Auriol, not just to consider touching the intangible but actually to do it. On 25 September the Poincaré franc was officially "revalued"—meaning devalued—by 34 percent. Conservatives had been howling since June about the "Ministry of Idleness," by which they concealed fears of economic ruin, and since July about the law dissolving all the right-wing leagues including the Cross of Fire, by which they concealed fears that only the Communists would have irregular shock troops. Now, they proclaimed, with a chorus of the many small investors in government bonds, that the Popular Front had broken faith with their patriotic sacrifices. When combined with a presumption of incompetence, the accusation of moral failing ensured that Blum and his cabinet lacked authority to compel a national consensus toward the new foreign policy crisis, a nightmare across the Pyrenees.

The Spanish Civil War transfixed France. Hitler's rearmament, even the remilitarizing of the Rhine, did not have the same effect. Along much of the German border, France had built a series of fortifications designed to withstand any attack. Behind this Maginot Line, named for the minister of war, a veteran and amputee, who had championed it, the army would wait in safety to finish off an exhausted enemy. Never mind that this strategy contradicted French promises to defend Eastern European allies: war so conceived was not terrifying and did not seem likely. Spain was different. Here was the first fighting in Western Europe since 1918. Memories from less than two decades past lurched into consciousness and generated fears for the future. Censorship had cushioned the realities of fighting in the trenches, but reporting and photography in every major newspaper now revealed the horrific impact of total war—tanks, tactical air support, the bombing of civilian targets. Would the fighting, or the refugees, spill over into France? Was civil war in Spain a precursor to civil war in France? The Popular Front Republican government in Madrid could be compared to Blum's in Paris, General Francisco Franco and his Nationalists to La Rocque and his Cross of Fire. Of course, the comparison was hardly valid: the French

Popular Front was utterly moderate compared to the Spanish version, while La Rocque was a Republican who had willingly complied with the law to dissolve his league. Yet the precedent was disturbing to minds already disturbed.

What should France do officially? Almost from the outset Mussolini and Hitler backed the Nationalists with armament, equipment, advisors, pilots, and "volunteer" infantry—the effort solidifying the ties between them. The Spanish Republicans had the money and the means to buy matching armament and equipment from France, if France were willing to sell. Communists fervently demanded at least this much support of a democratically elected government that included their Spanish counterparts and was under attack from fascism. Equally fervent in their opposition were the extreme Right, because they admired Franco and Mussolini, and some of the conservatives, because they detested the Republicans for their anti-Catholic policies. The moderates and the Radicals feared a Nationalist victory that would add a new hostile border to the Rhine and the Alps, yet they feared that any French support of the Republicans could lead to war with Italy or Germany or both. The Socialists were divided, but Blum, citing the authority of Jaurès, declared that war had to be avoided at all costs. His pacifism was genuine, and he had an ulterior motive, coordination with Great Britain. From the outset of the fighting British leaders—many of them leaning toward Franco—had decided that the Spanish problem was to be isolated through a policy of "nonintervention." Germany and Italy would promise not to assist the Nationalists and would do so anyway. France might well have done the same for the Republicans. But if the French refused to counter the remilitarization of the Rhineland without British support, they were not likely to go it alone in Spain. By adopting nonintervention, Blum could follow the policy that appealed to most of France, do nothing and hope for the best. And so France rebuffed the Republicans in Madrid. With that decision Blum definitively proved his failure of leadership.

On 24 February 1937 Blum announced a "pause" in the program of the Popular Front, not a retreat but a consolidation of the "ground conquered" during the first nine months of his ministry. Some conquest: although the level of industrial production climbed from 87 to 93, up 6.9 percent, and unemployment dipped slightly from 422,000 to 410,200, down 2.8 percent, the devaluation of the franc had utterly failed to stimulate exports, which at the end of 1936 remained at the 15.7 million franc level of 1935. By contrast, devaluation drastically raised the cost of imports, their total rising 22 percent, from 21.1 million francs to 25.8. The combination of higher prices and higher wages along with the restoration of cuts in civil service salaries and pensions pushed the cost of living index to 468. There was also a huge increase in the budget deficit, from 10.3 million francs in 1935 to 16.9 million in 1936. The Communists especially, but elements of the Socialist Party as well, felt that the Popular Front government should have meant more—exactly what was unclear but certainly more than the forty-hour week. And that was increasingly all, as the first months of 1937 saw prices rise steeply and the franc begin to fall from its September peg.[22] More and more, the Left began to lose faith in its experiment of governing. As a telling proof of pessimism, the construction trades delayed and delayed finishing the building for the Great Exhibition originally scheduled to open on May Day for fear that there would be no work to follow. When the police restrained violent left-wing demonstrators, sometimes with death and injury, Blum was denounced as no different than any other bourgeois politician. When a new series of strikes broke out, Auriol had to plead that labor strife was undermining the recovery. The foreign minister, Yvon Delbos, was embarrassed by questions about why the Popular Front in France refused to save the Popular Front in Spain.

Uneasy since the 1936 voting diminished them, the Radicals decided that a year of Blum proved not only that he was on the wrong track but that he was the wrong symbol. Late spring brought a precipitous decline in confidence abroad and at home about the cabinet's ability to manage France's economy. As the franc fell and the budget deficit ballooned, Blum asked for decree powers to devise a solution. The Chamber agreed, although more than thirty Radicals deserted the majority. The Senate, where the Radicals ran things and had not made any promises in 1936, refused. The Popular Front under the Socialists was over, but given the composition of the Chamber, there was no alternative to a government sustained by the Popular Front majority. By default leadership fell to the Radicals—as if they had planned the events since Blum announced the pause four months earlier. Yet who could want to assume power under these conditions: polarization greater even than in 1934, financial crisis, open questioning of foreign commitments? The answer was Chautemps, who had his reputation to remake after the Stavisky affair and whose acceptance as premier was melancholy testimony to how much else, how much worse, had gone on since 1934.

To maintain the facade of the coalition, Chautemps made Blum vice premier of the cabinet he formed on 22 June 1937, but Popular Front recast it was not. Because the new finance minister, Georges Bonnet, was said to be of the deflationary school, the senators hastened to give Chautemps the decree powers they had denied Blum. Now regarded by the Radicals as unwelcome allies, the Communists found themselves ostracized. They tarred themselves with more rounds of bitter strikes and violent demonstrations. They were then further tarred by the Moscow purge trials, especially after executions eliminated most of the military high command—Laval's failure to initiate staff talks with the Soviet Union was now called "inspired." But the Chautemps cabinet was also not in any way bold. Held over as foreign minister, Delbos took comfort that, being busy with Spain, Hitler and Mussolini did not do anything *more* and that Franco had not won *yet*.

Bonnet cut both the budget, to reduce the huge deficit, and some business taxes, to revive production, but in fear of ever greater social strife, he dared not tamper with the now sacrosanct forty-hour week. When he had little to show for his efforts, he took advantage of Blum's having breached the psychological barrier a year earlier and further devalued the franc, letting it float on currency markets, where by December it had declined from the Poincaré franc value 92 percent against the pound and 94 percent against the dollar. The economic results were mixed but arguably presaged improvement to come. The level of production held steady at 92, while unemployment finally plummeted 44,800 to 365,400, the lowest since 1934. The new devaluation made French exports much more attractive, raising their total 56 percent, to 24.4 million francs, but drove up the price of imports even more dramatically, by 71 percent to 44 million francs. Pending a curb on the appetite for imports, prices would rise in some proportion, and by December the cost of living index reached 585, up 25 percent in a single year. Likewise, pending a sustained recovery, budget deficits would remain but certainly not be as enormous as the nearly 24 billion francs that the combination of Blum spending and Bonnet tax reductions generated for 1937.[23] In six months the Chautemps cabinet had not done much, had not changed much, but the crises appeared to be easing. Politics as usual remained a dream, but there was always hope.

So, if you, like Delbos about to leave for the circuit of Eastern European capitals, wanted to keep your eyes closed and wish hard enough, you could be excused for believing that everything was all right or would be all right or would be better eventually or was at least not any worse. But if you opened your eyes, you would see only too clearly that Fitzgerald's desolation was applicable to France: "The big sudden blows . . . from outside"—the war and the depression—had done "the dramatic side of the work" on the Third Republic. "Another sort of blow that comes from within"—failure of nerve, absence of character, cynical internecine hatred—had not been truly felt until it was "too late to do anything about it." In 1938 France would "realize with finality that in some regard" it would "never be as good . . . again."

1 Winter

January to March

Some stories are quintessentially French. In January 1938 François Fache, from alpine Châteaurenard, went on trial for attempting to murder his former best friend, Louis Meynaud, seventeen months earlier. Coming between them was, of course, a woman. When he was twenty-eight, a dozen years ago, Fache fell in love and married sixteen-year-old Jeanne, "pure and proper and beautiful," as he testified. Because "certain diseases" had made him sterile, he was surprised a few months later when Jeanne announced that she was pregnant. Asked how, she replied, "Since it isn't the priest's, it must be yours." Curiously, Meynaud took him fishing soon after and suggested that he arrange for an abortion. Fache refused and became an enthusiastic father to a daughter, Juliette. If the geometry of this triangle seems obvious, it was not so at first to Fache, but in succeeding years he did notice that Juliette more and more resembled his friend. In February 1936 Jeanne became pregnant again and, a month later, desperately ill. On her deathbed with husband and daughter beside her, she moaned: "I have been wicked! The child is not yours, she is Louis Meynaud's. You must know, Juliette, that your true father is Louis Meynaud. And I have done worse. I tried two times to poison you, François." She went on that Meynaud had urged her to kill him and that she was now dying from Meynaud's attempt to provoke an abortion of this new pregnancy.

Although Fache reported the confession to the police, they refused to take any action, even when he five separate times requested an autopsy of his wife. Meynaud, he supposed, had influence with the authorities, perhaps because he had grown rich as a vegetable wholesaler and was one of the larger employers in the region. Finally deciding that justice was his to impose, Fache took a revolver, sought out his former friend, and shot him three times. Given their history, Meynaud was certain to survive these grievous wounds, but he had clearly suffered and was suffering yet. How would the jury react? Fache's attorney, the illustrious Henry Torrès come all the way from Paris, knew exactly how to incite animosity against a wealthy, powerful libertine and to provoke sympathy for his victim. Juliette, now eleven years old, came forward accompanied by a nun and confirmed her mother's dying words. To which Fache cried out, "Whether she is his daughter or mine, I cherish her." Of course, the jury declared him not guilty of attempted murder, but he did receive a sentence of six months in prison for the illegal use of a weapon.[1]

A trial that opened in early March at Paris was more to the point of the 1930s than any timeless working of the Emma Bovary plot. Between June and November 1936 the soap factory of the Cusinberche family in Clichy, on the northwestern edge of Paris, had four successive strikes. The last one ended in riot and the death of a strike leader, Arab immigrant Tahar Acherchour, allegedly shot by Paul Cusinberche, the factory manager. The charge before the court was murder, but the jury was actually deciding the responsibility of the Popular Front.

According to many accounts, the June 1936 strikes so lacked acrimony that the workers more often sang "Auprès de ma blonde" than "The Internationale." Not so chez Cusinberche. An outsider, a Communist labor agitator, stalked into the factory and announced: "You are no longer the boss. We are the masters now. Give me your keys." The 130 employees obeyed his order to stop work, some out of fear because there was no shortage of threats. The family settled "under terror" by granting everyone an additional fifteen francs an hour. The second and third strikes were a replay but with ever-greater political overtones—the third called in support of the Spanish Republicans, a *grève à l'espagnole*. When the fourth began in mid-November, only half the employees supported it, and Cusinberche obtained an injunction ordering the police to clear the factory. Perhaps fearful of offending the Popular Front's minister of the interior, Marx Dormoy, the Clichy police commissioner refused. Unwilling to abdicate before what he called "Bolshevism," Cusinberche then led the non-striking workers back to the factory on the morning of 23 November demanding a return to work. Armed with pickaxes, shovels, and iron bars, the strikers attacked them. Thinking to quell the riot, Cusinberche fired his pistol twice into the air. Other shots followed. Acherchour fell mortally wounded. Finally, the Clichy police arrived and arrested Cusinberche for murder.

In fact, the evidence was overwhelming in Cusinberche's favor. Many witnesses testified that he shot into the air, and when detectives examined his revolver, only two bullets had been fired. They also discovered numerous shell casings on the factory floor, proof that more than one weapon had been discharged, as well as another revolver of the same caliber, an 8 mm. There were bullets in Acherchour's trousers, strongly suggesting that he had a weapon himself. Seemingly embarrassed by the efficiency of his men, the police commissioner refused to explain why he did not apply the injunction. The prefect of police for Paris, Roger Langéron, declined to appear and was excused. Dormoy could not be subpoenaed because he could not be found. Cusinberche's attorney, Maurice Ribet, explained to a stupefied court that when a bailiff sought out Dormoy's address first at the Chamber of Deputies and then at the ministry of the interior, the official response came back that his "domicile in Paris is unknown." By quickly declaring Cusinberche not guilty, the jury was at least implicitly laying the blame on the Popular Front.[2]

The heart and soul of the Popular Front was Léon Blum, but a more unlikely leader of the working class would be hard to imagine. Blum had no experience at a job more physically taxing than reading and writing, not a callus unless it was from holding a pen too long, not a day wearing the *blouse bleu* (blue overalls) of a laborer, not a day in military uniform, no illegal or even clandestine activity, no running from the authorities of a capitalist bourgeois government, no leading a strike, no possible sense of what living a working-class life might mean or what sacrifices working-class political activity had cost. Instead, he had led the comfortable life of the bourgeois society he called the enemy, educated at its best schools, reviewing its cultural expressions in expensive publications, pontificating from its highest administrative court (the Conseil d'Etat), and, because of his myopia, excused from serving in its military even during the Great War. He had not the bona fides of a Lenin, Trotsky, Stalin, Mussolini, Hitler, or even his hero and mentor, Jean Jaurès, who although bourgeois himself was at least robust, vigorous, earthy. Blum was slender, delicate in gesture, a drooping mustache not entirely concealing a weak mouth, his rimless pince-nez exaggerating the mien of an intellectual, impeccable tailoring and gaiters making him seem overdressed. His speeches in a high-pitched voice were too precise to be inspiring, and he had neither the florid eloquence that distinguished Jaurès nor the charismatic assertion that elevated Clemenceau. Even Blum's partisans acknowledged that he was perceived as sensitive and precious. His detractors called him effete, even effeminate. Léon Daudet, coeditor of the right-wing *L'Action Française* and the most accomplished vilifier of the time, dismissed him as "the revolution in pearl-grey gloves." [3]

Blum's detractors were wrong. A dilettante he may have been when younger, but the Dreyfus affair made him lay on the armor of principle. And that principle he took from Jaurès: democratic socialism is the defense of Republicanism, the logical offspring of the French Revolution, the next step and what every reasonable man of conscience would eventually support. Blum's socialism was more Kantian than Marxian, although no less compelling, and became the substitute faith for a Jew who disdained religious practice while exalting the historical role played by the revolutionary tradition in the Jewish heritage of toleration and assimilation in France. Perhaps he would not have turned to active politics but for the assassination of Jaurès as the Great War began. Although the Socialist Party had always refused to serve in "bourgeois" cabinets, it made an exception for the "sacred union" of the nation during wartime. Marcel Sembat became minister of public works and Blum his principal secretary from the fall of 1914 until the end of 1916. Soon after, the crisis of 1917 created the context for the French Left during the next two decades.

The desperate course of the fighting and the Bolshevik revolution in Russia tore the Socialist Party in two, leading inevitably to the schism at Tours and the creation of the French Communist Party in December 1920. The rump retaining the name Socialists struggled to define themselves—reformist or revolutionary, national or international. Blum, elected to the Chamber of Deputies for the first time in 1919, found himself the heir to Jaurès, seeking a unifying middle ground. In a balancing act, he defined the parameters of the "loyal" Left in France: the Socialists did not formally renounce the goal of revolution but would act as reformers; they preached international brotherhood but granted their ultimate allegiance to France. In practice the critical issue was the basis on which to accept ministerial responsibility. Blum envisaged two situations justifying the assumption of cabinet office and in carrying the party with him ensured his leadership. There was, of course, a "conquest of power," the—highly unlikely—possibility of a Socialist electoral victory and the opportunity to transform the existing order. There was also an "exercise of power," the—more plausible—victory of a coalition in which the Socialists had the dominant voice and, while unable to carry through their entire program, could enact essential elements.

Viewing national and international issues through the prism of this strategy, the Socialists saw Germany under the German Socialists as more congenial than France under the National Bloc, the Ruhr occupation as hostile and illegal, the Poincaré franc as rescuing the bourgeoisie at the expense of the proletariat, the demonstrations of 6 February 1934 as an attempted fascist coup d'état, the danger from Hitler as a rationale for French militarism. Three times, in 1929, 1930, and 1933, Blum spurned Radical offers for Socialist participation in a cabinet and so pushed both the Radicals to the Center and the Chamber as a whole toward the Center-Right. Despite Nazi rule in Germany and depression in France, he continued the party's ritual of voting against the "bourgeois" budget and against the appropriation for "militaristic" national defense. Even in the aftermath of 6 February, even after the Left sponsored impressive counterdemonstrations on 9 February and a "counter-fascist" general strike on 12 February, he rejected Doumergue's invitation to join the national union cabinet and refused entreaties to refrain from open opposition.

When the April-May 1936 legislative elections gave a majority to the Popular Front and made the Socialists the largest party in the Chamber of Deputies, the conditions necessary for an "exercise of power" had finally been achieved. In the party newspaper, *Le Populaire,* Blum demonstrated the unity of parliamentary custom with personal ambition through his assertion, "We are ready to accept the role that has fallen to us—to form and to assume direction of the Popular Front government." A certain cynicism apparent, the centrist newspaper *Le Temps* warned, "Monsieur Léon Blum will now have to take responsibility for the inviolability of the national frontiers, the prosperity of France, the integrity of our currency and foreign exchange, the state of the Treasury, the recovery of business, the absorption of unemployment, and many other things."[4] Custom and ambition aside, the cynics had it right: Blum was now in charge, but he was in every way the wrong choice. Even he had misgivings, saying two years later: "I asked in June 1936: am I a leader? I did not know the answer and, to tell the truth, I do not know the answer any better today. But, perhaps, if I committed errors it was because of not having been enough of a leader and not because of having been too much of one."[5] Blum was sixty-four years old when he stood before the Chamber of Deputies on 6 June 1936 to present his cabinet, to receive the vote of confidence guaranteed by the victory of the Popular Front, and to become thereby the first Jewish and the first Socialist premier in the history of France. His character and manner were long since formed and set, beyond any changing merely from the elevation to power. He was an intellectual drawn into politics and the leader of his party more by the power of his argument than by the force of his will. Clemenceau had been sixty-four when he became premier for the first time in 1905 and through his ferocity vindicated the nickname "Tiger." From the first day Blum proved that he was the anti-Clemenceau.

A deputy from the far Right, Xavier Vallat, who would earn infamy under the Vichy government as director of the Commission for the Jewish Question, served up an insult both anti-Semitic and anti-intellectual. "I have the special duty here," he proclaimed, "of saying aloud what everyone is thinking to himself: that to govern this peasant nation of

France it is better to have someone whose origins, no matter how modest, spring from our soil than to have a subtle Talmudist." Although
described as incensed, Blum let Edouard Herriot, the president of the
Chamber, call Vallat to order. From the Center-Right Paul Reynaud,
who knew his economics better than most, attacked the most vulnerable
point of the social reform plans advocated by the Popular Front. The
increased costs to production would cripple French imports without a
prior devaluation of the franc, and that, he reminded the deputies, the
Popular Front had ruled out. Rather than confront this argument, Blum
simply dismissed it as an attempt to frighten the middle class with a
threat to the Poincaré franc. But of course, he wound up devaluing in
September, and under worse conditions. By his declarations about the
sit-down strikes, Blum generated more fear among the middle and
upper classes than anything he might have said about the franc. While
admitting that occupation of the factories was clearly illegal, he cate-
gorically refused to force their evacuation: "If you expect that from the
government, I can tell you that you will wait in vain."[6]

And this equivocation continued in foreign affairs. When the Spanish Civil War began in July, Blum initially favored providing all possible
assistance to the Republicans until he learned that his Popular Front
partners, the Radicals and, more important, British leaders, were opposed. Although Blum would say of the decision that "my soul is torn
asunder," he adopted the nonintervention policy that he, largely, and the
British respected and which the Germans, the Italians, and the Soviets ignored. He even convinced himself that this charade was necessary to prevent the outbreak of general war—a defensible point. But indefensible
and pathetic was his self-pitying comparison of the moral dilemma to a
crucifixion—"I have known, I can assure you, some very cruel stations"—and abject lying about its effect: "To my knowledge, not a single
proof nor even a solid presumption exists that any of the respective governments has, since the promulgation of the enforcement measures, violated the engagement."[7] Clemenceau never shied from a fight; Blum re-
coiled from all of them, all except an exchange of nastiness—no getting
dirty or risking injury—with Italy. After successfully defying the League
of Nations over Ethiopia, Mussolini implied that a rapprochement was
possible if French leaders recognized the new Italian Empire in Africa

and accepted the inevitability of Franco's victory in Spain. Blum refused to take the offer seriously, convinced, as was British Foreign Secretary Anthony Eden, that Mussolini had already been drawn into Hitler's orbit. Or perhaps not: Italy's interests were by no means entirely congruent with Germany's. Blum could not forgive how the Fascists consolidated their power through the crushing of the Reform Socialist group and the assassination of its leader. "You forget that I was the friend of [Giacomo] Matteotti," he said in explanation.[8]

Even with the fate of his cabinet, even with the meaning of the Popular Front at stake, Blum found reasons not to fight. When his request for decree authority to deal with the economy was approved by the Chamber of Deputies but rejected by the Senate, he accepted the end to his "exercise of power." He could have provoked a constitutional crisis by asking Albert Lebrun, the president of the Republic, to dissolve the Chamber and hold legislative elections, which might have confirmed the Popular Front majority and led the Senate to back down. But dissolution required as well the consent of the Senate, which might have refused, and Lebrun himself had never been a friend of the Popular Front. Blum might instead have called on the members of the working class to demonstrate and manifest their will—as the left wing of the Socialist Party, led by Jean Zyromski and Marceau Pivert, demanded. He refused either option, defending the decision as necessary to prevent massive disorder at a critical time in French and European history. To persuade the party to accept the new Chautemps cabinet in which he would serve as vice premier, Blum argued irenically: "We cannot refuse to participate in a Popular Front government under Radical leadership, for we must keep intact the Popular Front majority. We must safeguard the social legislation we have enacted. We must preserve the past and prepare for the future." With much trepidation the Socialist Party did so. But better measuring its leader's state of mind was Blum's exclamation to American Ambassador William C. Bullitt: "I have had enough! Everything that I have attempted to do has been blocked."[9]

The spirit of the Popular Front did not dwell within Camille Chautemps. As a *ministre d'état* in the Blum cabinet—meaning minister without portfolio—he had been along for the ride, and now he had the reins. Like more than a few of the Radicals, he was relieved that the character of the Popular Front experiment had now changed decisively. From a government of the Left with an extension toward the Center, it had become a government of the Center with an extension toward the Left: a reversion to the palmy days of Radical tradition. If Blum was the anti-Clemenceau, Chautemps was the anti-Blum. He was thirteen years younger, and instead of coming to politics reluctantly and from principle, he had assumed it as a birthright. For Radical politics was the family business: his father, Emile, a former deputy, minister, and president of the Senate; his uncle, Alphonse, a former deputy and senator; his brother, Emile, a former deputy, who died heroically in the war. Camille Chautemps worked on his first political campaign when he was seventeen, and although he took time out to get a law degree, it was politics he would practice. Elected to the Chamber of Deputies in 1919, to the Senate in 1934, he had by June 1937 and age fifty-two been a minister thirteen times and premier twice. When the Radicals were in control, Chautemps most often held the ministry of the interior, at the Place Beauvau, where maintaining domestic order was only slightly more important than parceling out patronage and making elections. That he was first entrusted with the keys to this kingdom in Herriot's 1924 cabinet is all the proof necessary that his excellence at balancing these various responsibilities was recognized early.

Angular, his temples balding, Chautemps was unprepossessing with his tidy mustache above a ferret mouth and furtive eyes, as if he had more than a little to hide. Of the last there was always more suspicion than fact, and the Stavisky affair provided no definitive conclusion. Chautemps was premier and minister of the interior when the scandal broke, and two members of his cabinet, Albert Dalimier, colonies, and Eugène Rainaldy, justice, were quickly implicated. Chautemps's immediate instinct was to contain the damage, which might be exponential because his brother-in-law directed the prosecutorial office that had granted Stavisky so many delays, and Stavisky was said to have sown his political contributions in Radical fields. The detectives who cornered Stavisky in Chamonix and oversaw his "suicide" were from the State Security Police headquartered at the Place Beauvau. But who could say how much Chautemps had known or abetted? And he was nowhere near power when assistant prosecutor Albert Prince was discovered dismembered by the Lyon-to-Paris express six weeks later.

Although despised by conservatives, for whom he epitomized corruption in the Third Republic, Chautemps remained a Radical wheelhorse who knew where too many secrets had been hidden. His return to prominence after Stavisky came as minister of public works—handy for pork-barreling—in the Albert Sarraut cabinet from January to June 1936, where he did not demand action against the German remilitarization of the Rhineland. Because a year in the Popular Front cabinet taught him that Blum was not a fighter, when he took over on 22 June 1937 he was confident that he could alter the Socialist economic program in almost any way as long as the forty-hour week was left intangible. Chautemps and Georges Bonnet, the minister of finance, reverted to the Radical program of retrenchment. Labor leaders and especially Communist labor leaders responded with renewed confrontations in the late fall and early winter, most spectacularly an occupation of the Goodrich tire factory at Colombes. There followed the general strike of truck drivers and the bus and Métro systems in Paris which greeted Yvon Delbos on his return from Eastern Europe at the end of the year. In January negotiations over a code of labor relations between the independent-but-Socialist-leaning unions in the General Labor Confederation and the owners and employers in the Confédération Générale de la Production Française (General Confederation of French Producers) broke down completely. Also broken was even the semblance of the Popular Front. When the legislature reconvened after its holiday recess, Chautemps told the Chamber of Deputies, "With sadness but firmness, I must say that if certain men persist in troubling the peace needed by this nation, the force of law must come down upon them." There was no doubt that he meant the unions. When the Communist deputies threatened to deny Chautemps their votes, he replied that he would make up the difference elsewhere and excommunicated them from his majority. Blum and the other Socialist ministers resigned in protest, collapsing the cabinet on 15 January.[10]

And the new premier was—Chautemps. Bonnet tried to construct a cabinet, but the Socialists recognized him as an antagonist and refused their votes. Blum then sought a not-so-national alliance from the far

Left to the Center-Right, from Maurice Thorez, leader of the Communists, to Reynaud, but found no one right of the Socialists willing to consider Communist participation. A reconstituted Chautemps cabinet—all Radicals and reluctantly supported by the Socialists—seemed the easiest alternative to a prolonged crisis of government. Edouard Daladier at war and Yvon Delbos at foreign affairs remained, but, to placate Socialist opinion, the slightly less orthodox Paul Marchandeau replaced Bonnet at finance. On 21 January Chautemps won a vote of confidence 501 to 1, with slightly more than 100 deputies of the Right and Center-Right abstaining. *Le Figaro*'s political columnist Wladimir d'Ormesson called it "unanimity in equivocation." One Radical, André Albert, quipped, "The bigger the majority, the shorter its life." Both meant that the cabinet was a stopgap and weak. Parliamentary gymnastics had little resonance and less appeal outside the Chamber when there already was so much trouble and more looming. The cold weather of New Year's had set in: ice skaters on the lakes of the Bois de Boulogne, the Marne River frozen solid near Châlons, the temperature five degrees Fahrenheit at Vichy and in the mid-twenties at Paris. The news was all bad. Leaks from the investigation of a shadowy right-wing terrorist group, the Cagoulard, turned up links to agents of Mussolini. The Japanese demands on China were ever greater. Viewing German rearmament, Romania considered itself a "land under menace." Desperate fighting continued in Spain. Hitler browbeat Austrian chancellor Kurt von Schuschnigg at Berchtesgaden and raised the specter of *Anschluss*, forcible annexation of Austria to Germany. Articles about military strategy, about tanks and antitank mines, further heightened apprehensions of war. So did upbraiding by the likes of d'Ormesson: "The nations which have retained their nerve must, as soon as possible, recognize their responsibilities, their duties, and their strength." Murder, the German serial killer Bruno Weidmann revealed under interrogation, was an utterly banal act. But not for Louise Habuterne: she came to work at a factory in Courbevoie dressed all in black, shot dead her former lover because he had married another, and then jumped to her death in the icy Seine River.[11]

By mid-February the focus for the threat of looming trouble could be located clearly in Germany. Since Hitler's accession to power in 1933, followed by his aggressive foreign policy and rearmament, the dominant French attitude toward Germany had shifted from hatred—traditional since 1870 and reinforced by the Great War—to fear. The Nazi government exploited this change by encouraging the French to see in Germany what they wanted to see. The Right, more or less openly anti-Semitic, suspected Jewish refugees of inciting France to fight Germany on their behalf and for the ultimate victory of communism. Not just the Right, almost no one wanted to fight. Veterans groups especially, but the whole country generally, had an overwhelming desire for peace and the belief that war, not Germany, was the great enemy. The more Germany was fearsome, the more France grew timorous. Some, most often among the Center-Right but spread throughout the Center as well, saw German vigor and thought France's best bet to be a junior partnership, a revival of the pre-1914 policy of Joseph Caillaux, still a senator in 1938. Pierre-Etienne Flandin was perhaps the most prominent of them, but Bonnet and Anatole de Monzie, both powers among the Radicals, were not far behind. Bribes paid to venal and corrupt French dailies and weeklies ensured that Germany got the coverage it wanted. A few journalists, including Pertinax (André Géraud) and Henri de Kérillis, a deputy as well, decried this "allure of treason" and the "crisis of French nationalism," but they were largely ignored, as the French tried to pretend that the whole German problem would go away.[12]

On 20 February Hitler gave notice that all the pretending was for naught. In an extraordinarily inflammatory speech before the Reichstag, he declared Germany's unwavering support for Franco in Spain, seconded Japanese demands on China, emphasized his determination to "defend the interests" of ethnic Germans—seven million Austrians and three million Sudetens in Czechoslovakia—separated from the Third Reich by the Versailles treaty, and spoke contemptuously of France as suffering from democratic decadence. Later that evening Eden, the most prominent British proponent of collective security, resigned as foreign secretary. Two days later the words of Prime Minister Neville Chamberlain made clear the meaning of the change: "We must try not to delude small weak nations into thinking that they will be protected by the League against aggression—and acting accordingly when we know that nothing of the kind can be expected." Given that France had obligations to Czechoslovakia and an interest in the survival of Austria, both small, weak nations, the violence of Hitler's words and the capitulation of Chamberlain's were hammer blows to the foreign policy elaborated since 1918. Absent British support, would France stand up to Germany? And if so, could Britain be counted upon as an ally if general war was the result? At least publicly, Delbos insisted to the Chamber's foreign affairs committee on 23 February that nothing material had changed.[13]

Because this assertion calmed no fears, there followed two days later a full-scale debate in the Chamber of Deputies on France's foreign policy, the only one during all of 1938.[14] One of the least impressed by Delbos's brave face was Ernest Pezet, a vice president of the foreign affairs committee and one of the Center-Right Catholic Démocrates Populaires (Popular Democrats). How, he asked, was it possible to imagine that nothing material had changed when everything was in flux? Referring to Chamberlain's warning about not deluding small weak nations, he recalled the course of French foreign policy since the Great War: "I can only say that these small nations have been deluded for nineteen years; they have been told to hold out, to resist, and to organize themselves. They have been told that they would be helped if the occasion arose. And now when the moment has come, are we to drop them? That is what I call 'deluding' them." And to conclude he raised the terrible question on everyone's mind. "If the same technique of pressure and interference that Germany is now applying to Austria is also applied to Czechoslovakia, will France carry out her obligations under the Franco-Czech treaties of 25 January 1924 and 16 October 1925? What advice did M. Delbos give the Czechs [in December 1937]? Did he advise them to resist or to yield and resign themselves?"

No one had spoken so bluntly on an issue of foreign affairs since Raymond Poincaré and the occupation of the Ruhr. With the psychological barrier down, there was more to come. For the Socialists, Salomon Grunbach quoted Hitler's *Mein Kampf* as a warning and then bitterly attacked Flandin, the partisan-in-chief of accommodation with Germany who two weeks earlier had recommended French "retrenchment" in Eastern Europe. "As a former premier, his responsibility is three times heavier than if he were an ordinary mortal like myself. . . . I am profoundly convinced that if the world is left with the impression that his statements command support, the danger to peace would be enormous, for it would be an encouragement to all the enemies of peace and to those who wish to demoralize the French nation. And if we were to follow M. Flandin's policy of retrenchment, France would disappear not temporarily but forever from the world chessboard." The Left cheered, while some of the Center and Right booed. But only some, for there remained a stridently nationalistic strain among the Right and Center. Jean Ybarnégaray, parliamentary leader of the Parti Social Français (French Social Party), the political group Colonel de la Rocque had formed when the Cross of Fire was ordered disbanded, quickly continued the assault on Flandin and his ilk. The words were scathing: "There is no lack of people who will crowd the waiting rooms of [Joachim von] Ribbentrop, [Joseph] Goebbels and [Hermann] Goering, and who, without any mandate and without any authority from the government, go there like so many pilgrims to collect promises and assurances. . . . But I shall venture to say to them . . . that in doing so they are not serving the interests of France. Peace? Yes. There is not a Frenchman who does not want peace passionately. But peace at any price—No! There are some blind or cowardly men who say, 'We shall never mobilize for Austria or Czechoslovakia.' At the risk of making myself unpopular, I reply to them that it is not for Austria or Czechoslovakia that we shall be mobilizing, but for ourselves, because it is on the Danube today that the fate of our frontiers is being settled."

If Pezet's words had echoes of Poincaré, Ybarnégaray's were a fair imitation of Clemenceau. The resemblance was all the greater when he confronted Delbos directly on the terrible question. "What are you going to do about Austria? . . . What will you do? What can you do? The independence of Austria has been guaranteed by the League of Nations. . . . Is it true . . . that collective security is dead? If so, say it. Better to be frank than cling to illusions. My question is a simple one: are you going to save Austrian independence? Can you do it? Do you want to do it? If I ask this question about Austria, it is because you are now in a far better position than you may be very shortly, when Czechoslovakia is, in turn, involved. . . . Are France and England ready to unite on the Danube as they have united on the Rhine, and to defend nations whose independence they have guaranteed? If yes, say so openly; everything may yet be saved. If no, say so just as openly. But in that case, it will be a different policy, a policy of weakness and abdication—a policy of retrenchment behind the Maginot Line. If that is your policy, declare it, M. Delbos!"

In using the word *retrenchment,* Ybarnégaray was shooting across Flandin's bow. To do so meant drawing return fire of varying caliber from his allies among the Center and Right. Jean Mistler, president of the foreign affairs committee, responded with counsel that promised only to deny: "In certain vital areas—the Rhine, the Mediterranean, and Central Europe—there is a point at which great risks begin and beyond which this country must commit itself entirely. Because we cannot pursue such a policy alone, we must certainly act in close agreement with Great Britain. And it would be a mistake hurriedly to adopt an attitude that would not be without danger." Monzie defended retrenchment en passant—"Shall we do nothing? I do not think that is M. Flandin's intention"—while shifting the ground of the debate from present decisions to past failures and future agendas. Italy, he claimed, was the key, and if only Mussolini had not been alienated, Hitler would not dare to threaten Austria; if only Mussolini could yet be won to stand side by side with France in Latin brotherhood, Hitler would never dare again. Launched in that direction of conjecture, successive speakers from the Right called for making up to Mussolini or to Franco or to both. They included even Louis Marin, in the 1920s bold enough to criticize Poincaré for hesitating to act alone in the Ruhr but now seeking safety in numbers.

André Albert, the youngest of the deputies and perhaps with the same impudence of youth that led to his quip about the Chautemps majority, offended all of them by daring to say that they apparently had no guts. In doing so, he was at least bringing the debate back to where Ybarnégary had left it: if merit there was to retrenchment, let the argument be made directly. Jean Matigny then offered the case for capitulation in the best tradition of Caillaux, whose spokesman in the Chamber he was: "Since, rightly or wrongly, we have not created an army fitted for our foreign policy, and since it would take years to create one, we must—unless we are mad—adopt a foreign policy compatible with our military possibilities." But there was a sense that the time for surrogates had passed, and Flandin himself stood to a raucous mixture of cheers and hoots. More than two decades earlier he had been a heroic pilot during the Great War. Now he was the very image of the wealthy bourgeoisie he represented in leading the centrist Alliance Démocratique (Democratic Alliance): tall, paunchy, pallid, disdainful, impeccably dressed in English woolens. Because he had denounced the demonstrations of 6 February, because although serving in Gaston Doumergue's national union cabinet he rejected the proposed reforms to strengthen the executive, he once had a certain trust among the Left. That disappeared when as premier in 1934–35 he adopted deflation to combat depression. Although he was said to support the League of Nations, he aligned himself with Pierre Laval in opposing sanctions against Italy for the invasion of Ethiopia, and, as foreign minister in March 1936, he was singularly unwilling to act against Hitler's reoccupation of the Rhineland. Fear that war would mean either the victory of the Nazis or the victory of the Communists but surely not the victory of France was behind his policy of retrenchment—as was the fear shared by so many of the French with money and property to lose.

Flandin began by declaring that the present unfolding of events made this debate truly grave because France was likely soon to be faced with the fateful choice of peace or another war. And the choice, he insisted, had to be for peace. Great Britain, without whose support France dared not move, was against involvement beyond the Rhine—he quoted extensively from Chamberlain's speech on 22 February as proof. French armaments were in disarray—he cited production figures to demonstrate. "Your policy is out of date," he proclaimed to Delbos. "It is based entirely on old-fashioned formulae about the League of Nations, collective security, and mutual assistance." Regarding Austria, he was dismissive: "In the circumstances, let us, for goodness sake, stop striking heroic poses. . . . nothing can be worse than not to look the facts in the face." And almost so of Czechoslovakia: "Far be it from me to suggest that we should repudiate our obligations, but we ought to make sure whether we are able to meet them." European hegemony might tempt Germany, he admitted, "but it was also the dream of Napoléon, and his imperialist attempt failed when it came up against a coalition." Here Flandin reached the essence of his argument: "Today we are sheltered behind the Maginot Line. If ever we are attacked, we shall be strong enough to hold out until the freedom-loving countries of Europe come to our aid as they did in 1914."

Although Flandin's history was wrong—France started with a coalition in the Great War—what had to be taken on was his spirit of abdication, but no one from the government bench rose to do so. Instead, it was Paul Reynaud, wealthy bourgeois himself, Center-Right independent, the soundest financial mind in the Chamber, vain with good reason, diminutive, feisty, and spoiling for a fight. "We all want peace," he agreed, "but it is a question of method." For France to abdicate the resources of Central and Eastern Europe to Germany would be fatal. "You say there is the Maginot Line, . . . but there is not a single expert who will claim that any line of fortifications can resist indefinitely against an overwhelming accumulation of tanks and artillery. . . . and what chance would France have if half of Europe was against her?" He insisted that, despite Eden's resignation, despite Chamberlain's words, Britain would not abandon France if French leaders took the initiative in Central Europe. "There are some," referring to Flandin and Caillaux and their followers, "who believe that France could save peace by surrendering her role in Europe. I maintain, to the contrary, that such surrender would lead to war. France has the choice between two policies. Either she maintains the balance of power in Europe, or she retreats to the Maginot Line to begin with. . . . There is only one way of killing France, and that is by isolating her. That is what some are proposing." Then he concluded, in the hope that the deputies might force the creation of a broad national cabinet, a new "sacred union" government, "The world will soon be startled to see that it is impossible either internally or internationally to speculate on France's lack of unity." Much of the Chamber erupted in cheers.

And, finally, Delbos stood to declare his position. He looked beaten down, but his words had a ring of tenacity. "Those advocating a policy of abdication forget that France has something more to defend than her own frontiers. Must we throw to the winds France's greatness, her history, and the ideals that inspire her, ideals which will not allow her to forget her mission to the world? Are we to throw to the winds the respect

for our signature, our loyalty to our friends, our feeling of European solidarity?" He was categorical about Czechoslovakia: "I wish to affirm
once again . . . France's affection for the brave people of Czechoslovakia
and their government, who combine, with so much wisdom, their will
for independence and their concern for peace. And I desire to say once
again that our obligations to Czechoslovakia will, if it comes to it, be
faithfully observed." He was evasive about Austria: "Austrian independence is essential to the balance of power in Europe." Chautemps immediately intervened, seconding Delbos: "It is my duty to associate myself with the statement of the foreign minister and to affirm clearly that
France cannot abandon Central Europe to its fate or fail in her alliance
which makes it an obligation of honor for her to protect the independence of Czechoslovakia. . . . France must remain faithful to her historical policy based on the union of peaceful nations, on human liberty and
on the respect of treaties. It is always a weakness to betray the moral principles which dominate both the collective life and the individual conscience." Fine words, all, but no mention of Austria. And Chautemps's
conclusion was ambivalent: "The French Republic will overcome not
through war but in peace the obstacles on the road to her destiny." But
it was enough for the day, and the cabinet was rewarded with a strong
vote of confidence, 439 to 2, and nearly 150 abstentions.

The echo outside the small political world was hard to assess. There
were, as always, so many distractions. At the end of January a powerful
windstorm struck the Paris suburb of Villejuif, killing a young girl and
leaving damage that was still being cleared two weeks later. New losses
on the American stock exchange were frightening the French investors
who had sheltered their francs on Wall Street for fear of the Popular
Front. Antoine de Saint-Exupéry, celebrated for the heroic in his flying
and the mystical in his prose, barely survived another kind of crash
when his plane went down in Guatemala. The annual automobile
show packed in buyers and would-be buyers. Fashion shows tempted
women—and men—with the most form-fitting dresses of the decade
in slimming stripes and set off by hats for day, hats for evening, hats with
bills, hats with gaudy bows, hats with chiffon scarves. A celebration
commemorated fifty years of Arthur Conan Doyle's Sherlock Holmes.
The serious said Charles Boyer's *Orage* (The Storm) was the movie not

to be missed, but the need to laugh led more to *Laurel et Hardy au Far West* (*Way Out West*)—because even with such distractions the essential peril of the moment kept barging into consciousness.

The sinking of the British freighter *Endymion* off Spain by an unknown submarine, presumably Italian, raised questions about the safety of all merchant shipping in the Mediterranean. The bombing of Barcelona, 155 killed and 30 buildings destroyed, by German planes flying for Franco led to fears of widespread attacks on civilians in open cities. The start of a new purge trial in the Soviet Union, this time with twenty-one "Old Bolsheviks" in the dock, revived all the suspicions that the Communist revolution was consuming itself. At the beginning of March, Chautemps and Daladier, anxious and apprehensive, requested new military appropriations: for the air force, 1,700 million francs; for the navy, 800 million; for the army, 700 million. The deputies and senators approved them unanimously. Were these votes only bravado, and were they in time? From all over, the foreign correspondents for the major Paris newspapers were sending in disturbing reports. Other than the small group around Eden, British leaders viewed Austria's fate as unimportant. Mussolini, for whom Austrian independence had been a national priority, now regarded its absorption by Germany as natural and therefore inevitable. Speculation about the effect upon Czechoslovakia became less guarded. Belgian leaders recognized the Italian Empire to curry favor with the new Berlin-Rome Axis about which Europe was increasingly rotating.

But their debate on foreign policy concluded, deputies and senators now turned to the economy. On 9 February Daladier complained to the Chamber's armed forces committee that the Popular Front's social legislation hampered rearmament efforts, citing especially that the forty-hour workweek in France was 30 percent less than the fifty-two-hour week in Germany. The differential was far more serious when comparing the results of production, especially of military aircraft, with France turning out 40 each month, Germany 180, Great Britain 130, and Italy 100. But was it politically possible—was it even conceivable—for the Chamber of Deputies elected in 1936 to abridge the forty-hour week, the sacred accomplishment of the Popular Front? Gestures of conciliation were an overture. From Reynaud, disliked by labor leaders as much as

Bonnet for his classical-liberal economics, came the offer of a truce in the national interest. On 10 February, before the centrist Cercle Républicain (Republican Club), he declared: "I am convinced that we are at the end of an era, the era of financial mistakes. If the economic machinery does not turn, the fault does not lie in the ill will of any one class. What is lacking is a policy and determination to carry it out. A three-year plan must be applied, because the country cannot be put back on its feet in less than three years." And immediately after the foreign policy debate, Chautemps introduced a broad proposal with the title *Statut moderne du travail* (Progressive Labor Statute) to codify issues of collective bargaining, hiring, firing, layoffs, and strikes. Called by the cabinet an attempt to create a "better social climate," the legislation was pitched toward working-class demands. What satisfied the Chamber would not, of course, appeal to the Senate. Chautemps therefore had the calculated opportunity to demonstrate the sincerity of his new labor consciousness by posing the question of confidence before the Senate for passage on 4 March of the first element in the bill, regulations governing all aspects of collective bargaining and binding arbitration. Then, without explanation, he abandoned the rest of the proposal as he asked for decree powers to deal with what he called financial emergencies. When both senators and deputies resisted, he used their hostility as the justification for resigning with his entire cabinet on 10 March.[15] Chautemps was in a hurry to leave office not because of this opposition but because he had fair warning that Hitler was about to move against Austria. If he were not premier, he would not have to decide France's response. If he were not premier, he could not be blamed for what happened—so he thought and would argue for the rest of his life. The man of the Stavisky scandal became the man of the *Anschluss*.

In Vienna on 9 March Schuschnigg announced a plebiscite to be held four days later by which he hoped to demonstrate Austrian resolve for independence. Enraged by this effort to frustrate him, Hitler decided to carry out *Anschluss* immediately and by force, he and his troops entering Austria on 11 March—to cheering crowds. From Berlin *Le Figaro*'s usually reliable correspondent, Bernard Millot, reported, "Many here suppose that the absence of a government in Paris has only precipitated Hitler's decision." In his memoirs General Maurice

Gamelin, chief of the general staff, repeated the charge. While Gamelin did use every possible excuse in covering his own reluctance to act, on 11 March he was not consulted when Chautemps, Daladier, and Delbos decided in accord with Britain to acquiesce in this latest violation of the Versailles terms. Even in 1938, the year of excuses, Chautemps's was rejected. The reaction in the press was immediate and visceral. Henri de Kérillis, Nationalist as deputy and journalist, wrote in *L'Epoque,* "There is not a Frenchman who does not sense that his country may soon no longer have the right to maintain a colonial empire, to retain the provinces of Alsace and Lorraine where German is spoken, or to live free and proud beside a Germany in control of Vienna, Prague, and Poznan." *Le Figaro*'s editor-in-chief, Lucien Romier, called Chautemps's resignation in the face of the German threat "a painful, humiliating spectacle," while its principal columnist, d'Ormesson, raised the alarm: "Enough politics—face up to things! Enough retreat—the hour of the political Marne has sounded!" *Le Temps* warned that Hitler's goal of a *Mitteleuropa,* a Central European empire, was unmistakably clear and that *Anschluss* represented "the end of a political order upon which for twenty years the peace of Europe had been founded." [16]

What was to be done? Nearly a hundred deputies petitioned President Lebrun to create a "ministry of national union to confront grave events." But who on the Left could lead such a ministry—*on the Left,* because the election results of 1936 had made a cabinet of the Center or Right impossible. With few options Lebrun turned to Blum, whose absence from public life for over a month following the sudden death of his wife on 22 January left him untarnished by Chautemps's performance. Blum immediately declared his intention to form a ministry reaching left to the Communists and right to the Catholic Nationalists—from Maurice Thorez to Louis Marin. On 12 March, after first obtaining a mandate from the Socialist Party's ruling council, he addressed a hastily convened meeting of the deputies from the Center and Right, convinced that their traditional nationalism would overcome their hesitation about serving beside Communists. As so frequently in his career, Blum misjudged the situation, surprised at their hostility to the record of the Popular Front and to himself. In reply he warned: "Take care. If you do not accept today, the nation will turn against you, and you may not be able to count on the Socialist Party in circumstances perhaps even more serious." He asked them to recognize "what appears to me to be the common interest of all the parties of the Republic because that represents the common interest of the nation itself." Some appeared convinced, especially Reynaud, Marin, Kérillis, and Clemenceau's disciple, Georges Mandel. Kérillis sprang forward to grasp Blum's hand and call him "a great Frenchman." [17]

Yet when the deputies of the Center and Right voted among themselves, their resentments, fears, and prejudices greatly counterbalanced their sense of national peril: 152 to 5 against participation in a Blum cabinet. Flandin's opposition was especially telling and revealed the degree to which *Anschluss* had altered opinions in the less than three weeks since the foreign policy debate. Rejecting what he called the Communist Party's "posture of war," which he attributed to the influence of Moscow, he called for a "Chamberlain policy," negotiations with Germany and Italy. To general applause he insisted in words defining French weakness: "I do not accept that France play in Central Europe, regarding Czechoslovakia or any other nation, the role of gendarme which she is in no position to sustain. I have always said French policy should be aligned with that of her ally, Great Britain. Where Britain will not act, we will not act." Weighing heavily against Blum was also the widespread belief that he had alienated Italy and thereby made *Anschluss* inevitable. Earlier that day Lucien Bourguès, the foreign policy specialist for the mass circulation *Le Petit Parisien,* had written that "the loosening of ties knotting us to Rome has borne bitter fruit." And the following day in the far Right *La Liberté,* Bertrand de Jouvenel, renegade Radical now seeking a national savior, recalled his famous interview with Mussolini in June 1936, three months after Hitler remilitarized the Rhineland: "With you," Mussolini had said, referring to France, "I will defend Czechoslovakia; with me, you will defend Austria. There is no other means of stopping the conquest of Central Europe by Germany." And for good measure Caillaux had made clear that he and his allies would oppose a Thorez-to-Marin cabinet in the Senate if only from fear of German reaction: "If tomorrow brings an ultimatum, will it be war or a new humiliation? To avoid this double risk, I prefer to resist with all my strength participation by the Communists." [18]

And so in the wake of the gravest foreign policy disaster since the Great War, France was still without a cabinet. Swinging wildly at all targets, *Le Figaro*'s d'Ormesson expressed the national frustration: "Let everyone take notice! We will not easily pardon those who are responsible for this scandal and this shame. In the face of a Germany which took five hours to conquer a nation and a people, France has, in five days, not managed to constitute a government worthy of herself." When Blum did form a cabinet of Radicals and Socialists on 13 March, d'Ormesson dismissed it as "not serious." More important, so did the Germans and the Italians and the British, according to foreign correspondents. Blum himself admitted that a cabinet "of the June 1936 type" was ill-suited to the moment because divisive, but he constructed it as if he knew that here was the last and losing stand of the Popular Front. Purposely offending the Center and Right, he took finance for himself while placing Marx Dormoy at interior and Joseph Paul-Boncour at foreign affairs. Daudet's reaction in *L'Action Française* was typical of the far Right, damning Blum as "this foreigner, because a Jew," who wants war with Germany "out of ethnic madness" and alleging Paul-Boncour a homosexual, a "Don Juan of the toilets." The stock market plunged and then plunged some more in a vote of no confidence. Because so divisive, the cabinet was the opposite of what Kérillis had praised Blum for only a day earlier. And, of course, Blum was not about to become the Robespierre Kérillis wanted, heading up a "government of public safety" which would dismiss the legislature, censor the press, dissolve the labor unions, and revise the constitution to make the Republic safe from Communists and Fascists alike.[19]

Give Blum credit: he did spend the twenty-six days of his cabinet seeking the essence of the Popular Front. That distillation meant above all the confrontation with fascism. Paul-Boncour was no Louis Barthou—none of the bitter astringency, hardly a modicum of the experience, nothing of the authority—but he shared Barthou's belief in an iron ring to contain Germany. Hard upon the debacle of the *Anschluss,* a display of French determination was mandatory: a burnishing of the ring. First, Blum and Paul-Boncour met on 14 March with the Czech ambassador in Paris, Stefan Osusky, to reaffirm France's alliance and the promise of military assistance in the face of German aggression.

Second, at the explicit direction of Paul-Boncour, Charles Corbin, France's ambassador in London, reported this reaffirmation to British officials and asked, with a bluntness uncharacteristic of French diplomacy since 1934, that His Majesty's government define their intentions if Hitler's next target was Czechoslovakia.

And none too soon, for the news from Gibraltar to Moscow, dire for months, was worse. In Spain Republican successes early in the year had been reversed, and Nationalist troops were now mounting an offensive along the Ebro River toward Barcelona. Already this Republican stronghold had come under aerial bombardment that during four days in mid-March led to nearly seven hundred dead, including two French consuls, and more than eleven hundred wounded. Anxious at its apparent exclusion from the strategic reckoning, the Soviet Union called for an international conference discussing the threat to peace from Germany. The effect was ruined when Maxim Litvinov, the people's commissar for foreign affairs, declared that the Soviets would stand on the letter of their alliance with Czechoslovakia—all military assistance contingent upon France's prior commitment of forces—and by reports of further purge trials involving the military high command. Poland had seized the city of Vilna from Lithuania in 1923, and the issue had poisoned their relations since and turned Lithuania toward the Soviet Union for support. Emboldened by Germany's example and clearly unafraid of any Soviet reaction, Poland now demanded that Lithuania accept the loss of Vilna as the price for Poland's respecting the remainder of its territorial independence. With this backdrop who could wonder that Johannes Baumann, president of the Swiss Republic, hastened to proclaim that his people would defend to the death the inviolability of their mountains.

The Swiss had only to look south and east to stoke their patriotic fires. Rewarded with a telegram from Hitler promising never to forget his support for *Anschluss,* Mussolini told Italians that Rome and Berlin—he always cited Rome first—would march side by side to forge a new equilibrium for Europe. The shape of that new balance was already apparent in Spain, where Italian infantry and German pilots were the difference in the war. Mussolini was promising to recast Italian relations with Great Britain and France to Italy's benefit in trade and colonial claims. But that was the future; the present was in Austria. The Germans were imposing Nazification with a vengeance. The Paris press recounted the horror of arrests, beatings, rapes, and murders. The series of suicides by Austrian Jews choosing death rather than submission to this persecution appears to have profoundly affected French opinion because the newspapers printed story after story. D'Ormesson in *Le Figaro* was one of many eloquently decrying the barbarism, but he was best in giving it a title: "After the Taking."[20]

Given these circumstances, on 15 March Blum called upon France's military and diplomatic principals in the Comité Permanent de la Défense Nationale (Standing Committee for National Defense) to consider France's strategic position. Coming straight to the point, Paul-Boncour asked how France intended to uphold its obligations to Czechoslovakia. Daladier, minister of defense since May 1936, replied that France could initially provide no direct aid, only the possible intimidation of Germany by mobilizing along the frontier. Gamelin, chief of the general staff since 1935, admitted that a French attack across the border would compel Germany to commit important forces that might otherwise be used against Czechoslovakia but warned that German defensive works would make for hard slogging—a reference meant to recall the long and bloody operations of the Great War. With the concurrence of General Joseph Vuillemin, the new chief of staff for the air force, Gamelin discouraged expectations that the Soviet Union could provide substantial assistance. Without a common border Soviet ground troops would require passage rights from either Poland, an enemy, or Romania, hardly a friend. To be effective the large and unproven Soviet air force would have to operate from the few usable Czech airfields, which the Germans would certainly destroy at the commencement of hostilities.

The assessment was pessimistic as well about Spain. The basis of the late winter offensive by the Nationalists was reinforcements from Italy and Germany. What, Blum asked, would be the effect of threatening a French intervention for the Republicans if Franco did not renounce these forces within forty-eight hours? Gamelin and Vuillemin immediately warned that no abrupt action could be envisioned because even the possibility of intervention required calling up substantial reserves. Daladier agreed: "One would have to be blind not to see that intervention in Spain would unleash a general war." Alexis Saint-Léger Léger, the secretary-general of the foreign ministry since 1933, plunged the decisive dagger through the proposal by predicting that any French intervention in Spain risked a British repudiation and thus would place in jeopardy the alliance essential to French security. But what would be the result of a victory by the Nationalists which they owed to Nazi and Fascist support? When Paul-Boncour dared to ask, Gamelin produced a memorandum just completed by his staff. His voice steady, he read out the tables of doom: Germany and Italy could threaten attack by land through the Pyrenees, air attack on southern France and France's north African possessions, and the cutting of French and British communications in the Mediterranean.

Was there anything short of direct intervention that might forestall this chimera? When Paul-Boncour suggested that the French army occupy Spanish Morocco, Gamelin replied that doing so would preserve passage through the Strait of Gibraltar and require only a partial mobilization. Encouraged, Paul-Boncour proposed adding the Balearic Islands. Admiral François Darlan, chief of staff for the navy since 1936, ventured that a single ground division could manage it. But his civilian superior, César Campinchi, the navy minister, posed the question that had been hanging unasked from the outset, "What would be the effect, on the conduct of the war, of Germany's total mastery in the air?" Vuillemin's answer was categorical and unforgettable: "In fifteen days our aviation will be annihilated." Guy La Chambre, the air force minister, amplified the point by comparing the French and German aircraft production rates. All eyes turned to Marshall Philippe Pétain, by now an almost mythical figure—savior of Verdun in 1916, sole surviving symbol of France's victory in the Great War, chief of staff until his retirement in 1932, and still a power in the military and political hierarchy— hence his presence. He shook his head gravely: military adventures could not be considered. Nor even something less: when Blum asked almost plaintively about the possibility of sending secret "intensified aid" across the Pyrenees, Gamelin replied with a dismissive comment about Republican "ineptness." The senior military and diplomatic minds of the Third Republic had declared that Prague and Madrid could go to the devil.[21]

And then where would France go? If that question had no answer, the fault did not lie in a lack of warnings from the Deuxième Bureau (intelligence service), which was second to none during the 1920s and 1930s in both counterespionage and spy networks. After the creation of the Communist Party in 1920, the Soviet Union began recruiting agents among French armament workers, especially in the aircraft factories. France was then at the forefront of aviation technology, which Soviet leaders hoped to steal. Even more important, the Great War had proven that the organization of industry was the key to victory, and Communists wanted their men to have hands on the levers. Among party leaders in France, Jacques Duclos played the critical role in directing these "special services." Although he was elected a deputy in 1926, he was on the run a year later because the Deuxième Bureau managed to penetrate almost every operation either the party or Soviet operatives, the Ob'edinënnoe Gosudarstvennoe Politicheskoe Upravlenie (OGPU), mounted. But the fate of Duclos illustrates the fundamental problem of any intelligence service: the acquisition of information is subservient to decisions about its use. As French political leaders worried more about Germany, they worried less about the Soviet Union. Although Louis Barthou was a man of the Center-Right, he began the negotiations that resulted in the Franco-Soviet alliance of May 1935 which confronted Germany with the possibility of a two-front war. As French political leaders from the Center leftward grew fearful that right-wing leagues threatened a fascist coup, they welcomed the support of the Communist Party that had previously sworn their destruction in revolution. Even before the creation of the Popular Front, the Deuxième Bureau found that its highly accurate reports about Soviet or Communist espionage were set aside. And so the damage went unchecked. Pierre Cot, a Radical and six times air force minister during the 1930s, was at least a Soviet sympathizer and likely a Soviet agent. Until 1936 he obstructed rearmament and afterward subordinated rationalization of aircraft production to union demands. Cot and André Labarthe, his principal scientific advisor, populated the staff at the air force ministry with men whose allegiance was to Moscow first and to France second. Perhaps even more valuable to the Soviet Union and therefore dangerous to France was Edouard Pfeiffer, the longtime aide-de-camp to Daladier as minister of war and later as premier.[22]

Politics led to deflating the dangers intelligence revealed about the Soviet Union. Politics likewise led to inflating the dangers intelligence revealed about Germany. The Deuxième Bureau and its sources came, therefore, to despise the national leaders who exploited their work. For about the German target the French achieved a record of accuracy rarely equaled in the history of modern intelligence. When Germany secretly violated the arms limitation terms of the Versailles treaty during the early 1920s, when its military experimented with the coordinated dive-bomber and tank spearhead attacks eventually called "Blitzkrieg," when Hitler began his massive rearmament, when the decisions were made to reoccupy the Rhineland and to effect *Anschluss,* the Deuxième Bureau provided early and ample warning. And of German efforts to penetrate France, it was equally on the mark: Paul Paillole, who commanded the counterespionage division recalled forcefully: "There were no German spies. We knew them all!" As in such intelligence work, this success depended on the synergy of capable analysts and well-placed agents. Major Paul Stehlin, serving as air attaché in Berlin during the 1930s, reported in great detail on the growth and potential of the *Luftwaffe* and, in March 1938, warned four days early of the *Anschluss.* Few spies have ever been better placed to obtain sensitive information than Hans-Thilo Schmidt (code name "H.-E.," pronounced as the individual letters are in French, thus "asché"), who had access to German cryptography and was recruited by the Deuxième Bureau in 1931. Yet, far from spurring the French to act, the intelligence reports of a powerful and increasingly dangerous German military were used instead to justify passivity. Although this policy led to disaster in 1940, there were sound arguments—convincing a majority of the political, military, and diplomatic leadership—for it during the 1930s. The French had bitter memories of the Ruhr occupation in 1923, when they attempted to compel German compliance with the Versailles treaty and were undermined by their wartime allies. Since then, neither Great Britain nor the United States had indicated the slightest willingness to hold Germany even to the spirit of Versailles, much less anything stronger. France would not go it alone again. More important, France *could not* go it alone against Germany.[23]

As early as 1919, the French government was fully aware of the twin demographic catastrophes wrought by the Great War. First, the fighting cost 1.3 million men, 3.3 percent of the total population and nearly 25 percent of males aged twenty to twenty-seven. Second, the absence of soldiers from home led to an estimated deficit of 1.4 million births. The implications for national survival were heartrending and terrifying. The deaths left behind 600,000 widows and 750,000 orphans. The distribution of the deaths left young women by the hundreds of thousands without hope of a traditional role as wife and mother. The males unborn left the years beginning in 1935 without recruits to fill the ranks, the *années creuses,* the five "hollow years." For a critical period France would not have enough sons to defend her. Negotiations undertaken in the "Spirit of Locarno" shortened the occupation of the Rhineland ordered by the Versailles treaty. French troops departed German soil in 1929, but even without this last gesture of Briandism, they were due to leave in 1934, just as the period of depleted ranks began.

Where bodies were lacking, fortifications would take their place. This response to the grim prospect of the hollow years came as early as 1922 from André Maginot, a minister of war whose war-destroyed leg gave him the credibility to speak of conserving what French blood remained. He commissioned studies comparing various forms of defensive works, and by the late 1920s the army reached a consensus that the power of modern explosives required reinforced concrete positions linked by underground transit and communications and supported by heavy artillery. After Maginot became minister of war again in 1929, he convinced the Chamber and Senate to provide an initial three billion francs, and the building began. When he died less than two years later from bad oysters at a *réveillon,* there was never any doubt that the line of fortifications would bear his name.

But the very decision to build begged important questions. First, and obviously, where should the beginning be made? In 1914 the Germans had come through Belgium, "letting the sleeve of the last man brush the English Channel," as General Count Alfred von Schlieffen had urged in drawing up the plan. He intended to catch the French by surprise, as he did, because the traditional invasion route from the east was through Lorraine. There, in the gap between the mountains of Alps

to the south and the hills of the Ardennes to the north, the land was relatively flat and no major rivers had to be crossed. The Maginot Line began in Lorraine and was strongest in Lorraine for the soundest of military reasoning. Construction of what was then—and for a long time
afterward—the ultimate in defensive works took time, of which there
seemed less and less after Hitler took power, but, more important,
francs, of which there were fewer and fewer in the budget as the depression took hold of the French economy. Completing a line of these *gros
ouvrages* (heavy forts) at least to the border with Belgium was the plan,
but the middle 1930s imposed compromises. Especially in the Ardennes
region, *petits ouvrages* (lighter works) were substituted and justified because the terrain promised a more difficult approach by the enemy.

As for the remaining distance to the Channel, that left a second
question begging. Pétain himself declared that "the northern frontier
can be defended only by advancing into Belgium," a pronouncement
that was utterly Delphic. By treaty dating from 1839, the European powers had collectively guaranteed Belgian independence and neutrality.
When Germany invaded Belgium in August 1914, ignoring what Chancellor Theobald von Bethmann-Hollweg infamously called "a scrap of
paper," Great Britain's hesitation about fighting alongside France disappeared. Concluding that neutrality had offered only a deceptive protection, postwar Belgian leaders concluded a military convention with
France in September 1920, assisted in the 1923 occupation of the Ruhr,
and were a full party to the Locarno Pact in 1925. Bold while Germany
was weak, Belgium grew fearful as Hitler rearmed and France did nothing to stop him, especially when German troops entered the Rhineland
in March 1936. On 14 October, after dithering for seven months, Prime
Minister Paul Van Zeeland used the excuse that France's alliance with
the Soviet Union might embroil Belgium with Germany to denounce
the 1920 military convention and return to neutrality. Until then,
French military leaders had planned to meet the threat of German invasion by linking up with Belgian forces and fighting behind the natural barrier of the Meuse River and the fortress cities of Dinant, Namur,
Huy, and Liège. Now, until the moment that Germany actually violated
Belgian territory, French troops themselves would be regarded as
invaders. But that moment would come, Pétain and the rest of the

military leadership were convinced, and when it did, they would flood their best armies into Belgium to fight the Germans before the battle, the fighting, and the horrific damage so familiar from the Great War could reach France itself. The rest of the border would be safe behind the Maginot Line. And, critically, the German invasion of Belgium would once again make certain Britain's joining with France.

Such a military strategy raised the third question, what came to be called the "Maginot mentality." If there were not enough Frenchmen to fight Germany along all the borders of France, how could there be enough Frenchmen to fulfill France's treaty obligations to Czechoslovakia, to Poland, to the Soviet Union? And if France felt secure behind the Maginot Line, and if France was convinced that any German attack would have to come through Belgium and therefore British support was assured, and if France believed that the combination of the British and the line were sufficient, then why would France even consider risking its security for Eastern European allies? Yvon Delbos learned only too well during his December 1937 circuit how seriously the Eastern European nations had been pondering this issue.[24]

The economic malaise of the 1930s strongly encouraged the Maginot mentality. Depression fought à la française with budget cuts meant fewer francs to spend on the military. Political leaders of the Center and Left applauded. As early as 1930, Pierre Cot, a Radical, urged, "Not another man, not another sou for defense!" Although most of the Radicals did not go so far, the Communists and many of the Socialists would have. In 1914 the term of required military service for a Frenchman upon his twentieth birthday was three years. After the war it was decreased first to eighteen months, then to twelve, and in 1932, as an economy, to eleven. The hurry-up-and-wait procedures of induction and basic training meant that recruits were only beginning to become soldiers when they— gladly—turned in their uniforms. In principle these citizen-soldiers were required to fulfill their reserve duties through periodic maneuvers and instruction. In reality many of them never handled a weapon again until the call-up of 1939. More cost cutting was behind the cancellation of these field exercises, especially the reduction of the army officer corps by 15 percent in 1933 which stretched training capabilities to the limit. Among Radicals and Socialists the nation-at-arms soldiery animated by the French ideal of *Liberté, Egalité, Fraternité* was an article of faith. They had never forgotten the Dreyfus affair, and to them career soldiers, and especially the officer corps, were suspect as anti-Republican. Inevitably, they greeted the seminal and prescient ideas of Lieutenant Colonel Charles de Gaulle with a hostility born from their antagonisms. In *Le Fil de l'épée* (*The Edge of the Sword*, 1932) and *Vers l'armée de métier* (*Toward a Professional Army,* 1934), de Gaulle argued for an elite career military, because short-term draftees were incapable of mastering modern weaponry, and for a mechanized armored strike force to take the offensive, because that modern weaponry had made static defense a dangerous illusion. He was as correct on the theory as he was wrong on the politics.

Of de Gaulle a fitness report at the Ecole de Guerre once read: "intelligent officer, cultivated and serious; has brilliance and facility; good deal of worth; unfortunately spoils incontestable qualities by his excessive assurance, his intolerance for the opinions of others, and his attitude of a king in exile." Naturally, his sole political ally was Paul Reynaud, who suffered fools as seldom and was as short as de Gaulle was tall. De Gaulle had to be wrong because he attacked not only the citizen-soldier but also the high command's belief in the defensive. The generals had been converted by the experience of the Great War, by the failure after failure of attacks that wasted the better part of a generation. In March 1935, when Germany announced a return to conscription, the minister of war, General Louis-Joseph Maurin, told the Chamber of Deputies, "How can anyone believe that we continue to think of offensives when we have spent billions of francs to establish a fortified barrier?" Pétain, who held Verdun in 1916 against everything the Germans shot, threw, lobbed, and charged at him, his successor as chief of staff, Maxime Weygand, who was once the principal aide to Marshall Ferdinand Foch, and his successor, Gamelin—all worshipped at the altar of fortifications. Generals, it is said, prepare for the last war, but the French high command had more than history to cite. The internal combustion engine that was to power a mechanized force was far from reliable in the 1930s. Automobiles broke down regularly—why not tanks and troop carriers? In 1934, when Hitler sponsored the attempted coup d'état in Vienna, German equipment failed massively as it was rushed toward the Austrian border. France's military observer in Spain, General Maurice Duval, reported that the German tanks sent to assist Franco could not break through well-prepared positions supported by antitank weapons and artillery. So much for the shock tactics advocated by de Gaulle. Better let the enemy batter himself to destruction against French defensive works than risk defeat through an offensive in the open field.[25]

And for transport, better rely on the horse, of which the French had many and much grain to feed them, compared with few mechanized vehicles and too little gasoline to run them. In the mid-1930s twice as many cavalry brigades were mounted on horses as were driven by motors. As late as 1937, the appropriation for transport petroleum was less than one-quarter that for horse fodder. Rural politicians liked it that way, as did hide-bound army brass. Gamelin believed in "motorizing" the army—slowly—but members of his staff, holdovers from Weygand's tenure, resisted. The inspector general of infantry, General Julien Dufieux, feared the softening of foot soldiers if they marched less, and the inspector general of cavalry, General Marie-Robert Altmayer, kept officers in spurs even when they were assigned to tanks. But beyond the problem of mind-set was the question of money. The depression meant that the funds were not available for a rapid modernization, and Gamelin feared that if he raised the alarm too loudly, he might make Great Britain, France's only hope in a war against Germany, question the value of their alliance.

When Daladier became minister of defense in May 1936, he quickly changed the tone of rearmament. By August he demanded and got from Blum's cabinet formal commitment to a four-year program of significantly increased spending that would not be subject to annual review. He assigned more than half of the new fourteen billion francs in appropriations to mechanized warfare, roughly an even division between the offensive, more tanks and troop transport, and the defensive, more antitank and antiaircraft weaponry. To mollify the antimilitarist sentiment of the Popular Front majority, he pledged to nationalize some of the armaments factories. For many of the Socialists the issue was ending the profits made by "merchants of death," but for Daladier here was the chance to rationalize production. Too much of tank and especially aircraft manufacturing was in small factories with antiquated machinery and almost artisanal techniques. Daladier found that their owners, whipsawed by high overhead and low profit margins, often welcomed nationalization. The resistance came from "not a sou" Cot, the air force minister, who opposed retooling because closing factories—even temporarily—increased unemployment. When La Chambre replaced Cot in January 1938, the disarray in the procurement and disposition of the French air force was finally acknowledged. Taking advantage of the psychological shock from *Anschluss,* he and Daladier won approval for a massive program to produce nearly five thousand new military aircraft utilizing the latest advances in aeronautics and weaponry within twenty-four months. By spring 1940 the air force would be six times larger and perhaps the equal of Germany's, but in March 1938 Vuillemin's verdict seemed unassailable: "In fifteen days our aviation will be annihilated." [26]

Certainly, that assessment was supported by the Deuxième Bureau. As an argument for rearming and for undertaking whatever modifications—social, economic, and legal—were necessary to speed the process, this intelligence was invaluable. For Daladier and Gamelin such a judgment, combined with all the other intimidating reports on German military strength, also led to a broad political and diplomatic strategy. About Gamelin the German military attaché General Erich Kühlenthal shrewdly concluded that he was so favorably viewed by most politicians "because he did not arouse their suspicions or give rise to the belief that he was making himself too powerful." Of course he did not: "like a silk shirt, the more he is crumpled, the more supple he becomes" was the contemptuous retort by some of his principal staffers. Yet Gamelin despised what was his own essence when he discerned this trait in Daladier, whose mind, he complained, "changes with the direction of the wind . . . an absolute lightweight." To these men, neither confident nor decisive, the defense of France was entrusted. The superb intelligence from the Deuxième Bureau they used to justify rearming but not acting. When ready, Gamelin and Daladier said, France would take up its responsibilities. To be ready, France had to repair its economy, soothe its social distemper, rebuild its military, and secure its alliance with Great Britain. Until then the rest of Europe could go to the devil. Blum and Paul-Boncour were distressed by this pessimism, but all they could contrive to do beyond it was letting the clandestine traffic in arms to the Spanish Republicans increase slightly: "relaxed nonintervention." Too little, too late, it was for Spain and for a Popular Front version of foreign and military geopolitics.[27]

Was it also too late for Popular Front economics?

The story is told of a university search committee charged with selecting the next chancellor from among three final candidates, a mathematician, an economist, and an attorney. The committee called in each of the three separately to pose a final question: "How much is two plus two?" The mathematician said immediately, "Four." The economist paused, then responded, "Four, plus or minus one." The attorney replied with his own question, "How much do you want it to be?" Of course, the attorney became the new chancellor. This anecdote probably originated with a historian, envious because all the characters are usually better paid, but is nonetheless revealing despite its conception in resentment. The answers portray a continuum of knowledge, from mathematics and physics at the pole of certainty to hypothesis and argument at the pole of conjecture. Between lies the broad range of ambiguity where dwell forms of thought, among them history as well as economics, which combine ineluctable fact with varying degrees of surmise. Economists are always explaining why their forecasts go awry, shifting, as they do so, the balance from more surmise in the forecasting to more fact in the explicating. Historians generally avoid this embarrassing mea culpa by shunning predictions. Casting the future is especially dangerous in a time of crisis, and the Great Depression was that. Economic theories, conservative or liberal, capitalist or Marxist, deflationist or inflationist, were inadequate either fully to explain the origin of the slump or clearly to indicate measures of amelioration. Only later, after a second world war and a hard-won recovery during the late 1940s and early 1950s, could performances be assessed dispassionately.

Of Popular Front economics the judgment is harsh: "After finally having found the key to the lock in the devaluation of September 1936, they then bolted the door." The Popular Front campaigned on a false promise and took power with a false assumption. The false promise was that France could emerge from the depression without compromising the Poincaré franc. The false assumption was that France could rearm to confront the threat from Germany while the workweek was cut by one-sixth. The false promise, broken by the September devaluation, cost the Popular Front and Blum significant moral authority but should have been the basis for an economic recovery that might well have muted criticism. The false assumption, set into policy by the Matignon agreements of June, made that economic recovery impossible. Thus, of Blum the judgment is harsher still—"a great man poorly informed."[28]

Between French bosses and French labor there was no love lost. The victory by the Popular Front seemed to workers and their political leaders the moment for turning the tables. And to make certain the political leaders understood that the moment was at hand, the sit-down strikes in May and June 1936 put them on notice as much as the bosses. The Matignon agreements bore the mark of leaders trying to catch up with their followers. There was no careful analysis of what the hastily drawn provisions would mean to the economy. Instead, there was an emotional insistence to make up for the past—and as fast as possible. More from the love of round numbers than from any rational calculation, the new rules imposed a workweek of forty hours upon an economy accustomed to a workweek of forty-eight and added the requirement for two weeks of paid vacation. Leaving aside overtime, the reduction in the workweek was 16.6 percent, the reduction for the paid vacation another 3.8 percent. If employers wanted to maintain their previous production, they had to hire additional workers and thus lower unemployment. Unfortunately, the Matignon agreements limited their ability to do so by requiring not only that the forty-hour week be paid as if it remained forty-eight but that wages be increased in a range from 7 to 15 percent. For the economy as a whole, approximately 150,000 new jobs were generated, an increase of 7.5 percent in the number of employees. Because some small inefficient businesses closed or were bought up by larger ones, the *hourly* productivity rate did rise slightly, 3.5 to 4 percent. But combining the large reduction in hours with the modest increase in workers, the *daily* productivity rate fell. Between May 1936 and May 1938, France's level of production declined from 87 to 82, halving an increase of 78 to 87 between May 1935 and May 1936 under the much maligned deflationary tactics. Close inspection reveals worse: at a time when rearmament was paramount, production of primary materials, especially steel, was down much further than for consumer goods (11 percent and 1.5 percent, respectively).

The two devaluations reduced the value of the Poincaré franc 129.6 percent against the pound and 133.5 percent against the dollar. Between May 1936 and May 1938 exports rose 7 percent in volume and 96 percent in value; imports fell 10 percent in volume, 88 percent in value. The increase in exports would certainly have been greater, most likely much greater, but for the limits on production imposed by the workweek. The combination of the devaluations and decreased productivity led inevitably to higher prices: up 75 percent at wholesale and 47 percent at retail (the latter artificially low because of rent controls). Yet because of the wage increases, purchasing power remained almost the same and for industrial workers rose slightly. Certainly, the decrease in imports would have been greater, most likely much greater, but for this maintenance of consumption levels. The hard facts of economics cannot be escaped. If the initial devaluation had not been accompanied by the new workweek and wage increases, the surge in exports combined with the limitation of imports would have substantially raised production. Here was the "key to the lock" which would finally have brought France out of depression. The Matignon agreements were what "bolted the door." The effect of Popular Front economics was to uphold the standard of living at the cost of solving the problem of production. The country remained in depression.

The cost of these policies spread widely. For industrialists production remained low and headed lower. They also suffered the serious psychological blow of watching helplessly as the government permitted their workers to seize, often through violence, effective control of wages and rules. Surveying this economic landscape, investors and lenders drew pessimistic conclusions about the safety of capital. Stock prices declined, and the cost of borrowing rose. Purchasing power did not suffer, but it remained stagnant. A recovery from depression would have raised it far more than the Matignon agreements. Let it be stipulated: Blum meant well. The judgment that he was "poorly informed" actually means that he was woefully ignorant. To measure the failure of Popular Front economics requires only a single statistic: while French production was falling 4 to 5 percent, German production was increasing 17 percent.

Given the failure of what was done, what might have been done otherwise? From the outset the Popular Front gave evidence of weakness. Although Blum and Vincent Auriol, the minister of finance, recognized the necessity of a devaluation, they hesitated until September to abandon their campaign promise. The failure even to control—much less crush—the sit-down strikes in May and June meant that the workers and their unions, not the cabinet, imposed what became the Matignon agreements. Weakness as well as ignorance begot the economic policies that failed. If, instead, the Popular Front cabinet had been determined to govern and had a better grasp of economic realities, there were two options that could have brought success. Leaning in the direction of its Radical members, the cabinet could have declared an immediate devaluation of at least 20 percent, stimulated exports, and ordered two weeks of paid vacation as a first installment of social reforms to be enacted fully after recovery from the depression. Or, leaning in the direction of its Communist members, the cabinet could have nationalized the large industries and banks, instituted exchange controls to stabilize the currency and to decrease imports, and then dictated wages and prices. The former worked in Britain, the latter in Germany.[29]

Because the first Blum cabinet and then the two Chautemps cabinets did neither and stuck with policies that had demonstrably failed, there was little confidence when the second Blum cabinet proposed something of each. The plan presented at the beginning of April asked for decree powers until 1 July to carry out a program of limited exchange controls and massive spending on rearmament. To pay for the new armaments, the middle and upper classes would have to accept substantial new levies: a progressive tax of 4 to 17 percent on wealth of 150,000 francs or more, a 7 percent tax on the interest from national bonds, and various increases to the taxes on income, import licenses, and public concessions. To build the new armaments, the working class would have to accept a lengthening of the forty-hour week. On 6 April, more brilliantly than he had ever spoken before, Blum challenged the Chamber of Deputies to recognize their responsibilities in confronting the present danger and yet also in maintaining for France and the world the ideal of *Liberté, Egalité, Fraternité.* "We shall prove," he concluded magnificently, "that free peoples can rise to their duties, that democracies are capable, through voluntarily accepted discipline, of a might that is elsewhere provoked only through blind obedience."

Blum needed every eloquent word because his program and his cabinet were in grave jeopardy. During the last week of March new sit-down strikes had erupted among the heavily Communist metallurgical workers, especially in the automobile and aviation factories. Their leaders, joined by Marceau Pivert from the far Left of the Socialist Party, were making a political statement: Blum had failed to intervene in Spain; Blum might well compromise the forty-hour week; Blum had betrayed the Popular Front. The presence of Marx Dormoy as minister of the interior was proof that no decisive action would be taken against the strikes. If Blum could not control his own coalition, how could he hope to govern the nation? That question hung heavy as the Chamber's finance committee gave the new program only halfhearted approval, 25 to 18, and the deputies did the same, 311 to 250, with numerous abstentions among the Radicals. Conservatives argued that decree powers should be granted only to a government that inspired confidence and that Blum had proved himself "blind to all realities and deaf to all warnings." Flandin decried the Popular Front's two years of "discouraging work and saving." Reynaud, whose economic expertise was at last grudgingly admitted all around, capped the debate with the only words that came close to Blum's: "After so many setbacks, can France afford the luxury of failing again? A nation cannot rearm while resting two days a week. The will of the people is simple: to pull through. We must give our friends in the world the news they await with anguish. And the news is that we have now understood, that we are united to pull through."[30]

Every augury promised disaster for Blum in the Senate. Its finance committee rejected the program dismissively, 25 to 6. Knowing their opposition, Blum was hesitant before the senators, awkwardly quoting a column in the London *Times* as evidence of British support for his plan and then warning that the Senate should not frustrate the popular will as expressed by the Chamber of Deputies. Caillaux, a plutocrat as well as a German sympathizer, declared that the proposed wealth tax would ruin small farmers. About the rest of the plan, British reaction, and the Senate's constitutional role, his expletive "Diable!" expressed utter contempt. So, along with Spain and Czechoslovakia, the Popular Front could go to the devil. Most of the senators agreed by voting overwhelmingly, 214 to 47, against the cabinet. Blum and his cabinet immediately resigned. The Popular Front was finished.[31]

2 Spring
April to June

Hypocrisy is the art of affecting qualities for the purpose of pretending to an undeserved virtue. Because individuals and institutions and societies most often live down to the suspicions about them, hypocrisy and its accompanying equivocations underpin the conduct of life. Imagine how frightful truth unvarnished would be.

In early 1937 robbers took nearly a half-million francs of jewels from a Mme Tillèse, who kept a shop on the Boulevard Haussmann. Police detectives quickly solved the crime, made arrests, and recovered most of the jewels. But, according to Mme Tillèse, when inspector Jules Bonnel returned her property, he said that she could have the remainder only after paying him 10,000 francs. Seventy-three years old, robbed three times before, and familiar with the cupidity of underpaid detectives, she offered 4,000. Bonnel, she said, took offense, left, and never came back. In late April 1938 she brought suit against the Paris police. In response to her charge, which was supported by a witness, Charles Meyer, head of the criminal investigation division, answered that he was shocked—shocked—at such unjust and cruel discredit cast upon one of his men when "in five days, the police tracked down 480,000 francs of stolen jewels, the robbers, and the fencers. That counts for something." So it did: the judges ruled against Mme Tillèse and required her to pay the expenses of the trial.

Three weeks later in Poitiers the case of Octavie Berzin offered a certain moral lesson. On 25 February she shot her lover of seven years, Jean Frié, then an officer candidate at the School of Artillery. He had broken with her to contract a marriage "conforming to the desires of his family," meaning a suitable young woman. Suitable, Berzin was not: reared in a state orphanage, formerly the mistress of a notary clerk, nine years older than Frié, thirty-six, and whatever beauty she once had fading. She claimed that he had promised to make her his wife, but how could she have seriously believed that the son of a retired army colonel would make a life permanently with the likes of her? Discarded, with a promise of money implying that she was no better than a prostitute, she shot him six times to make certain he was dead. Such a woman had to be condemned, and the jury did so, but, recalling that she had attempted suicide three times in her life and the testimony by a psychiatrist that she had acted in a "state of passion," the judges sentenced her to only seven years.

In Bordeaux at the end of June another crime of passion came to trial, this one by the son of Léon Jouhaux, head of the General Labor Confederation. Paul Jouhaux had an unsavory past, four misdemeanor convictions for fraud and arrest in Belgium for smuggling arms to the Spanish Republicans. Somehow the social and economic discrepancies of the capitalist economy so resolutely denounced by the father had been reconciled in favor of the son. He bought a large property outside Bordeaux, traveled about in splendid automobiles, and had for his arm and his bed Mme Simone Lacombe, daughter of an old Parisian bourgeois family gone bankrupt. The ruin of this idyll came when Lacombe could not resist the charms of a young and athletic butcher. According to her, Jouhaux reacted violently to his cuckolding, slapping her, threatening to slash her with a razor, menacing her with his revolver. Jouhaux admitted angry confrontations but denied the razor and the revolver. A witness told the police and prosecutors of seeing him wave the revolver at her, but in court he recanted. Reminded of his previous declarations, the witness merely smiled. Jouhaux was acquitted.

For two decades Geo London had been reporting such cases while providing brilliant and cynical commentary. A fellow journalist, Marcel Montarron, revealed just how cynical. London was in western France covering the trial of a parricide that began in mid-afternoon. Because he had an early deadline, he telephoned a story that he was certain would take place: an angry crowd cursing the accused as he was marched to the courthouse from his holding cell at the police station. London then relaxed over lunch until he saw with dismay the guards and the prisoner coming but "not even the shadow of a gawker." His reputation at stake, he stalked to the door, cried out "Kill him!" and returned to his table.[1]

Geo London's fictive reporting was a mere indiscretion compared to the cynicism displayed by the Paris press reacting to the return of Edouard Daladier as premier on 8 April. For the Center and the Left he had been the man who failed, who took fright, on 6 February 1934. For the Right he had been *le fusilleur* (leader of the firing squad), on whose authority that night the police shot at the veterans and the fed-up who were protesting the corruption of politicians like him. Now he was the strongman, *le taureau de Vaucluse* (bull of Vaucluse). Although the Socialist Party declined to participate in the new cabinet, its newspaper, *Le Populaire,* and Léon Blum, who after all had made Daladier his minister of war, declared that government by the Popular Front majority continued. Speaking for moderates in general, *Le Temps, Le Figaro,* and *Le Petit Parisien* more correctly recognized that Blum's second defeat meant the end of Popular Front dominance and celebrated the new cabinet as a restoration of sense in not only economic but diplomatic policy. As such, Daladier was praised for having maintained "our magnificent and powerful army," and Georges Bonnet, made minister of foreign affairs, was described as "prudent, firm, and wise." Further to the Right, in the French Social Party's *Le Petit Journal,* which had good reason to despise Daladier, relief at Bonnet's return outweighed the resentment over 6 February, with the new premier called "a son of the common folk and a soldier from the trenches." The far Right of *L'Action Française* and its ilk was glad to see the end of Blum and Joseph Paul-Boncour but criticized the cabinet's inclusion of Paul Reynaud and Georges Mandel, *bellicistes* (warmongers) both, and Mandel a Jew. On 12 April the Chamber of Deputies gave the Daladier cabinet a vote of confidence 576 to 5 and then decree powers for the economy 508 to 12. The following day by unanimity, 290 to 0, the Senate authorized the decree powers it had refused Blum. Almost the only observer to decry how Daladier had been so transformed into the savior of France was Henri de Kérillis, a deputy himself, who wrote in *L'Epoque* that the votes ignored a record of "equivocation, hypocrisy, and deceit."[2]

Kérillis meant to discredit: he should have written "ambiguous." Born in 1884 to a modest baker's family in Carpentras, Daladier never forgot his origins and rarely failed to mention them. When as minister of war he accepted the invitation of an old noble family to stay at its château because army maneuvers were being held in the vicinity, he added that he had once entered by the back door when delivering bread. Yet he always said, "Je suis *sorti* du peuple" (I *arose* from the common people), by which he meant that he had "escaped" from them. He helped himself: a series of scholarships secured his education. He had a helping hand: Edouard Herriot, soon to become a power in the Radical Party, was his mentor at the lycée Ampère. He was diligent: passing the tough *agrégation* examination for history in 1909. He was ambitious: elected mayor of Carpentras in 1911 and then to the Chamber of Deputies in 1914. He was brave: during the war he was decorated three times for valor and promoted to lieutenant. He was lucky: he survived serious wounds, and his *marraine de guerre* (soldier's pen pal), Madeleine Laffont, daughter of a wealthy Parisian physician, married him in July 1919. Four months later he was reelected to the Chamber as one of the nation's heroes.[3]

For a time fortune continued to smile. Daladier was prominent in constructing the Coalition of the Left, which won the 1924 elections. When the Radicals were in power, he was minister for the colonies, minister of war, or minister of public works. When they were not, he opposed any cooperation with the Center-Right or Right and pushed the Radicals leftward toward the Socialists. He was increasingly at odds with Herriot, who was more moderate and more compromising. Because Daladier was combative and because he cultivated a glowering silence, his colleagues dubbed him the "bull of Vaucluse." He affected a Napoleonic stance, his chin tucked almost into his collar, one hand disappearing into the jacket of his dark double-breasted suit. It was the dour Jacobin Napoléon, not the expansive emperor, for Daladier's fortune was turning. His wife developed tuberculosis and, after seven years at a sanatorium, died in November 1932. Their two sons, born in 1922 and 1925, were sickly and confined away from Paris. His projects for an alliance of the Left foundered on Blum's refusal to accept participation in any cabinet short of a Socialist "exercise in power." When Daladier finally became premier at the end of January 1933, he was able to accomplish little before his cabinet collapsed in October over wrangles about the budget. The conservatives returned the contempt he had shown them, and the Socialists refused to save him. When he got a second chance the following January as the Stavisky affair convulsed the nation, he lost his nerve and resigned the morning after the 6 February demonstrations. The Communist daily *L'Humanité* denounced the "regime of slime and blood." The right-wing press assailed him as *le fusilleur,* and *La Victoire* repeated a slogan chanted by the fed-up, "Daladier au poteau! Au poteau Daladier!" (Lynch Daladier!). Its editor, Gustave Hervé, drew a deadly comparison: "Despite his determination, he reminds me of the pitiable Louis XVI." [4]

But even in disgrace Daladier had a means of recovery because he had made himself one of the Chamber's experts on military matters. After Paul-Boncour sent him to head the ministry of war in December 1932, he stayed on until February 1934, twice while premier himself. There in the offices on the rue Saint Dominique, he sat long hours over the dossiers he compiled compulsively all his life. Short, a bit stout, square-faced, his forehead high from early balding, about to enter his fifties, he was solitary as much by nature as from the disease that had robbed him of his family. His close associates treasured his quiet humor and his dedication. They also recognized in his detachment and a certain lack of confidence the very antithesis of a strong man. He never completely escaped being a *boulanger boursier* (baker scholarship boy). Eventually, the pose of strength fell away and led to the sad witticism that the bull of Vaucluse had the horns of a snail. Daladier's experience in the trenches of the Western Front made him loathe war as only a sergeant or lieutenant, close to the troops he orders to die, can loathe war. He also came to believe that France alone could not carry off victory over Germany, not in the Great War, not in any other. He agonized over possibilities and consequences, what could be risked, militarily and diplomatically, and what could not.

Two years later, in May 1936, when the Popular Front swept to power, Daladier returned to the ministry of war. The remilitarization of the Rhineland confirmed the excellent intelligence of the Deuxième Bureau that the threat from Hitler's Germany was dire. With General Maurice Gamelin, the chief of the general staff, Daladier now urged Blum to hasten rearmament. He pushed the army to mechanize and to add tanks, although he refused Charles de Gaulle's prescription of special fully armored units. He reinforced cooperation among the army, navy, and air force. He made progress and would have made more except for the limitations imposed by the forty-hour workweek and by disruptions from strikes. But he rejected using this force prematurely. When Blum sought to aid the Spanish Republicans, Daladier made common cause with Alexis Léger, the secretary-general of the foreign ministry, who shared with him an obsessive fear of France's standing alone. Together they argued strenuously against any policy that might separate France from Great Britain and stayed Blum's hand. The same reasoning was behind his assessment of the alliance with the Soviet Union. The Deuxième Bureau concluded that in combination with the Little Entente powers—Czechoslovakia, Romania, and Yugoslavia—the Soviet Union and France could present Germany with the credible threat of a two-front war. Active pursuit of these military dispositions would mean breaking definitively with Poland, which feared Moscow more than Berlin, and trusting the Soviet government that had betrayed France in 1918 through a separate peace with Germany and ruined French investors through repudiation of the czarist debt. For Daladier and Léger the most important argument against a Franco-Slav strategy was its risk to the relationship with Britain, which was utterly opposed to commitments in Eastern Europe and might even be reassured that the German menace was now contained. When British leaders made clear their refusal to oppose the *Anschluss*, no one in the Chautemps cabinet was willing to act alone, no matter what they might subsequently claim.[5]

By the time of the Popular Front, Daladier's political resurrection was well under way, propelled not only by his ambitions but by those of his Egeria, the Marquise Jeanne de Crussol. Born to the bourgeois Breton family Béziers, made wealthy by the canning of sardines, she gained her title through marriage to an aristocrat in need of a hefty dowry, no less than the grandson of Duchess Marie d'Uzès, social lioness among the French nobility when she was not sculpting and writing novels. Such vertiginous social climbing gave rise to a play on the pronunciation of her new surname, that she was *la sardine qui s'est crue sole* (the sardine that took itself for a sole), yet there was no mistaking her new status in society. Her husband's preference for country living suited her perfectly as she established a glittering salon in Paris. Because her politics, taken from her family, not her marriage, were slightly left of center, she invited Daladier early. They became friends and soon enough lovers. For him the liaison gave entrée to the social elite and so made him more attractive to conservatives. For her, as Daladier's sun rose again, she could bask in the glow of presumptive influence. In 1935 a popular song was "Tout va très bien, Madame la Marquise" (Everything Is Going Very Well, Madame la Marquise). How well and how much influence was never clear. Jeanne de Crussol was no empty-headed socialite. She had taken courses in political science and had opinions—solidly Radical—on economics and foreign policy. Some thought her attractive, her hair auburn and curly, her nose gracefully arched, but no beauty. She affected the dress of the bourgeoise she had been and resembled more a schoolmistress than a fashion plate. She was both discreet and frequently at Daladier's side. A man of hesitations, he must have sought her counsel.[6]

That counsel was ill toward the ablest member in the cabinet, Paul Reynaud. They were close in age, Reynaud six years older at fifty-nine, and height, Reynaud even shorter, but in almost every other way they were opposites. Daladier had won his way upward; Reynaud, the son of a wealthy textile manufacturer, had been there all along. Daladier was instinctively a man of the Center-Left, Reynaud of the Center-Right. Trained as an academic, Daladier's preference was to ponder; trained as a lawyer, Reynaud's was to act. Compact, brooding, square-jawed, the very image of the French common people, Daladier stalked; lithe, flamboyant, hair slicked back, squinty eyes and arched brows that looked almost Asian, Reynaud preened. Daladier, a widower, had a marquise for a mistress; Reynaud, married to the daughter of legendary barrister Henri Robert, had a countess. The occasions for antagonism were legion.

Reynaud spent the war in the medical corps and then entered politics as a member of the National Bloc in 1919, conspicuously supporting the occupation of the Ruhr. Between 1930 and 1932 he served as minister of justice, minister of finance, or minister for the colonies under André Tardieu and Pierre Laval. From 1936 on, he was the outspoken and lonely proponent of de Gaulle's idea for the creation of armored divisions. Perhaps inevitably, de Gaulle converted to his theories of modern warfare the politician who was most like him, a lone wolf mistrusted for brilliance, energy, and independence. Both recognized how much their contemporaries were prisoners to thinking that time had outrun, and both were too eager to say so. Reynaud was disliked by the Right for having been correct about the necessity to devalue the franc, and he was despised by the Left for being correct that the Popular Front's forty-hour workweek was the major impediment to economic recovery. If Daladier was to demonstrate that a new firmness had come to government, he could hardly refuse Reynaud a place in the cabinet, especially with its axis moved rightward of the Socialists. But for reasons political and personal the place would be minister of justice. Daladier refused Reynaud either ministry he deserved: finance, because his economic prescriptions would deny the cabinet needed votes from the Left, and foreign affairs, because his strident determination to uphold France's pledge to Czechoslovakia might fray the relationship with Great Britain.

The political reasons were certainly enough to leash Reynaud. The personal reasons are harder to judge. In the middle 1930s Tardieu introduced Reynaud to Countess Hélène de Portes, whose ambition was the kind of influence over the Third Republic which the Marquise de Pompadour had exercised over the French monarchy during the 1750s and 1760s. Pompadour had Louis XV; de Portes would have Reynaud. After befriending and thereby taking the measure of Mme Reynaud, she then became his mistress. Shortly, she demanded that he choose, and he left his wife and house for an apartment near the Chamber of Deputies. She never doubted that she would be victorious, for she was accustomed to winning. The daughter of a Marseilles shipbuilder, Hélène Rebuffel had married another aristocrat in need of a substantial dowry, Count Jean de Portes. Leaving him behind to work for her father, she set her sights on Paris. What Reynaud saw in her can only be guessed. Although some contemporaries granted her sex appeal, almost no one thought her even comely, remarking instead about her sallow complexion, slightly protruding teeth, untidy hair, and too-large mouth. Many considered her ill-bred, her braying voice, compulsion to be noticed, and pleasure at finding fault provoking them to recall her origins. In conversation she revealed intelligence but used it to cultivate a coterie whose taste in politics ranged much farther right than Reynaud. Her ambition was utterly naked: by whatever means, with whatever allies, she would make him premier and rule behind him. In a play on her name she was called *la Porte à côté* (side door). Because Daladier and Jeanne de Crussol stood in her way, they were the enemy. How obvious that they should return the sentiment and block Reynaud.[7]

A second strongman who had to be limited because he might eclipse Daladier was Georges Mandel, whose talents were wasted overseeing the colonies. As minister of foreign affairs, he might have been the resurrection of Louis Barthou in both policy and character: they were both great haters, especially of Germany. Mandel left behind his Jewish birth as Louis Rothschild while making a career in journalism beside Georges Clemenceau at *L'Homme Libre.* He then became the executioner in the Tiger's cabinet that led France to victory in 1918. Thin, hard, cold-eyed, nose slightly askew, implacable, Mandel imposed his master's will upon a nation almost too tired to go on fighting. Afterward he became a deputy sitting with the Center-Right but was never popular because he continued to manifest icy authority and vindictiveness. He had been a minister only once, running the ministry of posts, telegraph, and telephone (PTT) from November 1934 to May 1936, where he negotiated an end to incessant labor strife, inaugurated airmail delivery, improved telephone service through automatic dialing, developed radio news programming, and, most dramatically, installed a radio antenna atop the Eiffel Tower. Because he was so effective where others had failed, he was needed, like Reynaud, as a symbolic presence among Daladier's ministers. But there was a significant difference: the revival of anti-Semitism stigmatized Mandel and made him a special target for those who feared war with Germany. By now he was heavier, but the invariable dark suit, old-fashioned high-collared white shirt, and black tie reminded all that he remained what he had been in 1918, politically Manichaean and fearfully so. General Sir Edward Spears, who knew France as well as any Englishman of his generation, called Mandel "a great patriot" and "a great man. His intelligence struck all who came in contact with him. His memory was prodigious, his courage astounding."[8]

Because Mandel was a lion, he was relegated. Because Georges Bonnet was a weasel, he got the Quai d'Orsay. As Daladier was forming his cabinet, he sought the advice of Paul-Boncour, Blum's foreign minister, who urged him to remain steadfast in Eastern Europe. Daladier demurred that he thought France not strong enough and that he was giving Bonnet charge of diplomacy. Paul-Boncour replied circumspectly that if Daladier meant to change French policy, he could not make a better choice. Mandel spoke more bluntly: "His long nose sniffs danger and responsibility from afar. He will hide under any flat stone to avoid it." Gamelin said worse: "a foul ferment without morality but with a taste for intrigue." William L. Shirer, who reported on France and Germany in the 1930s, judged him to be "this vain, tricky, conniving Radical politician." Paul Nizan, the Communist novelist and friend of Jean-Paul Sartre, described the "enormous nose," which overpowered a long sly face, agreed with the accusation of vanity, and added, "extremely ambitious, very touchy, very susceptible to flattery; and can be very spiteful and resentful if you rub him the wrong way." Alexander Werth, the well-connected correspondent for the Manchester *Guardian,* uncovered a strange story. During the war Bonnet had defended a German officer sentenced to execution by court-martial and risked a charge of treason by smuggling the man's few possessions back to his family. All concurred that Bonnet was not especially likable and that his political career had flourished only because of his marriage to the niece of Camille Pelletan, a great power in the Radical Party during the early 1900s. Her charm manifest and her political contacts legendary, she was known as *la soutien-Georges* (George's support), a pun on *soutien-gorge* (brassiere).[9]

To his wife's influence Bonnet added an economic expertise rare among the Radicals. By April 1938 he had been a member of thirteen cabinets, always charged with budgetary or commercial responsibilities. Because he had been Daladier's minister of finance in 1933, when he reestablished the national lottery, he was blamed—unfairly—for failing to recognize the illegal enterprises that culminated in the Stavisky affair.

Like other Radicals, he recovered through the victory of the Popular Front but was profoundly uneasy about its economic program. As minister of finance in the Chautemps cabinet from June 1937 to January 1938, he began the return to more orthodox policies. Daladier now wanted him for foreign minister. Bonnet did have some diplomatic experience, as France's representative to the 1932 Stresa conference (to discuss a Danubian customs union) and the 1933 London economic conference (to discuss currency stabilization) and as ambassador to the United States from late 1936 to mid-1937, despite complete ignorance of English. But the experience was not auspicious, for both conferences were failures, and the American Congress passed the Neutrality Act. The best explanation for the choice is a version of Paul-Boncour's: Bonnet's personality of equivocation matched well with Daladier's of hesitation.

Following the massive votes of confidence in the Chamber of Deputies and the Senate and the grant of decree powers, the plan of the cabinet was to concentrate on the economy and rearmament. Daladier began his ministerial declaration by proclaiming, "a great and free country can be saved only by itself," and then defining that salvation as "a healthy currency and a healthy rhythm of production, above all in the war industries." But the ambiguity of his language about foreign policy set newspapers, and thus public opinion, ablaze: "Some countries are disappearing while new empires are coming into existence. . . . In all cases—whether strengthening the bonds with our friends or proving our loyalty to pacts and treaties we have signed, or entering into equitable negotiations—the unity of national energies is indispensable." Already, the fact of *Anschluss* had raised the issue of how France was to fulfill its treaty obligations to Czechoslovakia. Moderates and conservatives, the direction in which the cabinet was now tilted, urgently called for a reconciliation with Mussolini, which would require not only recognizing Italy's new African empire but acquiescing to Franco's victory in Spain, and for abandonment of the ties to the Soviet Union which exacerbated relations with Great Britain. Here was the very opposite of Popular Front diplomacy, but the argument was still over honoring the commitment.[10]

Much more dangerous was a questioning of whether to do so. Czechoslovakia had been in existence only nineteen years, and, despite its alliance with France, not many French appeared to know much about it. A series of articles in the right-wing and widely read *Le Journal* made the country out to be part of some great Danubian morass. In Jean-Paul Sartre's novel *Le Sursis* (*The Reprieve*), set during the last days of September 1938, Mathieu Delarue, professor of philosophy at the lycée Buffon, has to sketch the boundaries of Czechoslovakia on the map of Central Europe in a pre–Great War atlas for the sometime medical student Ivich Serguine. Although its many ethnic varieties—Czech, Slovak, Ruthene, German, Magyar, Polish—lived in relative harmony, the accusation "artificial" and "fissiparous" was easy to make. As an excuse to leave them to their fate, it was easy to believe. The people of Czechoslovakia were far away, unknown, perhaps a burden, and—decisively—not French. Should France risk "our own tomorrow," as Colonel de La Rocque asked, by defending them? Yes, replied Henri de Kérillis, "for all that Europe is lacking is the word and the will of France."[11]

On 12 April *Le Temps,* the most respected of French newspapers, published an analysis of France's treaty obligations to Czechoslovakia by Joseph Barthélemy, an august legal scholar at the Paris Faculty of Law. Were three million Frenchmen to be sacrificed for the maintenance of three million Sudeten Germans under Czechoslovak rule? Was France bound by an alliance established to supplement the Locarno Pact now that Germany, in reoccupying the Rhineland, had denounced it? Was there any cause other than invasion of France itself that would justify the national suicide war would mean? No to all, he answered unequivocally. Such was Barthélemy's authoritative stature that Bonnet had to dissociate the cabinet from this editorial. He called in the Czech ambassador, Stefan Osusky, to declare formally that "the position of the French government in relation to Central Europe has not undergone any change" and charged the Quai d'Orsay's jurisconsult to refute Barthélemy in a brief that *Le Temps* published on 17 April. But damage had been done. In Paris the Maginot mentality was strengthened. In other capitals, especially London, Berlin, and Prague, questions about French determination became more insistent. Former premier André Tardieu, who had been at Clemenceau's side as Czechoslovakia was created and the Treaty of Versailles negotiated, answered the unwilling and the wavering on

6 May in the weekly *Gringoire:* that in fighting for Czechoslovakia, France was fighting for itself against the menace of a German colossus, a cause that Great Britain would certainly join, as in 1914; that Germany's claim for the Sudeten Germans of Czechoslovakia would be followed by a claim for the Alsatian Germans of France; and that Germany's denunciation of the Locarno Pact did not free France of an obligation willingly assumed. Refusing to accept official and semiofficial repudiation, Barthélemy then replied in *Gringoire* that the proper historical analogy to 1938 was not 1914 and the alliance that barely won the Great War but 1870, when France faced Prussia alone and met disaster. This exchange had the potential to deepen anxieties.[12]

Bonnet thought that reassurance could come through reconciliation with Italy. He sensed an opening because the British were making up to Mussolini in an agreement signed on 16 April and because the French chargé d'affaires in Rome, Jules Blondel, reported that the *Anschluss* had shocked a public that was already anti-German. When Blondel met with the Italian foreign minister, Count Galeazzo Ciano, on 18 April, he learned that any negotiation had to follow Hitler's state visit in early May. Yet because the conversation was cordial, Blondel and Bonnet were confident of eventual success. The demarche would please the British, with whom Bonnet and Daladier were to meet in London at the end of April. And pleasing the British was by far the most important aspect of French diplomacy.

Five months had passed since the foreign policy principals of the Western democracies had sat down together, and of the four only Prime Minister Neville Chamberlain remained from November. Much had happened since. Anthony Eden, regarded as a supporter of collective security, resigned as foreign secretary in February, succeeded by Edward Lord Halifax, whose thinking was similar to Chamberlain's, that small nations were on their own. The Popular Front team of Camille Chautemps and Yvon Delbos was long gone, and in their stead Daladier and Bonnet were supposed more willing to shelter behind the Maginot Line. Of course, by more than doubling Germany's border with Czechoslovakia, the *Anschluss* placed Prague in great danger. Hitler's willingness to provoke a crisis was more clearly recognized, and thus the alarm over the speech by Konrad Henlein, political leader of the Sudeten Germans, at Karlsbad on 24 April. There could be no mistaking that Berlin inspired his denunciation of the concessions the Czech government proposed to mollify its German minority. When the Anglo-French talks began four days later, on 28 April, Daladier sought unambiguous responses from the British about opening general staff consultations to prepare for war and about opposing possible German aggression in Central Europe, meaning especially Czechoslovakia. Chamberlain resisted. On the coordination of military preparations he promised nothing more than air defense support and declared that only two ill-equipped divisions would be available for ground combat. On Central Europe he argued that Britain and France were not strong enough to fight Germany and that Czechoslovakia would do well to meet whatever demands Hitler made and might thereby ensure its survival. As a means, he proposed Britain's urging Berlin to seek a peaceful solution and France's pressing Prague to concede quickly.

The official communiqué of the conference cited the British-French "general agreement in the action that might most usefully be taken" to preserve peace in Europe. Stripped of diplomatic language, that meant utter French accommodation to British policy and the first step toward betraying Czechoslovakia. All was not lost: Daladier and Bonnet spent one night as the guests of King George VI and Queen Elizabeth at Windsor Castle, dinner on gold plate and music by the band of the Grenadier Guards—the experience so delighting Bonnet that he was reported to talk of nothing else. Back in Paris, Daladier bluntly told the American ambassador, William C. Bullitt, that "he had considered the position of Czechoslovakia entirely hopeless since the annexation of Austria by Germany" and, to the question of whether France would go to war, retorted contemptuously, "With what?" In fact, two weeks earlier Kérillis had written presciently in *L'Epoque,* "Dear M. Hitler, France is the ally of Czechoslovakia, but she is determined not to keep her promise and her solemn understanding to defend her."[13]

The French foreign policy apparatus generally rejected this pessimism but was deeply divided over how best to realize a policy of strength. At the Quai d'Orsay, Léger, the secretary-general, sought diplomacy à l'Aristide Briand, his mentor. He hoped to surround France with friends who shared democratic ideals—thus, his support for the

League of Nations, for close ties to Britain, for mutual assistance pacts with Eastern Europe, and for rejecting Mussolini and Franco—but if France had too few friends, he would grudgingly appease Germany. The political director, René Massigli, was sterner. He regarded Czechoslovakia as the rock on which German aggression would run aground, and to make certain of the shipwreck he recommended prodding Great Britain to accept a role for the Soviet Union, conciliating Italy, and seizing the moral advantage of having the League take Prague's side. Pierre Comert, who headed the Press Office, was a version of Paul-Boncour. Perhaps the only high official at the foreign ministry still favoring a clearly Popular Front policy, he called for opposing German Nazis, Italian Fascists, Spanish Nationalists, and their like everywhere else by combining the Western democracies with the Soviet Union through the League. Given his pronouncedly Maginot mentality, Bonnet was uncomfortable with all three of his top subordinates but least so with Léger, who was, again like Briand, at heart a compromiser. Anthony Eden admired Léger the poet, who wrote exquisite lines under the name Saint-John Perse, but less so the diplomat, whom he claimed lacked the strength of character to impose his ideas. Of Massigli, Bonnet in his memoirs criticized a "difficult temperament," meaning the refusal to acquiesce. In October 1938 Bonnet resolved the internal debate by appointing Massigli ambassador to Turkey—effectively to exile—and dismissing Comert.

Among the principal French ambassadors André François-Poncet at Berlin came closest to Bonnet's views. Sleek, ample, born to wealth, steeped in German culture, he found Nazism alternatively seductive and repulsive. Perhaps because of his fluent Germanophilia, he entertained illusions about the regime. If France and Great Britain distanced themselves from the Soviet Union, made limited concessions, but also took a firm line, Berlin, he argued, might be won to moderation. The opposite advice came from Robert Coulondre at Moscow. Quiet and supremely conscientious, he came to understand that the convulsions of Stalin's rule had made the Soviet Union stronger, not weaker. He urged military staff talks to give the Franco-Russian alliance reality but even more so to prevent a sense of isolation among Soviet leaders which would, he predicted ominously, make them turn to Germany. From

London, Charles Corbin, courtly and dispirited, had almost no advice at all. He concluded early on that British leaders were not going to be firm and were not going to check their anti-Soviet attitude. If France wanted a more aggressive policy, it would be on its own. Bonnet rejected that option absolutely, and dispatches arguing for it from Léon Noël in Warsaw and Victor de Lacroix in Prague he disregarded almost entirely. What he called their excessive sympathy for Czechoslovakia was instead a protest against his increasingly disingenuous diplomacy.[14]

In the meantime, while there was a meantime, the mirage of security created by the London consultations granted Daladier the moment to announce his prescriptions for the economy. The context was already propitious with the franc firmer and stock prices higher. For the financial world the new cabinet was the first of the post–Popular Front, and Paul Marchandeau, who returned to the ministry of finance he had directed from January to March under Chautemps, was reassuringly bland, willing to do what was necessary but not go too far. And that was the tenor set by the first set of decree-laws, announced on 3 May. To cover the budget deficit there was new rigor: an 8 percent increase to all taxes direct and indirect; revised customs duties and a special surtax on defense industries to prevent profiteering would add 3.7 billion francs; denying a planned 10 percent raise to government workers and curbing abuses in war pensions would save an additional 0.7 billion. To pay for rearmament there was a new bond issue of 5 billion francs at 5 percent for thirty years. To stimulate production there were limitations on the new taxes for manufacturers of exports, subsidies for constructing new housing, and low-interest loans for improvements by landlords. One day later, as a further spur to exports, Daladier announced the equivalent of a third devaluation: permitting the franc to float as low as 179 to the British pound. Over the next two months the franc would fall 11 percent against the pound (from 160.54 to 178.17) and 11.5 percent against the dollar (from 32.33 to 35.93). The reaction by investors to this program was immediate and overwhelmingly positive. They moved an estimated 17 billion francs back to France from foreign markets and bought up the rearmament bonds in only a few hours upon their issue on 16 May.[15]

The *Guardian*'s Werth noted a new optimism in France during the first three weeks of May, but his always acute perception was hardly necessary to draw this conclusion. Department stores and shops fairly blossomed with clothing and equipment for the spring and for summer vacations, now the right of all. Au Printemps advertised a full range of travel bags, from expensive leather to economical fiberboard. Galeries Lafayette featured tennis outfits, camping outfits, beach outfits — everything youthful and sporty. Guerlain announced a lighter eau de cologne inspired by spring. In the tony newspapers women's pages advised "how to match your makeup to your gown," called fox the "fur of today," urged "going strapless," and declared a "return to nature" the "attitude in 1938." Military analysts allayed fears of war by writing of "the Czechoslovak army, shield of Central Europe," and "the lesson of Verdun underlining the importance of fortifications." Unemployment declined 3.1 percent from April to May and would decline another 4.7 percent from May to June. Diplomat and mystically Catholic poet Paul Claudel described the Shroud of Turin as bearing the imprint of Jesus Christ.[16]

But the problems of the day kept intruding. Production remained flat and then all but flat: the level at 82 for April and May, 83 for June. As a stimulus, the cabinet prepared a decree on permissible exceptions to the forty-hour week which it issued on 24 May. Management gained thereby the right to recoup all the hours lost through strikes and, upon authorization by the minister of labor, add up to an hour of work per day or eight hours per week but only with the concurrence of the labor unions, which almost invariably refused. The minister of the interior, Albert Sarraut, too timid to oppose the German reoccupation of the Rhineland, demonstrated a certain ferocity in rounding up "undesirable aliens" and issuing restrictive rules for foreign workers. At the end of April the marriage in Tirana of Albania's King Zog to Countess Geraldine Apponyi became another occasion to celebrate the influence of the Berlin-Rome Axis, Hitler sending a deluxe Mercedes Benz as a gift and Mussolini flying in many of the guests—flying out, one of the planes crashed amid the Apennines. In Spain Franco's forces isolated Republican-held Barcelona by their victory at Vinaroz on 15 April and launched a massive attack along the Ebro River. But most of all the question of Czechoslovakia reached a crisis.[17]

On 24 April, with much vehemence, Konrad Henlein had made demands upon the government of Czechoslovakia on behalf of its

Sudeten German minority. By the terms of this "Karlsbad program" self-described German-speaking regions were to have full autonomy, compensation for alleged damages since 1918, and the right to proclaim their Germanism and pursue the "ideology of Germans," meaning National Socialism; furthermore, Prague was to revise completely its foreign policy, meaning to abandon the alliance with France and to align itself with Germany. Because the British and French still believed— even after the *Anschluss*—that what Hitler and his henchmen within and without Germany demanded was subject to negotiation, they enjoined Czech president Eduard Benes to be accommodating. Knowing better but dependent upon the Western democracies for his nation's survival, Benes offered talks. Henlein instead traveled to London and Berlin pretending to a moderation that was credible only through elaborate self-deception. His return was the signal for a succession of violent incidents in the German region against government officials and installations. Ahead of everyone else this time, *Le Figaro*'s Wladimir d'Ormesson warned on 16 May that the rising tension could lead to a general war and its attendant horrors. He was prescient or had excellent sources because during the next days rumors of German troop movements near the border of Czechoslovakia caused enormous alarm. On 20 May, recalling that similar rumors had preceded the *Anschluss,* Britain's ambassador in Berlin, Sir Nevile Henderson, sought an explanation from the German foreign ministry and received an anodyne reply. Early the next morning at Eger a Czech border guard shot dead two Sudeten motorcyclists speeding through the frontier crossing. In Prague the government called up several thousand reservists, using as a pretext the preservation of order. But this action could easily be interpreted as the first step in a mobilization to secure the nation's defenses against sudden German attack.[18]

No such attack was planned—yet. Hitler was volcanically angry that Czechoslovakia appeared to have called his bluff. His subordinates, especially Foreign Minister Joachim von Ribbentrop, communicated this fury to the diplomatic representatives of Czechoslovakia, France, and Great Britain. The response Hitler anticipated was craven; what he got was resolute. In Berlin on 21 and 22 May François-Poncet declared to the German government that France would honor its commitments to

Czechoslovakia in the event of German aggression. Henderson delivered two messages from Halifax starkly warning that "His Majesty's government could not guarantee that they would not be forced by circumstances to become involved" in that instance. Emphasizing the gravity of the situation, he ordered the preparation of a special train to evacuate British embassy personnel if diplomatic relations were severed. In Paris Daladier stressed to the German ambassador that France would fight to prove her honor and predicted darkly that the war would be the end of European civilization. When the "May Crisis" ended without an attack, without a war, the credit went to this vigorous attitude.[19]

The self-satisfaction, the chest puffing, of the Paris newspapers and of the public opinion they registered was at first remarkable. On the Right, where criticism of Prague had become almost endemic, *Le Journal* lauded the "unanimity, calm, and courage" of the Czech people, and *Le Matin* celebrated France's "wise and virile friends" in the heart of Europe. Prague's constant defenders went much further. Emile Buré in *L'Ordre* called Czechoslovakia "an exemplary democracy, the last obstacle to the *Drang nach Osten* (Germany's "eastward expansion"). In *L'Epoque* Kérillis compared the Czechs to the Belgians in 1914: "Destiny sometimes reserves the highest and noblest of missions for the smallest of nations." And although he acknowledged the calamity of a war— "There is not a Frenchman who does not recoil from it in horror"—he asserted, "there is also not a Frenchman who is unwilling to do his duty if eventualities require it." The Socialist *Le Populaire* and the Communist *L'Humanité* predictably praised the sangfroid of the Czech government and claimed that peace had been safeguarded through the respect of treaties, meaning France, and commitments, meaning Great Britain. For La Rocque's *Le Petit Journal* the essential lesson of the May Crisis was that Britain kept its word to France. For *Le Figaro* it was the Franco-British "unity of action." But writing in *L'Europe Nouvelle*, Pertinax (André Géraud), the most respected of the foreign policy columnists, warned, "it is not certain that our British friends who saved the peace by an act of firmness the other day will not try at some other critical moment to save the peace by an act of weakness." "British policy," he argued, "is empirical with no fixed rules, and France's internal disorder, if not stopped in time, may send the 'Chamberlain experiment' off in a different direction." For Pertinax the essential lesson of the May Crisis was that the "French system"—meaning Barthou's iron ring around Germany—be reconstituted through the addition of Russia before Hitler created the next emergency.[20]

Pertinax called 21 May a "turning point" because the danger of war suddenly became more reality than potentiality. Germany was threatening Czechoslovakia; Czechoslovakia was determined to resist; France was bound by treaty to Czechoslovakia; and Great Britain had made a dramatic decision to back French action. If events played out in this fashion, and if France honored its commitments, the French decision would be the key to a new European war. One manner of understanding the transformation of accepted ideas or habits is in comparison to an epidemic: the altered perception becomes contagious, little changes have enormous impact, and the transformation happens suddenly—reaching what has been called the "tipping point." Recent reports about the civilian casualties in Spain and China—from air raids, artillery bombardment, and ravage—and accounts of Nazi atrocities in post-*Anschluss* Austria, where by mid-May thirty-nine Jewish lawyers had committed suicide rather than suffer arrest and sentence to concentration camps, were a litany of fear. More important, here was a preview of what might well be France's fate in any war. And so war had to be prevented, even wished away. *Le Temps,* since April said to reflect Bonnet's views, insisted on 23 May that Hitler had many times affirmed his desire for peace and that "nothing permits doubting his sincerity." *Le Figaro* was usually steadfast and anti-German, but one day later its editor, Lucien Romier, offered the reassurance that, while Hitler might seek "a violent adventure, . . . he has thus far shown that he does not behave like a blind man." In another species of wishing and not far from Bonnet's thinking, Pierre-Etienne Flandin wrote in *Le Petit Parisien* on 29 May that France and Great Britain would most serve the cause of peace by negotiating with Germany and Italy "their return to a concert of Europe where force would serve only as the sanction of law and justice." Writing such words two months after the *Anschluss* and only days after the May Crisis required either cynicism or delusion.[21]

Maybe both, because upon close inspection the May Crisis revealed France's allies and friends to be something less than allies and friends.

Late in the evening on 22 May, at the very moment when their nations were supposedly demonstrating a common resolution, Sir Eric Phipps, Britain's ambassador to Paris, presented Bonnet with a note from Halifax that all but sent him into vertigo. Bluntly, the French government was informed that it should have no "illusions": Britain would come to France's aid upon an unprovoked attack by Germany against French territory but would not assist in the defense of Czechoslovakia under any circumstances. Because French commitments to Czechoslovakia could lead to a war between France and Germany, Britain expected—meaning demanded—to be consulted before any French mobilization. The note warned further that in the judgment of British military analysts even the joint intervention of Great Britain, France, and the Soviet Union could not save Czechoslovakia. The news from the Poles was worse. On the same day, 22 May, Bonnet met with Ambassador Juliusz Lukasiewicz to ask formally what the reaction of Poland would be if France and Britain defended Czechoslovakia against German aggression. The reply from Warsaw two days later by Foreign Minister Jozef Beck was cold and arrogant: Poland would "reserve the right of examination and decision" while demanding that any concessions granted to Sudeten Germans be matched for Teschen Poles. Worse still came from Brussels, where the French ambassador, Paul Bargeton, was told, "if you enter our territory to aid the Czechs, you will confront the Belgian army." The ambassador of the United States to Paris, William C. Bullitt, was a Francophile but perhaps not a true friend of France. Although he counted both Blum and Daladier among his confidants, politically he was closer to Caillaux. His prescription for European harmony was Franco-German cooperation, and he regarded the Soviet Union with horror and thus also the Franco-Soviet pact. Indiscreetly, he told the Poles that French assistance to Czechoslovakia would be "illusory." And to make his prediction true he dared suggest to President Franklin D. Roosevelt, "I think we should attempt to find some way which will let the French out of their moral commitment." Lafayette he was not: when Guy La Chambre placed orders for aircraft in the United States, Bullitt reminded him that the Neutrality Act might prevent their delivery.[22]

By contrast, the Soviet Union, which Bullitt loathed, clamored to fulfill its responsibilities. At Geneva on 9 May Maxim Litvinov, the people's commissar for foreign affairs, pressed Bonnet to acquire permission for Russian transit rights from Poland and Romania, both fearing and mistrusting the Soviet Union. He reminded Bonnet that the French alliance with Poland and friendship with Romania presented the opportunity to make Soviet intervention possible if there were German aggression against Czechoslovakia. When Bonnet took no action, Litvinov drew the conclusion that France was wishing away the danger and slipping the bonds of their alliance. His suspicions aroused, a month later, on 5 June and two weeks after the May Crisis, Litvinov had the Soviet ambassador in Paris, Jacob Suritz, pose a tortured question to the Quai d'Orsay: if Poland took advantage of a German attack on Czechoslovakia to seize Teschen and if Russia then attacked Poland in defense of Czechoslovak territory, what would France do, because by treaty France was required to defend both Czechoslovakia and Poland? The French answer implied that the question was straightforward: Soviet defense of Czechoslovakia was dependent upon the prior commitment of French forces, and, thus, France and the Soviet Union would be fighting together. Instead, Litvinov was already considering permutations. At Moscow he told Coulondre that the Soviet Union might intervene even if France did not. Coulondre understood that comment literally as an insinuation that France would not defend Czechoslovakia and potentially as a threat that the Soviet Union might have to reach an accommodation with Germany.[23]

France had let Europe go to the devil, and now that the devil was stalking France, France was all alone with Czechoslovakia. For the Czechs the French were their only hope. For the French the Czechs were either the keystone of resistance to German domination or the trap by which France would be forced into a new and terrible war. Blum, Delbos, and Paul-Boncour had tried unsuccessfully to establish a foreign policy based upon the keystone. Daladier and Bonnet would base their foreign policy on escaping from the trap. The first evidence was their anger and frustration at the Czechoslovak mobilization. Bonnet complained that Czech leaders had completely ignored the arbitration treaty between Germany and Czechoslovakia which dated from the Locarno Pact, but he was far more exercised by their conduct on 20–21 May. They had acted without consulting Paris and without informing even Lacroix, the French ambassador in Prague and as much a friend as Czechoslovakia had in Europe. To French leaders the implication was that the Czechs had used reports of threatening German troop concentrations to generate the illusion of an emergency by which France and Great Britain could be brought to condemn Germany. Reeling from the Halifax note, Bonnet called in the Czech ambassador, Osusky, to make clear France's insistence that Prague make "generous and speedy" concessions to the Sudetens and rescind the mobilization. And so began French scrambling to escape the trap—but leave the Czechs behind. On 24 May Bonnet complained bitterly to Bullitt of Benes's "pigheadedness." On 27 May the ministry's jurisconsult issued an opinion that Czechoslovakia would have to invoke the arbitration treaty with Germany before requesting French assistance and that such assistance would be determined by "the circumstances of the time." On 29 May, claiming pressure from the British, Bonnet told Osusky that Prague should conclude an agreement on Sudeten demands within "two weeks." When Osusky dared reply that French foreign policy risked becoming hostage to British demands, not just Bonnet but Léger warned him that close coordination with Great Britain was France's paramount objective and that Czechoslovakia would interfere at its peril. The devil was knocking on the door.[24]

Did that sound drive the thousands who packed theaters to see Marcel Carné's new movie, which opened in Paris on 17 May? *Le Quai des brumes* (*The Port of Shadows*) was the darkest of films noirs. "Right-thinkers"—political as well as moral—were disgusted by the offhand portrayal of decadence, Suzanne Chantal in *Le Journal de la femme* denouncing its "bitterness, atrocious despair, ugliness, discouragement, and sadness." *Le Figaro*'s reviewer, Jean Laury, agreed that it was "among the most despairing ever" but then pronounced unequivocally "and among the best. Its technique is faultless, its interpretation incomparable." The belletrist Francis Carco used his *Figaro* column to praise how "the ancestral, the eternal combat of man with his conscience appears to us here in all its implacable brutality." The story is of an army deserter, Jean (played by Jean Gabin), hiding out in Le Havre, who meets a young woman, Nelly (played by Michèle Morgan), anxious to escape her oppressive guardian, Zabel (played by Michel Simon). In a movie where every character is a *raté* (failure), the dream of Jean and Nelly to flee

France and make a new life grants them a single moment of joy before they are enveloped again by an inescapable past. In 1938 audiences so embraced this desire to get away combined with pessimism about the chances that they made *The Port of Shadows* the year's most commercially successful French movie and a close second to *Blanche-Neige* (*Snow White*), the Disney animated feature from the United States which was boosted by children's repeated attendance.[25]

From their two previous movies, *Jenny* (1936) and *Drôle de drame* (*Bizarre, Bizarre*) (1937), director Carné and poet-screenwriter Jacques Prévert already had a reputation for chiaroscuro lighting and for developing scenes and dialogue tailored to the specific talents of their actors. In both respects *The Port of Shadows* was an advance of significant magnitudes. Apart from two scenes the action takes place in shadows, smoke, and fog, literally darkening the screen and figuratively preventing the characters from accurately assessing themselves or their possibilities. A trucker on the road to Le Havre picks up Jean, a hitchhiker in army uniform, who takes a proffered cigarette but deflects a question about being on leave. When a dog suddenly darts into the road, Jean grabs the steering wheel and forces the truck to the shoulder. The driver is angry, wants to fight, but then backs down, saying he fears Jean has a gun. "Using a gun is easy," Jean replies. "You fire and the guy gives a little cry and clutches his belly, making a face like a kid who's eaten too much. Then, his hands go all red, and he falls down. You're left standing there, not understanding anything any more. It's like everything has melted away." The trucker senses that he is speaking from experience and leaves as quickly as possible. We have just met Jean Gabin, playing the quintessential loner, the tough-yet-tender outcast, the good-guy-in-trouble, a type and part he had perfected during the last two years starring in Jean Renoir's *Les Bas-fonds* (*The Lower Depths*), Jean Grémillion's *Gueule d'amour* (*Love Mug*), Julien Duvivier's *La Belle équipe* (*The Good Team*) and *Pépé le moko* (*Pépé the Gangster*). But soon enough Carné and Prévert would reveal his raw carnal magnetism and then the romantic hero he had played as Maréchal in Jean Renoir's *La Grande illusion* (*The Great Illusion*).

Jean walks the rest of the way to Le Havre, where he meets a genial drunkard, Quart Vittel (played by Raymond Aimos). Recognizing from the uniform that Jean needs a refuge, he takes him to Panama's, "the safest place on the coast," a lonely bar on the edge of town. The dog, a white spotted short-haired terrier, has trailed along, but Jean declares, "I like no one who seeks a master." The bar owner (played by Edouard Delmont) takes his name from a white suit, a guitar, and a panama he has owned since 1906. He cares not a whit what Jean may be running from but warns: "Don't bring the fog in with you: no trouble, no sob stories. There's no fog here. It's always fair weather." He indicates the barometer above the bar, the indicator showing high pressure, but the joke is that the needle is nailed down. Otherwise, the reading would be for storms because everyone but Quart Vittel is dour—especially the well-dressed man carrying an artist kit, Michel Krauss (played by Robert Le Vigan). "I can't help painting the things behind things," he says. "To me, a swimmer is already a drowned man. . . . I have to live in this sort of anguish. . . . Some people go hunting, fishing. Others fight wars, commit their little crimes of passion. Some commit suicide. You have to kill someone." Noticing Jean, he adds, "If I were to do your portrait, I'd paint you in the fog, hands in pockets." Jean reacts angrily to these "fine phrases" and then excuses himself by confessing that he has not eaten for two days and has no money: "When you're hungry, you're supposed to say so but you don't. Funny, but there's such a thing as pride."

Panama takes him into a back room to offer bread, cheese, and sausage, but what Jean notices is a young woman standing at the back door dressed in a trench coat and a beret. She is a blonde gamine with a pageboy, a tight smile, and a stance like a wary cat. As Jean devours the food, his eyes are all over her. He says: "You're beautiful, and I'm attracted, no kidding. Though there isn't much of you. It's like the movies. One look and I like what I see." But he has taken her for a prostitute: "You're on the game, hawking your meat. You're not here to visit your old grandmother, like Red Riding Hood. More's the pity, because I'm the Big Bad Wolf." Then, with less bravado, as if from sad experience, he continues: "A man and a woman can't get along. They don't understand each other. They don't speak the same language." She responds, "Maybe they can't understand each other, but they can be in love." Jean asks, "Have you ever been in love?" She holds his gaze briefly then turns away, "Not truly." He does not yet know her name. He thinks he has been chatting up a whore, and she realizes what he thinks of her. The sexual tension, the sexual chemistry, between Jean and Nelly is manifest and, in reality, tangible. Gabin, thirty-three, and Morgan, seventeen, barely restrained their passion for each other during the filming; in 1939 he left his second wife for her.

The attraction becomes a bond when Panama's is suddenly no longer the safest place on the coast. Pistol shots announce that local gangsters have taken their feuding this far out of town. Lucien Legardier (played by Pierre Brasseur) and his henchmen are after Zabel because they think he killed a pal of theirs, Meurice Brevin, and then tipped the police that they did it. Zabel, who hides his illegal enterprises behind the facade of a trinket shop, did indeed kill Meurice, but from jealousy, not any falling out of thieves. For Zabel is Nelly's guardian, and Meurice was her lover. Zabel lusts after her, perhaps has already molested her. When Panama fires back from inside and shoots out a headlamp on Lucien's car, the gang drives off. That saves Zabel, but he is quickly sent away before he can see either Jean or Nelly, who have remained in the back room. They sense that they have both gone to ground here. As the sun rises, Nelly muses: "Each time another day dawns, you think something new is going to happen. But the sun goes down and so do you. It's sad." In the barroom, when Jean asks where he can get some civilian clothes, Panama concludes that he must be on "indefinite leave" and promises something by the evening. Jean, Nelly, and the dog then head back toward Le Havre, their alliance contingent and tenuous. Watching them go, Michel says to Panama: "As it happens, I have a set of clothes and papers I don't need. My own. I'm going for a swim. It's rough and it's foggy and that's fine. I don't swim very well, but I feel I shall swim to the utmost." He walks outside. Panama follows, calling: "Michel! Don't be stupid! What's the use?" There is only a heap of belongings.

The next scene is the first without fog, as if to imply that the way out can be found. Jean and Nelly sit on an old pier, their legs dangling over the water as they banter. Nelly says she is seventeen; Jean replies that he was seventeen "once." They have just promised to meet later at Panama's, and Nelly has slipped some money into Jean's pocket, when a car with a broken headlamp pulls up. Lucien, his gang behind him, sneers at Nelly, "It's a bit much, the way you go with anyone but turn up your nose at me." He reaches for her, and she cries, "Don't touch me!" Lucien mocks her: "Meurice didn't touch you, I suppose? Or the others? Or this one [indicating Jean]? Anyone at all but me, is that it? Instead of shaking it about at the Petit Tabarin, you should have stuck to the shop with your guardian!" When he grabs at her, Jean rushes forward, slaps him twice across the face, and warns him to stay away from them. Humiliated, Lucien rushes to his car and drives away with his equally cowed gang. Nelly asks Jean why he intervened, saying, "You don't know that I'm worth it." Then she tells him she must return to Zabel, but "after running away, it will be awful whether I go back or not." To himself as much as to Nelly, Jean agrees: "I ought to go back somewhere, too. But as you say, it would be awful." The way out is closing fast.

At Zabel's trinket shop Lucien brandishes a pistol, insisting, "I am a man!" He wants back "all the papers" and accuses Zabel of murdering Meurice. Calmly, Zabel denies any knowledge of Meurice and claims that the "papers" will wind up with the authorities if he should die suddenly. Overwrought and fearful, Lucien again threatens to shoot Zabel, and as his gang prevents him, he shouts, "Some day, I'll show you I'm someone!" One of the gang explains that a soldier has just knocked Lucien down in a fight over Nelly. As soon as they leave, Nelly enters the shop. When Zabel disingenuously asks why she ran away, she answers, "Because I was afraid of you." If so, he says, why return? "Because others frighten me, too. Where would I go?" He puts his hands around her waist, murmuring, "still a child yet already a woman." When she frantically pushes him away, protesting that he not look at her "that way," he accuses her of trolling for soldiers. She stares at him coldly.

As the weather turns darker with fog, Jean wanders the docks until he finds a ship leaving the next day, the *Louisiana,* bound for Venezuela. He thinks his decision made and wants to square accounts. Walking up from the port, he notices a music box displayed in a shop window. He goes inside to find both Nelly and Zabel behind the counter. When Zabel leaves them briefly, Nelly asks whether Jean has followed her and why buy her a souvenir? Embarrassed, he answers, "I don't like taking a woman's money." Shrewdly, Zabel has guessed everything and returns, suggesting Jean stay for a drink. Nelly goes to the basement for cognac and stumbles upon a cufflink—Meurice's—implying that Zabel killed him. Upstairs Zabel tells Jean that Nelly runs off occasionally, "just little escapades, nothing serious." Nelly faints coming up the steps and drops the cufflink. Zabel pockets it quickly and then takes her away to lie down. On his return he is quick to the point. Quoting Jean's army number at him, he says: "You've done something silly, and now you need to get away. I can help. If you need money, papers, a passport." In return all Jean has to do is kill Lucien—he'll be doing society a favor. Jean angrily refuses and grabs Zabel by the throat: "In Indochina, I saw a disgusting thing that made you sick to look at it. A centipede, they called it, and you're just like it. You have a filthy voice, too, sounds like you're crawling through slime. I am what I am. Anything I've done was done in anger because there's always some filth like you around to muck up anything decent. You disgust me. I don't like killing lice." Jean stalks out, the dog ever with him. Nelly comes from a side door and catches him in the street. They agree to meet that night at a small fair outside the city.

In the late-afternoon fog Jean walks to Panama's. Michel's possessions are waiting for him, and everything fits more or less, even the description on the passport—"Incredible how alike people sound on paper." The wallet contains 850 francs, and Panama assures Jean: "That won't make any difference to him. He won't need it." Jean takes Michel's kit to complete the disguise and leaves his uniform, which Panama casts into the sea weighted by a rock. At the port Jean makes friends with Molène (played by René Génin), ship doctor for the *Louisiana* and artist manqué. Over a drink at the bar-hotel Au Rendez-Vous de la Marine, Molène offers to arrange Jean's passage in return for discussions about painting. Knowing nothing else to say, Jean repeats Michel's words, "I usually try to paint the things hidden behind things." When Molène learns that Jean has only a single case, he exclaims: "Wonderful! That's how I always imagined artists to be. No luggage, independent, free. How fine to be free. . . . I mean, have you no personal attachments?" Jean answers, "None."

In the second scene without fog Jean and Nelly meet at the fair. She buys a leash for the dog: "It would be awful to lose him now that I'm used to him, and you." Feeling guilty, he replies: "You're a strange girl. Looking at you, listening to you, makes me feel like crying." She takes his arm: "You can't imagine how happy I am when I am with you. I can breathe. I feel alive. Being happy must do that." Is Jean taken by love or by pity? He says, "You've got great eyes, you know." And she sighs, "Kiss me." And then, "Kiss me again." There is a fade to the bumper car arcade. Lucien and his crowd have broken in line to get tickets—"Down peasants. Make way for your betters." He tries to impress his girlfriend by swiping at passing hats and knocks off Jean's. When Lucien tries to escape, Jean again slaps him hard across the face twice: "I warned you!" Everyone laughs, including the girlfriend. Lucien screams, "I'll kill him—him and Zabel both. I'll kill them, I tell you." Calmly, Jean leads Nelly away. At a table beside the merry-go-round she confesses: "It was so awful at Zabel's. I couldn't breathe. At the Petit Tabarin, at least people danced and had fun. And Meurice was nice to me. He told me he loved me, so I said I loved him too." When Jean comforts her, she continues: "When you call me Nelly like that, I feel like a little girl again. . . . I grew up too quickly, saw too much. I'm damaged goods." He protests: "Damaged goods! Don't be crazy. You're the most unspoiled girl I've ever met. When a girl is pretty and wants to live, it's like when a man wants to be free—everyone gangs up on them." Here is the moment she has sought consciously or not: she becomes the focus of his honor and his pride. "I'm sure I really do love you, Jean. You mustn't leave me. What would become of me without you? I won't go back to Zabel's again and be afraid all the time. . . . If you go, maybe you'll take me, too. . . . Keep me with you, Jean." There is no fog, and for the moment the path is clear.

The following morning in a small sordid room at the Au Rendez-Vous de la Marine, Jean is dressing as Nelly lies sleepily in the bed. "Do you remember?" she asks. "You woke me last night and told me you loved me. . . . I'm smiling because I was wrong in thinking life was so awful." Jean has been staring out the window at the *Louisiana*. He begins, "Listen, I really must talk to you," when he is interrupted by the delivery of breakfast and the newspaper. Nelly sees the headline and screams: Meurice's body has washed up at the port and, near it, a soldier's uniform. Nelly sobs, "I didn't love him, and he did hurt me, but why kill him?" To Jean's question, "You know who did it?" she is firm, "I'm sure I know." As Nelly dresses quickly, Jean says: "Listen, I was about to say something. . . . there's a ship leaving soon for Venezuela, and I'm taking it. . . . You must think I'm a louse . . . because I could have told you last night. But you seemed so happy, so carefree. I wanted you so much. So I said nothing." She embraces him: "I'm glad you didn't. It wouldn't have changed anything. Even if you were bad, maybe I'd love you just the same." Jean explains that his arrangements are made, Michel's papers are in order, and he will get away unless Zabel talks. Nelly assures him: "If he hasn't already, he won't. Because I know how to keep him quiet." He promises her, "If I get out of this, I'll write, and you'll join me." After watching her leave the bar-hotel, Jean crosses the dock to the *Louisiana,* boards, and finds Molène's cabin. He ties the dog's leash to a support and paces a few moments then strides out determinedly.

Nelly has rushed to Zabel's shop and finds him in the basement. He asks if she has heard the news about Meurice and says there is talk a soldier killed him, "maybe yours." She is no longer cowed: "I won't have him mixed up in this. You know I can prove who the killer was. . . . I tell you I know! . . . You don't frighten me anymore. I'll never be frightened of you again. I want Jean to go free." But Zabel is used to having his way: "No point shouting, no one will hear you. . . . He was no good, Meurice, and I couldn't bear the idea of you and him. I killed him because I was jealous. . . . I horrify you, but I horrify myself sometimes. Even so, I have to go on living." He puts his hands on her, and she screams as Jean appears at the top of the stairs. Jean calls out, "Let her go, you bastard!" Taking up a knife, Zabel answers contemptuously: "You don't think you're getting away, the pair of you? Hoping for a miracle? You believe in Santa Claus? I'll kill you!" But Jean slugs him with a brick, shouting, "You're disgusting, you filthy rotten louse. You don't deserve to live." Nelly looks on, her hands at her mouth, saying nothing until she is certain that Zabel is dead. Then, smiling slightly with satisfaction, she takes Jean's arm and says, "Come away from here."

At the shop door Nelly asks why he came back. Jean replies, "I wanted to say that thanks to you I'd been happy at least once in my life." She pleads with him: "The ship hasn't left yet, maybe you can still go. . . . Please Jean, you must get away." When they step from the shop onto the sidewalk, Lucien is waiting in his car, pistol at the ready. Once Jean has turned to walk toward the docks, he shoots him in the back.

Jean turns staggering, and Lucien fires four more times. Nelly rushes to his side as Lucien drives off. She looks into his eyes, and he murmurs, "Kiss me," and because he knows he is lost, "Quick." She sobs: "You can't do this, Jean. You can't leave me all alone. You mustn't die. I love you so much." Her wail of anguish as she realizes that he is dead is matched by the whistle of the *Louisiana* announcing its departure. Inside Molène's cabin the dog strains at its leash and finally breaks free. After jumping to the dock before the ship casts off, it runs back to the outskirts of Le Havre, where it was first seen along the road in the fog.

Of course, *The Port of Shadows* is a melodrama. The action, covering only forty-eight hours, is replete with murder and revenge. The cinematography is moody, literally reeking of smoke and fog. The plot balances between escape and destiny. Seven decades later the star-crossed lovers, Gabin and Morgan, are so convincing as a couple because of their infatuation for each other. Nelly is a fallen damsel in distress. Jean is a not-so-white knight. They know instinctively that they are each other's second—perhaps last—chance. But in film noir redemption comes to few because would-be, reluctant heroes often fail. For this reason and many others *The Port of Shadows* had analogies to France in 1938. It could be regarded—and to judge from allusions in the reviews was regarded then—as allegory: Jean (France) attempts to rescue Nelly (Czechoslovakia) only to be shot dead by Lucien (fascism). Panama and Quart Vittel define varieties of escapism. Michel is the essence of accepted defeat. Zabel represents the corruption lurking beneath the profession of virtue from every authority figure. If this destiny awaits France, who would not seek escape? But how and where and at what cost? Even the dog races to its former haunts rather than risk the sea journey. Yet the final chance to get away will disappear when the *Louisiana* steams out of the harbor. Was there any hope left of climbing on board? [26]

Just as the French were crowding to see *The Port of Shadows,* British leaders appeared to offer exactly that possibility. Chamberlain and Halifax had never shown the slightest sympathy for the Spanish Republicans and now were making up with Italy. Their note of 22 May clearly demonstrated a low regard for Czechoslovakia. Could an accommodation with Germany be far behind? Like the whistle from the *Louisiana,* this diplomacy signaled to France the exigency of decision. Ambassador Phipps urged Bonnet to threaten Czech leaders with the withdrawal of France's guarantee unless they came to agreement with the Sudetens. Abashed, he did so on 9 June, although more ambiguously than London wanted. Bonnet was also feeling pressure about Italy and Spain. On 15 May at Genoa, Mussolini had vehemently criticized France's relaxation of controls at the Spanish border which allowed the Republicans enough arms and matériel to withstand—barely—the Nationalist offensive. Ciano repeated the attack in a speech at Rome on 2 June: as long as France left the border porous, there was no possibility of reconciliation. Ten days later in a speech at Vienne to a meeting of his Democratic Alliance, Flandin declared that "the greatest menace to the peace and security of France is the war in Spain. It is incredible that a political minority, more or less inspired by Moscow, should impose on France risks contrary to her evident interests." By "political minority" Flandin meant the Popular Front. France had permitted limited covert assistance to the Republicans since early in the fall of 1937 and especially since mid-March 1938, when Blum and Paul-Boncour increased the aid. Because Daladier personally supported this policy, he had left it in effect, but now, on 13 June, he ordered the frontier with Spain closed "hermetically" and so signed the death warrant for Republican Spain.[27]

Typically, Daladier was vacillating. Only a week earlier in a major speech at Lyon, he had declared eloquently: "France is resolved to remain France. She will renounce none of the grand hopes which have animated men and nations throughout the centuries and to which she has contributed profoundly during the march of history. She will not succumb to the fevers of an epoch that turns all values upside down. She will not say that liberty is vain, that dignity is illusory, that justice is deceitful. She will not permit force to become the arbiter of all human relations." Well said, if meant—Bullitt, at least, believed so. And there was the brief exhilaration when France's Davis Cup team crushed its Italian opponents at the end of May. But the signs pointed toward a diplomacy that was altogether less ringing. On 14 June Jean Mistler, chairman of the Chamber's foreign affairs committee, and Joseph Caillaux stopped at the British embassy to assure Phipps that "France would never fight for Czechoslovakia." Three days later before Mistler's committee

Flandin argued that France should go to war only if her very soil were attacked and even then only if all negotiation had failed. There had been a portent: Charles Maurras, founder of *L'Action Française* and progenitor of the far Right, was elected one of the forty "Immortals" composing the Académie Française (French Academy) on 9 June. The editorialists scrambled along this route of escape. Both the right-wing *Le Journal* and the left-wing *La République* called for a "party of peace" to oppose the "bloody ideologies." Louis Marin, leader of the Catholic conservatives, used *La Nation* to promote amity with Mussolini. *L'Epoque,* the paper of firebrand Kérillis, endorsed opening relations with Franco, as did *Le Figaro.* Only Geneviève Tabouis, writing in the Radical newspaper *L'Oeuvre,* remained adamantly opposed to doing business with dictators—but as the niece of Paul Cambon, France's ambassador to Great Britain from 1898 to 1920, she had the right genes for a Cassandra. So much to tell, so few to believe: in mid-June Daladier quietly canceled a long-planned visit to France by Benes and his chief of staff, General Ludvik Krejci. Bonnet left unanswered requests from the Soviet Union to begin military assistance talks and did not even ask Poland to grant transit rights for Soviet forces. In Berlin on 22 June Ribbentrop asked François-Poncet why France supported Czechoslovakia, "which presents no fundamental interest to her." In Prague on 25 June Benes, "sad and weary," asked Lacroix "whether France was now considering Czechoslovakia a burden."[28]

These two questions framed the essential issue for France: the costs of freedom and responsibility. Almost as if he heard them posed, Jean-Paul Sartre decided at this moment to examine the consequences through fiction and thus was born the idea for *L'Age de raison* (*The Age of Reason*), set in mid-June 1938. After the Munich conference at the end of September, Sartre decided that the week of crisis preceding it should be the subject of a second novel, *Le Sursis* (*The Reprieve*), with the same characters. Although the writing would take him until 1944—late 1938 to summer 1941 for *The Age of Reason* and summer 1941 to late 1944 for *The Reprieve*—he retained the mentality of 1938 by reading and rereading the newspapers from that June to September as he wrote. He was determined to portray what he believed to be its ethos: abulia, cowardice, escapism, insincerity, futile lucidity, succumbing to the course of events.

So often in these more than seven hundred pages the characters ensnare themselves in desperation, missed opportunity, self-loathing, and betrayal. Fragile and poignant, they await their portion as the time grows feverish and crepuscular. So like France.[29]

Born in 1905, Sartre grew up lonely and introspective, as he described in his autobiographical *Les Mots* (*The Words*). After preparation at the lycées Henri IV and Louis le grand, he entered the Ecole Normale Supérieure in 1924, where he rapidly acquired a reputation for brilliance. And for brattiness: he ridiculed the Nietzschean pose of older students by throwing water bombs with the shout, "Thus pissed Zarathustra!" He explained his shocking failure of the *agrégation* for philosophy in 1928 by alleging that his idiosyncratic interpretations went unappreciated by the examiners. The following year, whether or not he stuck to rote explanations, he finished first. Simone de Beauvoir, with whom he began a lifelong intellectual and romantic relationship, was second. She knew from the start that "he would not resign himself to having a career, colleagues, superiors, rules to observe or impose; he would never be a family man or even marry." From November 1929 to February 1931 he performed his required military service, the army training him in meteorology, far from the threat of combat, because of his weak vision. In 1933 and 1934 he studied the phenomenology of Edmund Husserl at the French Institute in Berlin. By 1937, after postings at various lycées, he and Beauvoir both wound up in Paris. Sartre was about to attract attention with the philosophy of existentialism he depicted through a short story, "Le Mur" ("The Wall"), which ran in the July 1937 issue of *La Nouvelle Revue Française,* and through his first novel, *La Nausée* (*Nausea*), published by Gallimard in April 1938. And they had attracted a circle of friends, lovers, and disciples who would appear as characters in Sartre's two new novels, especially Paul Nizan (as Brunet), Olga Kosakiewicz (as Ivich Serguine), Jacques-Laurent Bost (as Boris Serguine), Stépha (as Sarah) and Fernando Gerassi (as Gomez), and Marc Zuorro (as Daniel Sereno).[30]

For long Sartre had scorned the established bourgeois society that made possible his life as a nonconformist intellectual. In 1936 he cheered the Popular Front but did not bother to vote. Two years later his attitude had changed: "the depression, the coming of Nazism, the events in

China, the war in Spain opened our eyes; we saw that the earth was going to open under our feet, and suddenly, *for us as well* the great historical swindle had begun: these first years of a grand world peace had to
be recognized as the last years between wars; each promise that we had
hailed was instead a menace, each day that we had lived now revealed its
true visage: we were marching toward a new war with untold speed,
with a rigor hidden behind nonchalance, and our lives as individuals,
which had appeared to depend on our own efforts, virtues, and failings,
on fortune and misfortune, on the good and bad will of a small number
of people, now seemed governed in even their smallest details by ob-
scure and collective forces and that the most private circumstances
reflected the state of the entire world." And so Sartre makes the quotid-
ian anxieties of his characters in *The Age of Reason*—too little money,
an unintended pregnancy, complicated romantic entanglements—a
microcosm of French society in mid-1938. The novel would exemplify
his mandate for fiction that characters define themselves at the moment
of moral extremity. It would demonstrate his profound philosophical
conviction that because this definition, this liberty of choice, was limited only by the choice of someone else, relations between human beings had to be the clash of one freedom against another.[31]

To test his mandate and his conviction Sartre created as his protag-
onist Mathieu Delarue, a thirty-four-year-old professor of philosophy
at the lycée Buffon—in effect, himself. *The Age of Reason* begins on
Tuesday, 14 June, at 10:30 P.M., and like *The Port of Shadows* covers
forty-eight hours. Mathieu is walking through the Latin Quarter on the
way to visit his mistress, Marcelle Duffet, who lives with her mother on
the rue Vercingétorix, a couple of blocks from his own apartment on the
rue Huyghens. A good-natured drunk—akin to Quart Vittel—begs a
coin and rambles on about wanting to fight in Spain for the Republicans. Mathieu finds Marcelle anxiously staring at a photograph from
ten years before and declaring how much older and fatter she has become. Petulant, she picks at him, "Your life is full of missed opportuni-
ties," and then complains that he is obsessed with Ivich Serguine, the
sister of his former student Boris. Finally, she announces that "it" has
happened: after eight years together he has made her pregnant. She
hopes that he will want to marry her, to form a family, but he says

immediately, "Well—I suppose one gets rid of it, eh?" She has prepared for this response. Abortion had always been illegal in France, and since 1923 cases were heard by three-judge panels because juries often refused to convict. The wealthy went to private clinics, their steep price of four thousand francs including a guarantee that no inquiries would follow. Anyone else had to seek out back-alley practitioners operating—literally—in constant fear of a police raid. Marcelle already has the address of an old woman who lives nearby and who will charge only four hundred francs, still a high price when the salary of a lycée professor was three thousand francs a year. Mathieu knocks on her door, but he is appalled at the squalor and raises her suspicions. That same night in the Montmartre district Boris Serguine is having dinner with his own mistress, Lola, a nightclub singer. He is twenty, she in her forties. Then and later at her hotel room she overwhelms him with her need: "You're all I have left. I'm in your hands, darling, don't hurt me: don't ever hurt me—I'm all alone." She is another version of Marcelle, and Boris is Mathieu in waiting.[32]

The following morning, 15 June, Mathieu confides Marcelle's pregnancy to his friend Sarah because he knows she once had an abortion. He expects her to recommend someone, but she tells him: "They gave me a little parcel after the operation, and they said to me: 'You can throw that down a drain.' Down a drain! Like a dead rat! Mathieu, . . . you don't realize what you're going to do." Although she mentions a Jewish physician who came from Vienna after the *Anschluss,* Mathieu blanches at the thought of his fee. The visit has gone badly. When he first arrived, their mutual friend Brunet, a Communist militant, was there with news of Sarah's husband, Gomez, who is serving with the Spanish Republicans in Barcelona. Mathieu considered going to Spain and considers joining the Communist Party, but he has commitment for nothing, and especially not his mistress. What he has instead is longing: "I must be free. I must be self-impelled, and able to say, 'I am because I will; I am my own beginning.'" He recognizes the fatuity in these words and adds, "I am waiting for nothing."[33]

Not quite nothing: there is Ivich, another longing. Mathieu is meeting her along the boulevard Saint-Michel before they go to a Gauguin exhibition, and she is late. He will excuse her; he will forever excuse her.

She has just taken the PCB (physics, chemistry, biology) examination to qualify for medical training. He fears that she has failed and fears more that her White Russian father will recall her to Laon—seventy miles from Paris—where he has done quite well for himself after fleeing the Bolsheviks. She is twenty-one years old, frail, pallid, somehow beautiful, acute, willful, often impossible. Mathieu adores her, and yet, "when he saw Ivich, he felt as though he were experiencing a catastrophe. Ivich was a voluptuous and tragic little embodiment of pain which had no mor-row: she would depart, go mad, die of a heart attack, . . . but Mathieu could not endure to live without her." As they have a drink together, he gets a message from Sarah with the news that the Jewish physician will require four thousand francs cash down. Disconsolate, he tries to kiss Ivich in the taxi on the way to the Louvre, and she reacts with utter dis-dain. "She sat by his side, stiff and silent, and there was this gesture be-tween them—'I hate being touched'—this clumsy, affectionate gesture already marked with the impalpable insistence of things past." After they see the exhibition she takes her revenge. He is no Gauguin: "You're settled, and you won't change for all the money in the world. . . . With you there's a sense of security, never any fear of the unexpected." [34]

Ivich and Marcelle have come to the same conclusion about Mathieu. The mocking continues that afternoon when he turns up at his brother Jacques's law office in the banking district of the rue Réaumur with this simple reasoning: Jacques is a well-to-do solicitor; he is a poor professor; Jacques should loan him the money for an abortion. Of course, Jacques has the advantage, and when Mathieu declares, "All I want is . . . to retain my freedom," he delivers a dagger's thrust: "I should have thought, . . . that freedom consisted in . . . accepting all one's re-sponsibilities. But that, no doubt, is not your view: you condemn capi-talist society, and yet you are an official in that society; you display an ab-stract sympathy with Communists, but you take care not to commit yourself, you have never voted. You despise the bourgeois class, and yet you are a bourgeois, son and brother of a bourgeois, and you live like a bourgeois." Jacques declines to make a loan but promises ten thousand francs if Mathieu will marry Marcelle. Humiliated, Mathieu returns to his apartment, where he finds Brunet, who argues that he should assert his responsibility by joining the Communist Party. Mathieu refuses, recognizing that he may have ended their friendship, and wonders whether everyone—even himself—has concluded that he is "a rotter . . . a lousy wash-out." Because others are eager to make decisions: Marcelle wants to have the child; her friend Daniel Sereno, a stockbroker and secretly a self-loathing homosexual, wants to ruin Mathieu because he envies his ability to attract disciples like the Serguines. They can each have their way if Mathieu is made to marry Marcelle. Daniel visits her late that evening and tells her that he has already turned down Mathieu's request for a loan, coyly adding that he could reconsider. When she hesitates, he is certain: "I've won, she's pining to lay an egg." He thinks to himself how much the female form repulses him and then rejoices that Mathieu might be made to embrace forever this woman he once desired and now does not. Marcelle agrees to let him approach Mathieu about marriage.[35]

As Daniel and Marcelle plot, Mathieu has joined Lola, Boris, and Ivich at the Sumatra Club in Montmartre. Ivich is getting drunk because, she says, "I shall be flunked, I'm certain, and I shall go away immediately." As she stares at the striptease dancer, Mathieu notices Ivich's "air of cruelty; when all was said, she was like the rest, the nasty little creature. . . . 'She is quite alone,' he thought; 'she is hiding her wrecked face under her hair, she is sitting with her thighs together, and having an orgasm! . . . And I love that girl for her purity.'" Boris says to Mathieu: "Don't you think it's a grand insult to say to a fellow: sir, you're a second-rater? . . . In my opinion a man *ought* not to live beyond thirty; after that he's a back number." Although not aimed at him, these words, even more than Jacques's derision, shame Mathieu deeply. He assails himself: "I have led a toothless life. . . . I have never bitten into anything. I was waiting. I was reserving myself for later on—and I have just noticed that my teeth have gone. What's to be done? Break the shell?" Looking at Ivich, he concedes, "She will never be mine, she will never come into my shell." Besides, there is the question of Marcelle. Boris tells Mathieu that Lola has seven thousand francs in her room and offers to ask her for it. But when he does she wonders whether her young lover is taking advantage and refuses. Ivich is now tipsy, and partly from self-destructiveness, partly to shock an older woman giving her a disapproving stare, she slashes her palm with a knife. Mathieu then sticks the knife into his own palm: "It was not only to defy Ivich . . . , it was as a challenge to Jacques, and Brunet, and Daniel, and to his whole life." Ivich suddenly rubs their hands together—to mingle their blood, she explains—and his hopes rise again.[36]

Late in the morning of the next day, 16 June, Mathieu meets Ivich at the Dôme Café on the boulevard du Montparnasse. The PCB examination results will be posted at 2 P.M., and, convinced that she has failed, Ivich thinks even being a scullery maid in Paris would be better than going back to Laon, a kind of prison. Boris appears suddenly, claiming that Lola is dead. Depressed because he asked her for money, she took a sleeping drug, and he awoke to find her eyes fixed and staring. Rather than call for help, he ran away, only to realize that all his letters to her will be found when the police come to investigate. If he is drawn into scandal, his father is "quite equal to calling me back to Laon and sticking me into a bank." Realizing abruptly that both Serguines are helpless, Mathieu volunteers to retrieve the letters and takes a taxi to Lola's hotel on the rue Navarin, at the southern edge of Montmartre. On the way he has an epiphany. He thinks about "the far-off days of childhood, the day when he had said: 'I will be free,' the day when he had said: 'I will be famous,'" and realizes that "his casual, cynical present was the original future of those past days. It was he whom they had awaited for twenty years, it was he, this tired man, who was pestered by a remorseless child to realize his hopes; on him it depended whether these childish pledges should remain forever childish or whether they should become the first announcements of a destiny." In Lola's room he finds the letters, but as he considers taking her money, she stirs, and he leaves quickly. Hearing this news, Boris declares that he cannot see Lola again. Ivich approves: "If he goes back to her it will be from a motive of pity. . . . You can't ask him to do it: there's nothing more repugnant, even to her." Unconsciously, she has described the dilemma of both men.[37]

All afternoon and without success, Mathieu tries his last sources for a loan. When he returns to his apartment at 6 P.M., a message awaits: "Flunked. So what? Ivich." Worried what she might do, he runs down all her usual haunts and friends until he finds her at the Tarantula, a dive on the rue Monsieur-le-Prince near the boulevard Saint-Germain. She is drunk and leaning on an elegant young man, who clearly expects to take advantage of her later. Seeing Mathieu, she calls out: "Take me away from here. I feel degraded." And so he does, to his own apartment, which she has never seen, his intention both lascivious and protective. She vomits out the window of the taxi but tells him, "I was hoping all the time that you would come." Once on his sofa, she falls asleep immediately. Looking down at her, Mathieu has another moment of lucidity: "'How young she is!' he thought. He had set all his hopes upon a child. . . . She could give no help to anyone; on the contrary, she would have to be helped to carry on her own life. And Mathieu could not help her. Ivich would go off to Laon, she would vegetate there for a winter or two, and then some man would come along—a young man—and take her off." When she wakes up, he offers, awkwardly, to support her if she will return to Paris in October. She curtly rejects the idea—"Quite impossible"—but warms to it after he says, "I can't endure the idea of not seeing you again." Then Sarah rings at the door with the news that the Jewish physician will not wait and will not grant credit. Mathieu then confesses his situation to Ivich. In a frozen voice she replies: "How sordid! . . . Excuse me, . . . I never really thought of taking your money: you will need all you have to start housekeeping." Afraid of his emotions, Mathieu rushes from his own apartment, leaving her standing in triumph.[38]

Abasement takes charge for the last few hours of the novel. "To think," Mathieu ponders, "I used to take myself seriously." Claiming to defend his freedom, he has importuned those he despises and alienated those he loves. With no values left to defend, he resolves to take Lola's money. Daniel, driven yet disgusted by his homosexual desire, returns from an encounter determined to resolve the contradiction. He considers cutting off his genitals—"*Dead the beast, dead the poison*"—but then decides on a remedy without blood, to ruin his life as he planned to ruin Mathieu's, to marry Marcelle. Mathieu gets to her first. Counting out five thousand francs, more than she needs, he promises that she will be safe in the hands of the Jewish physician. But from Daniel she had thought Mathieu would be proposing marriage. She throws the money in his face: "Because I no longer respect you. And also because you don't love me any more." Glad to go and leaving the money on the floor, he returns to his apartment, where he finds Ivich has never left.

She apologizes for her outburst. Mathieu explains that he has broken with Marcelle, that he left her money he stole from Lola, and that he is filled with remorse. The thought of his anguish is what finally touches Ivich's heart. She comes to him, her head tilted a little, her lips parted. He kisses her lightly only to realize, "Why, she's nothing but a child." As he pulls away, she is furious again, "You looked so proud of having made a decision that I thought you had come for a reward." Pathetically, he insists, "But I love you, Ivich." She answers, "I—I don't love you," yet looks at him with "something like affection." They are interrupted by ringing and banging at the door. Lola is looking for Boris, whom she accuses of robbing her. Although Mathieu admits taking the money, she will not believe him. She threatens going to the police when Daniel appears with the five thousand francs from Marcelle. Eventually pacified, Lola leaves. Ivich has already gone. Daniel and Mathieu are alone. The only unfinished business is between them.[39]

Coolly, Daniel announces that he is going to marry Marcelle, that they will keep the child, that he is a homosexual, and that none of it is Mathieu's concern: "You have your hands full dealing with your own conscience." Indeed, when Mathieu calls Marcelle, she hangs up on him. Daniel insists that he will make a good husband and father, although "it is agreed that any emotional relation shall come gradually." Mathieu recognizes that he will never see Marcelle again, never see again the woman with whom he shared all his thoughts for eight years. And so when Daniel says, "In this affair, . . . you've been a winner all around. . . . You are free," Mathieu answers ruefully, "No . . . it isn't by giving up a woman that a man is free. . . . The truth is that I gave up Marcelle *for nothing*." This conclusion is far more dismal than Jean's murder in *The Port of Shadows*. Jean rejects the temptation of escape to act—even Daniel acts—and in doing so neither can go back. For Mathieu "everything happens as though I could always play my strokes again." Jean accepts responsibility; Mathieu flees from it. If he had died at that moment, surely the conclusion would have to be that he is a wash-out.[40]

In late 1945, when *The Age of Reason* and *The Reprieve* were published simultaneously by Gallimard and his existentialist philosophy was all the rage, Sartre told an interviewer: "We say that there is no human nature, that there is no eternal and immutable essence of man. . . . We say that for a man, freedom precedes essence, that he creates his essence in acting, that he is what he makes of himself by his choice, that he must choose good or evil, and that he is always responsible for that choice." These words condemn Mathieu, who at the close of the novel thinks over the last two days and concludes, "Various tried and proved rules of conduct had already discreetly offered him their services: disillusioned epicureanism, smiling tolerance, resignation, flat seriousness, stoicism—all the aids whereby a man may savor, minute by minute, like a connoisseur, the failure of a life. . . . 'It's true, it's really true: I have attained the age of reason.'"[41] Mathieu has squirmed to evade his responsibilities. He has sought to make others pay his bills. He has escaped the consequences through the intervention of another. He has chosen by refusing to choose and calls that reason. So like France in 1938: Marcelle's imprecation is close to Benes's question. The French were squirming to evade their responsibilities. They were seeking to impose the cost anywhere else. They were desperately hoping for some saving intervention. They did not want to choose, and they could still claim that their policies were righteous. Hypocrisy is the art of affecting qualities for the purpose of pretending to an undeserved virtue. The truth unvarnished, for France as well as Mathieu, was offensive.

3 Summer
July to September

In the late 1930s an accusation sometimes whispered by French leaders about themselves and their nation was *écroulement morale*. The literal translation is "moral collapse." Figuratively, the meaning is to act and to justify the act, in full knowledge of doing wrong.

Consider the most pungent murder trial of 1938, held in the stifling oven of a courthouse on two July days at Perpignan in the Pyrenees Mountains. Four months earlier, on the night of 21 March, Suzanne Delaris broke into the apartment of her husband, François, from whom she had been separated since January 1937. When he came home a few minutes later, she was hiding in ambush behind a sofa, but he was not alone. For the next three hours he "entertained" a Mme Gratia then saw her out and fell exhausted to sleep. Suzanne Delaris had waited patiently and now crept to his bedside. She fired twice at close range into his skull and left the revolver at his hand to imply suicide. Back at her mother's house, she wrote a note to her solicitor asking that he inform her husband that she would soon be taking their daughter to visit him. Neither of her schemes deterred the police investigation. Suicides rarely fire two bullets, especially into their heads; Suzanne had never permitted François even to see the daughter, who was born several months after their separation. Interrogated, she confessed almost immediately, and before the court she even managed to say, "I'm sorry." No one present believed her.

Born Suzanne Garrigue, she was thirty-four, tall, slender, attractive, aloof. To the embarrassment of the three judges and the prosecutor, she was also a barrister who had practiced before them. Given the evidence of premeditation, they were inclined to be harsh against one of their own, and a further motive was making an example of her for behavior defining a *garce* (a malicious and scheming woman). Certainly, her private life had been a scandal. She engaged in what might be called ephemeral marriages: in her late twenties for three months to a Monsieur Combacal, from whom she obtained an advantageous divorce, and soon after, for nineteen months, fourteen of them in separation, to Delaris, whom she lured from his first wife. He was in his late thirties, a successful businessman, and helpless before her wiles. After they married, in August 1936, any happiness must have been brief because she left him in December and obtained a formal separation a month later. When their daughter was born, in May 1937, Suzanne was granted custody, and François agreed to pay five hundred francs a month in support pending the final arrangements of a divorce. He asked for visitation rights, which the Perpignan district court granted and which Suzanne ignored. François finally retaliated by demanding control of all marital property. When the district court agreed on 15 March 1938, Suzanne decided to kill him and did so six days later.

The trail of her retribution was easy to follow. She wrote in a letter to François, "I am ferocious, and to avenge myself, I would kill with all the refinements of cruelty." She asked a friend, "Do you know of a gypsy who would take him down for 20,000 francs?" She was neither intelligent in planning nor cautious in execution. At her trial she offered no defense beyond a plaintive excuse: "I lost my head. I thought of our little girl. I no longer knew anything." She did sob and groan to much effect, once falling to her knees. The task of the prosecutor was merely to describe the defendant: "You cowardly devised a horrible crime against the man whom you had conquered and carried it out mercilessly. . . . taking the life of this unfortunate father who has been lowered to his grave without ever seeing his child." The jury, he insisted, had to convict and to convict without lessening her punishment by declaring extenuating circumstances. Disregarding this admonition and ignoring the evidence of premeditation, the jury found—unspecified— mitigating conditions to their verdict of guilty. Suzanne Delaris was condemned to five years in prison.[1]

Such "moral collapse," then and later, Edward Spears blamed on "the mud accumulated during decades of . . . inefficient and often corrupt regimes . . . coming to the surface . . . and bursting in fetid bubbles. All this was . . . so obvious that only the willfully blind could fail to observe it"—and he was a great friend of France. Georges Mandel, minister for the colonies in Daladier's cabinet but deserving the Quai d'Orsay, recalled a wholly different attitude before the Great War. With the stone clarity Clemenceau had taught him, he recognized that the psychological spring of the nation had broken, that there was, as he told Spears, a general *défaillance* (breakdown). But in July 1938 part of moral collapse was to be "willfully blind," made all the easier by the pageantry of a royal interlude.[2]

Yes, the British were coming. Premier Edouard Daladier extended the invitation during the London talks in late April. Newly crowned King George VI and Queen Elizabeth were to make France their first foreign travel, breaking the recent tradition of going first to one of the Dominions. British sovereigns had last been to France twenty years ago, and this visit at this moment of crisis in world affairs was highly symbolic of their solidarity. Originally, the date was set for 28 June, but the death of the queen's mother, the countess of Strathmore, forced postponement to 19 July in accordance with ritual mourning. The change meant that Paris became the cynosure of European eyes twice within a week, for Daladier was determined to make Bastille Day a spectacular demonstration of French might.

Whatever their intentions and progress on rearmament, the Popular Front had significantly lowered the martial tone. In 1936 the sound of "The Internationale" sometimes drowned out "La Marseillaise." In 1937 the only cabinet member present was Pierre Cot, minister of the air force, who read a statement from Premier Camille Chautemps. This 14 July brought back the éclat. Heralded as the "Grand Procession of the French Army," thirty thousand men marched down the Champs-Elysées from the Arc de Triomphe to the Place de la Concorde, giving their salute to the president of the Republic, Albert Lebrun, the premier and minister of war, Daladier, the minister of the navy, César Campinchi, and the minister of the air force, Guy La Chambre. A huge and enthusiastic crowd cheered in acclamation. The parade took more than two hours: the cadets from Saint Cyr and the Ecole Polytechnique, the Garde Républicaine (the Republican Guard, special security forces commanded by the prefect of police), the Marines, the Chasseurs (regiments of infantry), the *troupes de forteresse* (fortress troops from the Maginot Line), the Zouaves (the Algerian infantry), the *Spahis algériens* and the *Spahis marocains* (the Algerian and Moroccan cavalry), the ceremonial regiments—the Third Cavalry, the Fourth Hussars, the Sixth Dragoons, the Eleventh Cuirassiers—and finally the new motorized formations, the Third Engineers with 75 mm cannons followed by rows upon rows of tanks. Above, the latest fighters and bombers from the air force flew low over this massive display of vigor, the largest since the victory parade of 1918.[3]

However impressive, Bastille Day was only a prelude to the royal visit. From the Eiffel Tower a Union Jack fifteen hundred yards square dominated the sky. On the ground almost every man, woman, and child either carried a British flag or wore one as a lapel pin. Street musicians played "Rule Britannia." The post office issued a new 1.75 franc stamp showing the Houses of Parliament linked to the Arc de Triomphe by hands reaching across the Channel. To secure the royal passage through Paris, a double cordon of soldiers lined the streets with another of police facing the crowd. Eight miles of wood fencing gave additional protection in the most vulnerable sections. The luxury in preparation for the king and queen would have made French revolutionaries take up arms. At the Quai d'Orsay royal apartments stood ready with tapestries and furnishings from the Louvre and with baths of gold and silver mosaic. In the Hall of Mirrors at the Versailles Palace a grand state banquet was being prepared: ten of the finest chefs, waiters in breeches and perukes, champagne from the birth year of the king, burgundy from the birth year of the queen, and entertainment by the ballet company of the Paris Opera. Chief among the special favors ready for presentation were Lyon silks woven specially for the queen and two exquisite dolls, each with a trousseau of forty-seven dresses made for the royal princesses back in London. So many British officials busied themselves with their own arrangements that sightings in Paris of grey flannel trousers increased significantly.

The performance was worthy of the preparation. On the morning of 19 July a French flotilla boasting a battleship, four cruisers, three destroyer divisions, and a squadron of submarines met the royal yacht *Enchantress* in the middle of the English Channel and escorted it to Boulogne. From there a special train decorated with the royal arms brought the king and queen, Edward Lord Halifax, the foreign secretary, and a party of twenty to the Bois de Boulogne station at the western edge of Paris. Awaiting them were Lebrun, Daladier, the cabinet ministers, the presidents of the Chamber of Deputies and the Senate, and the members of the British embassy. When George VI stepped from the train, the British flag was raised above the station, a military band struck up first "God Save the King," then "La Marseillaise," and ten thousand pigeons were released to fly suddenly upward like a cloud of white smoke.

In a cavalcade of automobiles preceded by mounted Republican Guards, the royal party and their hosts entered Paris on the avenue Foch, passed the Arc de Triomphe, and proceeded down the Champs Elysées. All along the route Parisians by the hundreds of thousands shouted "Long live the king!" and jockeyed to use cardboard periscopes to see over the security cordons. At the Quai d'Orsay Foreign Minister Georges Bonnet bowed almost to the floor in welcome. That evening at the Elysée Palace there were ceremonial conferrals, President Lebrun awarding the queen the Grand Cross of the Legion of Honor, the king granting Lebrun the Knight Grand Cross of the Bath. At the first of the splendid banquets, this one for nearly three hundred guests, George VI offered, in French, a toast using words the leaders of France longed to hear: "In spite of the strip of sea which separates us, our two countries have seen their destinies inevitably drawn together with the passage of centuries, and it would now be impossible to recall a period in which our relations were more intimate. . . . It is the ardent desire of our governments to find, by means of international agreements, a solution to those political problems which threaten the peace of the world, and of those economic difficulties which restrict human well-being."

On and on went the ceremonial visitations. The royal couple began 20 July by laying a wreath upon the Tomb of the Unknown Soldier beneath the Arc de Triomphe. Without so much as a gesture from anyone, the large crowd became absolutely silent in homage as the king stepped forward with the Flanders poppies. There followed in rapid succession a reception at the Hôtel de Ville (City Hall), a luncheon at the British embassy, a viewing of the British Exhibition at the Louvre, a garden party at the Bagatelle Palace on the fringe of the Bois de Boulogne, the second of the grand banquets, this one offered by the king and queen at the British embassy in honor of President and Mme Lebrun, and to complete the evening, a gala performance of "Salammbô" at the Opera.

On 21 July the special train carried royals and dignitaries to Versailles. Before the palace of Louis XIV fifty thousand troops marched in review, as George VI sat with Marshall Philippe Pétain and the heads of the French armed forces, General Maurice Gamelin, Admiral François Darlan, and General Joseph Vuillemin. Afterward came the much-anticipated third banquet, the gastronomic tour de force in the Hall of Mirrors and then a promenade through the grounds, where a concert of chamber music complemented the staging of mythological scenes. Still to come after the return to Paris was the final banquet, with Bonnet as host at the Quai d'Orsay and a musical program including Maurice Chevalier. As final proof of the entente between Great Britain and France, the king and queen announced that President Lebrun had accepted their invitation to visit London the next spring.

One last ceremony remained. On 22 July George VI and Elizabeth traveled with Lebrun to Villers-Bretonneux, in northern France near Amiens and the Somme River, along what for almost four years had been the trench line of the Western Front during the Great War. They came to unveil a memorial to the nearly fifty thousand Australian soldiers who died in the fighting, a quarter of whom lay in mass graves or were never found. After a service of dedication, Lebrun declared, "Our nations still stand shoulder to shoulder in maintenance of the ideals for which so many of our people laid down their lives." First the king and queen, then Lebrun, laid wreaths of poppies on the memorial, and the British military band played "Land of Hope and Glory." The royal visit was over. To the glittering brilliance of display in receptions, banquets, performances, and reviews had been added the poignancy in memory of shared sacrifice. One train took Lebrun back to Paris, another, George VI and Elizabeth to Calais, where the *Enchantress* waited for the voyage home.[4]

As this moment so critical to French morale had begun, Jules Sauerwein in the mass-circulation *Paris-Soir* made his column an equation: "England + France = Peace." For the Socialists Léon Blum welcomed the "head of British democracy" and derived the same answer. Among the Center-Right Emile Buré in *L'Ordre* could hardly contain himself: "Long live England! Long live her king! Long live her queen!" Neither could *Le Figaro*'s Wladimir d'Ormesson, "The English Channel is no more!" Usually clearheaded, Henri de Kérillis in *L'Epoque* imagined a new Anglo-French cooperation in Central Europe. More cautious and more apprehensive, Colonel de La Rocque's *Le Petit Journal* warned, "we can count on them, but we must above all count on ourselves."[5] That counsel was all the more appropriate once the party was over, for the cleaning up was left to do and the bills to be paid.

The signs and portents were not favorable. On 4 July France's greatest tennis champion, Suzanne Lenglen, died from aplastic anemia. The Wimbledon tournament, which she had dominated the previous decade—six times winner of the women's singles, three times winner of both women's doubles and mixed doubles—had concluded two days earlier without a single French player in the finals. Three weeks later the French Davis Cup team, who had crushed the Italians at the end of May, were themselves decisively eliminated by the Germans. On 10 July President Lebrun, the papal legate, and forty-seven cardinals, archbishops, and bishops assembled at Reims to celebrate the restoration of the grand cathedral all but demolished by German artillery during the Great War. Although this pious labor of twenty years was called "symbolic of France's resurrection," the ceremony, entirely opposite of triumphant, raised the question of whether, with renewed war looming, the rebuilding had been in vain. With good reason: that same day rumors ran through Paris of military preparations in Germany. Stocks and bonds on the Paris Bourse fell sharply. Investors were so spooked that to sell a new issue of short-term bonds—eighteen months at 3.5 percent—the treasury had to offer the interest up front. Additional evidence proving

Mussolini's embrace of Hitler came in a declaration by faculty from the University of Rome that the Italians were of pure Aryan stock and that the government propose a doctrine of racism. Roger Martin du Gard, awarded the Nobel Prize for Literature the previous December and a writer of immense influence among the middle class, defined the fears of many by predicting the horror of "aerial bombardments that decimate innocent civilian populations" and then dared, in the perpetual idealism of pacifists, to dream that "in the face of the approaching cataclysm, peoples can bind themselves together, in spite of their governments, to create against war a vast movement of defense and fraternal cooperation to assure the common safety."[6]

Of course, the Bastille Day virility was calculated to deter this temptation, and Daladier provided the proper preface with a major speech on 12 July. Regarding the vital question of peace or war, he was firm: "The French contribution to the task of conciliation has been . . . active, sincere, and constant, for we do not believe in the fatality of war. . . . Our engagements to Czechoslovakia are inescapable and sacred. We have no wish to carry them out, but we will not repudiate our word if this hope is disappointed." To both the fainthearted and the sellers-short, he was stern: "The inciters of panic will not prevail, and the dupes who follow them will be their first victims. The government has already taken important steps in financial redress and has given the nation the means necessary to restore productive growth. . . . We are resolved to defend the value of our currency, to impose respect for domestic order, and to ensure the normal operation of all public services."[7] But as always, the question was whether Daladier meant what he said and how long he would mean it.

Especially about Czechs, for the British were applying new pressure. If the government in Prague settled with its Sudeten minority, Germany would have no more quarrel with Czechoslovakia, France would not have to honor her guarantee, and Britain would be spared the agonizing decision of whether to intervene or not—so went the argument of Prime Minister Neville Chamberlain, Foreign Secretary Halifax, and Ambassador Eric Phipps. France, they insisted, should do more to pressure its ally to accommodate Sudeten, meaning German, demands. Bonnet had done so to a point, but he recognized how unseemly—even

deceitful—was such conduct toward an ally. To overcome this reluctance Phipps now presented the Quai d'Orsay with various schemes to
convert Czechoslovakia into a neutral, the borders of which would be
guaranteed by all its neighbors, once the Czechs had settled with their
minorities. The plural was important: at a minimum the Poles and
Hungarians within Czechoslovakia would insist on the same concessions granted to the Sudeten Germans. Czechoslovakia as a nation and
the French system of security in Eastern Europe would then be finished.
The British pressure on France was unseemly, even deceitful, treatment
of an ally. For Bonnet here was an exquisite and memorable experience
in irony. An Anglophile, he adopted the English public school tradition
of passing blows downward by amplifying the pressure on Prague.

On 17 July, through French ambassador Victor de Lacroix to Czech
president Eduard Benes, and on 20 July, personally to Czech ambassador
Stefan Osusky, Bonnet warned that France could hardly expect public
approval for a war to preserve Czechoslovakia from Germany if French
territory were not attacked and British support was uncertain. London,
Bonnet insisted, wanted evidence that Prague was sparing no principle
short of its sovereignty in seeking an accommodation with the Sudeten
Germans. Paris, he added, needed that proof as well to rally Frenchmen behind any military action. The timing of the Osusky interview
was quickly evident. On the same day Halifax revealed to Bonnet
the British plan of arbitrating the Czech and Sudeten dispute, with
Walter Lord Runciman, former chairman for the Board of Trade, going
to Prague as the mediator. Daladier was suspicious, recognizing that, although France had the treaty responsibilities to Czechoslovakia, Great
Britain was taking over the negotiations that could either actuate or ob-
viate this guarantee. For Bonnet the British expropriation of this diplomacy was the escape he had sought. If Czechoslovakia refused Runciman's embassy, Britain would declare that by spurning a chance for a
peaceful solution, Czech leaders were unworthy of any support. France
could then, with only slight bad conscience, agree and annul the treaty.
If Czechoslovakia accepted the arbitration, Britain became bound by
its own plan. If the Czechs became the aggrieved party and France
came to their assistance, Britain would have to lend its support. But the
French government's position on the Runciman mission was, in fact,

meaningless, for the British were determined to pursue it—so much had France become dependent on Britain, and so much was Britain willing to take the advantage. Although there was no immediate announcement of the plan, more than a hint of something came on the following day at the Quai d'Orsay banquet for the king and queen. About the time Chevalier was singing and dancing, Halifax found a moment to talk privately with Pierre-Etienne Flandin, who was afterward smiling smugly. By contrast, Osusky did not look so happy. Soon unhappy as well were Czechoslovakia's leaders in Prague, but they recognized that with their only ally supporting this scheme, resistance to it was futile, even dangerous. Putting up a brave face, Osusky conveyed his government's formal acceptance on 25 July and was rewarded by reassurances from both Bonnet and Alexis Léger that France was not using the Runciman mission to evade its treaty obligations and would actively monitor the mediation.[8]

The reaction of French opinion was closer to the worries of Daladier than to the cynicism of Bonnet and Flandin. *Le Figaro* had long reflected the hopes and especially the fears of the upper middle class, with its editor, Lucien Romier, writing darkly on 26 July, hours before the public announcement of the Runciman mission, "The truth is that a cult of force has grown up which promises much but delivers little because it offers no destiny to mankind other than to die like a wolf among wolves." At first *Le Figaro*'s principal columnist, d'Ormesson, reacted by proclaiming it "Wisdom" and, with *Le Temps,* willing to believe that the mediation could open the way to a "general appeasement"—meant only as a calming of tensions—in European affairs. But soon enough, at least for *Le Figaro,* there were suspicions, especially in reaction to an interview Flandin granted to *Le Petit Parisien.* There he argued that France's leaders should put aside any idealism of opposing dictators and caring about the "Jewish question" to concentrate on the country's "essential interests"—a grand economic partnership with Britain, Germany, and Italy, and if that meant German domination of Central and Eastern Europe, France would still have an overseas empire to exploit. D'Ormesson retorted that the development of markets might be one matter, but if Flandin meant to grant Germany a "blank check to wage war" and create a Germanized Europe, "we affirm that not another Frenchman would approve."[9]

In a rare concordance Léon Blum in *Le Populaire* and La Rocque's *Le Petit Journal* noted Runciman's reputation as a Germanophile and worried that the British entente was becoming the British *tutelle* (tutelage): France risked the role of "brilliant second." As acid as ever, his column's title "They Have Lost Clemenceau's Peace," André Tardieu in *Gringoire* warned that French prestige had been severely damaged and that Czechoslovakia was about to be bullied. Although never a friend of Clemenceau and never much one of Tardieu, Louis Marin and his Fédération Républicaine (Republican Federation—the Catholic conservatives) agreed that "the Czechs could hardly let the mediator go home empty handed." Among the firmest of Prague's partisans Kérillis rejected in advance any "solution" that might threaten the existence of Czechoslovakia because that in turn would "indirectly provoke the ruin of France." The keenest critique came from Pertinax, who insisted on the inescapable realities of the Runciman mission. First, whatever the diplomatic pressure upon them to do so, by submitting questions of domestic order to the arbitration of a foreign state, Czechoslovakia's leaders had gravely compromised their sovereignty. Second, the very mechanism of arbitration weighed heavily against Czechoslovakia because Great Britain and France would expect concessions even as Germany encouraged the Sudetens to demand more. Third, because Runciman's past made him almost as much a representative of British business interests as British foreign policy, his recommendations were likely to have a bias toward the maintenance of conditions favorable for trade— meaning peace at almost any price. Fourth, and most important, this mediation had transformed the foreign policy context: "The *essential fact* has been France's determination not to allow Czechoslovakia to be invaded. Now the reins have been taken from France's hands, and the *essential fact* is no longer the Franco-Czech alliance but the results of the Runciman mission." His eyes clear, Pertinax saw the potentially disastrous implications of a policy Bonnet gladly and Daladier reluctantly had embraced as further proof of the entente with Britain and as a means to avoid the hard choices themselves.[10]

Because the Runciman mission at least temporarily postponed further decisions about Czechoslovakia and because the traditional August vacations were upon France, a certain languor descended. Paris all but shut down, senators and deputies gone since mid-July, President Lebrun away to Avignon, Bonnet just across the Swiss border to Vallorbe, and Daladier himself taking an eight-day cruise on the Mediterranean. The newspapers ran photographs of families filling the train stations to head for the countryside, the mountains, and especially the beach. No one could recall greater crowds along the Côte d'Azur. As one hotel owner guilelessly explained: "The international situation is doing us a world of good. People who used to go to Austria no longer like to go there since the *Anschluss;* Spain is closed to tourists, Switzerland is expensive, in Italy the food is bad and a lot of people don't like the Fascists—so where are tourists to go except to *la belle France*–with 175 francs to the pound?" Italy was certainly inhospitable, in early July border guards shooting at two French alpinists and at the end of the month the government banning travel by Italians to France. In the crush their absence went unnoticed.[11]

Without visiting monarchs or international crisis, journalists could indulge in the silly season, even if the stories had a sharper edge this year. To recall the royals, women's fashions for the fall had a British theme, tailored, conservative, worn with pearls, and described as *à l'entente cordiale* (Franco-British amity). As if to demonstrate Nazi hypocrisy, Germany banned all photographs or film from the heavyweight championship fight between black American Joe Louis and Aryan German Max Schmeling—for good reason: Louis knocked out Schmeling at Yankee Stadium on 22 June in round one after only two minutes and four seconds. In Italy the Fascists were embarrassing themselves with talk of imitating the German racial laws, proposing that the percentage of Jews in any profession not exceed that of Jews in the general population, one per thousand. No summer was complete without a good crime, and the State Security Police provided that, breaking a heroin smuggling ring led by Isaac Leifer, a Hasidic rabbi from Brooklyn, New York, born in Poland and a naturalized American. With two accomplices, a Hungarian, Herman Gottdiener, and another Pole, Abraham Kantorovitz, Leifer arrived in France with forty prayer books, each containing a sachet filled with 160 grams of heroin, the total worth 600,000 francs. Within days the Security Police made three more arrests in Paris, two in Beirut, Lebanon, and one in Alexandria, Egypt, rounding up the rest of the conspiracy. Pope Pius XI, unpopular in France because he had treated with both Fascists and Nazis, made one of those papal pronouncements that inspire devotion from the faithful and jeers from anticlericals: "Be warned! Whoever attacks the action of the Catholic Church attacks the pope, and whoever attacks the pope dies. History demonstrates this truth." Everyone left in Paris was going to see *Vivacious Lady,* starring Jimmy Stewart as a small-town college professor who marries New York nightclub singer Ginger Rogers with predictably hilarious consequences.[12]

The gentle climate of the silly season changed drastically after the first week in August, when a harsh cold front from Germany collided with a storm system from southern France. On 7 August Germany announced large-scale military maneuvers for which 750,000 reservists were to be mobilized. On 8 August dockworkers in Marseille declared a strike and left six ships stranded with perishable goods. French security without and within was under threat. The German maneuvers immediately recalled a little-noticed article two days earlier that the catacombs beneath Paris, which amounted to almost one-tenth of the city surface and had been proposed for air raid shelter, were unsuitable because of their narrow corridors and difficult entry. During the next week the reports from Berlin were increasingly grim. With the reserves integrated, the German army would number 1.35 million men, sufficient for war. More than 300,000 German workers were transferred to military construction projects, especially a feverish effort to build the Siegfried Line in the west, defensive works to hamper any French invasion and behind the shelter of which Germany could launch an invasion to the east. As if in preparation for war, all Germans sixty-five years or younger were forbidden to leave the *Reich.*[13]

Even so, the moderate newspapers counseled moderate thinking. *Le Temps* refused to believe that Hitler "would resort to force without waiting for the result, one way or another, of the Runciman mission." *Le Figaro* excused the maneuvers as "moral revenge" for the Czech mobilization in May. Pierre Dominique, Joseph Caillaux's ally at the principal Radical paper, *L'Oeuvre,* even declared that Hitler did not want war and that the maneuvers were too costly to maintain for long. But this anodyne view was distinctly in the minority. Once again, Blum and La

Rocque's *Le Petit Journal* were in agreement, with their language eerily similar. For Blum: "By making French and British opinion, which desires peace, aware of the war danger, Hitler surely reckons to bring new Western pressure on Prague, . . . but I remain confident that neither London nor Paris will succumb to this maneuver." For Léon Boussard: "Against a Hitler who sees himself as a thunderbolt in the night, France and Great Britain are invincible because they draw their essential strength from the will of free peoples." Kérillis in *L'Epoque,* Buré in *L'Ordre,* and Marin in *La Nation* said much the same less eloquently, Marin citing the danger of a population imbued with the madness of *Mein Kampf.*[14]

While Germans were brandishing their weapons and flexing their muscles, French factories were mostly closed for vacation, and the dockworkers remained on strike. His face deeply tanned from the sun, Daladier was back in Paris on 9 August sounding optimistic. The trouble in Marseille, he insisted, was merely a dispute over the refusal to work overtime which had been exaggerated by the press, and whatever the rumors, "the financial situation is not at all disquieting." Four days later, with the strike continuing, Daladier appointed an arbitrator, whose ruling that the dockworkers could not refuse overtime work was ignored. Four more days later Daladier threatened to mobilize the dockworkers if they did not accept the arbitration ruling. That kind of talk quickly generated more rumors of financial instability and a brief panic on the Paris Bourse. Daladier had to call a press conference on the following day, 18 August, to declare that "the government is resolutely hostile both to exchange controls and to a new devaluation of the franc." He also promised a proposal by the cabinet to end the dock strike. The dockworkers unanimously rejected the cabinet's terms. At the same time, Ambassador François-Poncet sent a detailed report from Berlin on the German mobilization, concluding that Hitler meant to impose the Karlsbad program on Czechoslovakia whether through intimidation or force. Prodded by Paul Reynaud, frustrated, alarmed, and convinced that the situation had become grave, Daladier then decided to address the nation by radio.[15]

The experience with politics via kilohertz in France was mixed. In 1934, when Gaston Doumergue imitated the American president

Franklin D. Roosevelt's "fireside chats," his thick meridional accent evoked derision. His generation of politicians, whose careers began before the Great War, was also accustomed to a florid oratory that made good theater in person but tedium for listeners straining to hear through the static of early radios. André Tardieu was better at the microphone, younger, smarter, able to adapt his ideas to brief phrases. Blum, almost the same age and smarter still, was not, because he retained the old speaking style. Daladier was quite good, not as smart as either Tardieu or Blum, never eloquent but always clear and concise and, most important, heard by the French as one of their own, a leader who had ascended from the people while never forgetting his origins. Given the context of impending crisis, the announcement that he would make a national broadcast on the evening of 21 August generated an apprehension ensuring a large audience.

Daladier began so forthrightly that the tenor of this speech, the utterance of unpleasant truth, was immediately obvious: "International conflict dominates our thoughts. War rages in Spain and the Far East. In Central Europe, great nations prepare their forces. For their soldiers and their reservists, there is no longer any limit to military service. For their workers, there is no limit to the workday. Most of the world's nations are also examples of intense activity. Such facts are a warning to France." And France had to take it to heart: "National defense is all of a piece. The strength of a country, the guarantee of its independence is maintained not only by the might of its armies but as much by the daily exertion in the factories, the workshops, in all the work sites, by the stability of its currency and the state of its treasury." And why? "We can uphold peace with honor and solidarity alongside the great democracies of the world only if we have the courage to avoid all monetary and fiscal crises. I am certain that a new devaluation of the franc or its variant through the establishment of exchange controls would immediately risk or ruin these endeavors. I am equally certain that such a crisis in France would be considered a moment of weakness to be exploited by those who want war."

What was to be done and how: "The road to salvation is to increase the gross national product," which, measured under the gold standard, was 38 billion francs in 1914, 49 billion in 1931, but only 22 billion in 1937.

"France must go back to work. No other country in the world lets its industrial plant sit idle one or two days a week. As long as the international situation remains so delicate, a workweek of more than forty hours must be made possible. It is not a question of abrogating the law of forty hours but of permitting certain firms to work longer without having to pay prohibitive overtime wages"—meaning an extension of the workweek for national defense industries to forty-eight hours. Recognizing that he had crossed the final line linking him to the Popular Front, Daladier concluded with a series of rousing injunctions: "Let all in France set aside their differences to do what is necessary for the safety of the nation. Let us put France back to work, and we shall save the peace. Let us put France back to work, and we shall be assured of maintaining the social laws that are founded on justice. Let us put France back to work, and we shall be able, through fiscal stability, to realize further generous reforms. For this defense of France, for this security of France, an energetic revival must be pursued with confidence and order through ardent attachment to French peace and national destiny." [16]

Daladier expected a political firestorm, but he faced only a brushfire. The following morning Paul Ramadier, minister of labor, and Ludovic-Oscar Frossard, minister of public works, both with close ties to the Socialists, resigned from the cabinet in protest. Daladier quickly replaced them with Charles Pomaret and Anatole de Monzie, centrist Radicals, and the balance of the cabinet shifted slightly farther away from the Popular Front. The Communist *L'Humanité* had complained for more than a month about how "sabotage by the bosses" was the cause of lagging production, especially their reluctance to make capital investments, although the manner in which Blum and his minister of the interior, Marx Dormoy, had acquiesced to the sit-down strikes was certainly a disincentive. After 21 August complaining became railing against the "abominable campaigns of the capitalist oligarchy" to overturn "the social conquests of the Popular Front" and against Daladier personally for his failure to impose exchange controls against the "deserters of the franc." But the Communists were already voting against the cabinet and could be disregarded. Not so Léon Blum, who still controlled the pivotal Socialist votes. By calling the speech "surprising and disturbing," he revealed Daladier's failure even to consult him beforehand. By claiming that labor was prepared to make concessions but that capital should make them as well, he gave his unbidden advice. By declaring that only "France of the Popular Front" could fulfill the "necessary patriotic duty," he gave reason to the snub. But by insisting that the Socialists stand with Daladier because in the "present state of Europe . . . a cabinet crisis would be a formidable event," he demonstrated a loyalty that Daladier did not deserve and a courage too often lacking during his own premiership.[17]

Among the multifarious Center and Right 21 August represented the final proof that Daladier was one of their own. For the Catholic conservatives Marin extolled the "Back to Work" speech as "an act." For the cultivated bourgeoisie d'Ormesson challenged: "Let the government govern. Heroically if necessary. France will be behind them." For nationalists La Rocque deemed it "the necessary preliminary to civic order and a sound economy," while to Kérillis it was the "measure of his worth." To the executive committee of the Radical Party Daladier insisted that "the maintenance of peace requires that France be strong without delay, not in six months or a year"; they unanimously voted their approval. Caillaux added his blessing. And they were all the more pleased when the cabinet issued a decree on 30 August by which the minister of labor could, on his own authority, establish the weekly hours for workers in defense industries or public security and could, after consultation with representatives of labor and management, order up to one hundred additional hours of work per month to accomplish other vital tasks.[18]

What exactly was the situation in mid-August 1938? Statistically, the economy was certainly not in crisis. After the May devaluation the franc remained essentially firm: dropping from 176.25 to 178.52 in August against the pound (1.2 percent) and from 35.47 to 36.57 against the dollar (3.1 percent). The number of unemployed declined significantly, from 380,800 in May to 338,400 in August (11 percent). But the index of production failed to rise—82 in May, 83 in June, 81 in July—and during the August vacation closings it fell to 70. The contrast with Germany was deplorable. Clearly, the issue had become less to shock the economy into revival than to shock the nation into sacrifice. Daladier could have called for a new "Sacred Union," but that meant a greater role for the

Left, including the Communists. He could have demanded government Clemenceau-style, a "Committee of Public Safety" in the best Jacobin tradition to confront enemies within and without, but that meant imposing blame and burdens all around. Instead, Daladier chose to impose them only on the working class. He could not have more cogently demonstrated the death of the Popular Front than through his gratuitous refusal to consult Blum or Léon Jouhaux, of the General Labor Confederation, beforehand. Afterward, he made no effort to restrain Ramadier or Frossard from resigning. Pomaret, the new minister of public works, was close to Caillaux, Monzie, the new minister of labor, to Bonnet, and thus both additional voices in the cabinet were against a firm policy toward Germany. Georges Mandel found Monzie repellently spineless, and he was coming to the same conclusion about Daladier. His mentor Clemenceau had loathed Caillaux, and Mandel instinctively placed men by the company they kept. The 21 August speech was Daladier's claim to be France's strongman. Instead, it was further evidence of his weakness.[19]

For the issue was what Daladier failed to do in mid-August. When Germany announced and then began its late-summer maneuvers with the massive call-up of reservists, Daladier did not counter this warmongering with a call-up of French reserves. Although meant to demonstrate French calm in the presence of German bluster, the absence of any riposte recalled France's failure to respond to the remilitarization of the Rhineland or the *Anschluss*. On 24 August the air force chief of staff, General Vuillemin, returned from a nine-day official visit to Germany, where military and industrial leaders made certain that he was impressed by the size of the *Luftwaffe* and even more so by the pace of new aircraft construction. Almost his first words to Daladier were that Germany was producing twelve times as many airplanes as France, and to everyone he repeated his prediction from March, "In fifteen days, our aviation will be annihilated." Vuillemin also confirmed reports from the Deuxième Bureau and from François-Poncet that Germany was now capable of launching a sudden attack on Czechoslovakia. Still, Daladier did not act. On 25 August René Massigli, the Quai d'Orsay's political director, asked Gamelin the status of French preparedness, and he replied, "our system is ready, to start it one need only press a button." Four days later, when Daladier had not yet pressed that button, Gamelin himself, hardly known for his initiative, recommended a limited mobilization to strengthen the Maginot Line and other fortifications—but not a single soldier who could come to the aid of Czechoslovakia. Four more days later, on 2 September, the cabinet approved this weak response but de-layed announcing it until 5 September.[20]

From outside, France appeared not calm but beleaguered. Since 1918 European leaders had believed that France could maintain the peace, but that belief, shaken since 1936, was increasingly untenable. With the threat of a new and cataclysmic European conflict looming, for just a moment hope glimmered of reconstituting the grand alliance of the Western democracies that had won the Great War. On 16 August, in a speech broadcast by radio and heard in Europe, the American sec-retary of state, Cordell Hull, decried the brutalities of dictators and de-clared: "When freedom is destroyed over increasing areas elsewhere, our ideals of individual liberty, our most cherished political and social institutions are jeopardized. . . . When the dignity of the human soul is denied in great parts of the world and when that denial is made a slogan under which propaganda is set in motion and armies take the field, no one of us can be sure that his country, or even his home, is safe." Here was no promise, nor was there one in President Roosevelt's speech at Kingston, Ontario, on 18 August: "We in the Americas are no longer a far-away continent to which eddies of controversy beyond the seas could bring no interest or harm. . . . The vast amount of our resources, the vigor of our commerce, and the strength of our men have made us vital factors in world peace, whether we choose or not." And likewise no promise was issued at Lanark, Scotland, on 27 August by Sir John Simon, chancellor of the exchequer, when he reaffirmed the warning by Prime Minster Chamberlain the previous March that in a war over Czechoslovakia, "it would be quite impossible to say where it would end and what governments might become involved." Were these words the illusion or the reality of support?[21]

Hoping for the reality, Le Figaro's editor Romier argued that sup-port of France by the United States would be the difference in a long war. L'Epoque agreed: the American people are prepared to consider military intervention beside the Western powers. Le Petit Journal exclaimed, "the hour has come to consider the entente of free peoples." Henry Bérenger, chairman of the Senate's foreign affairs committee and ambassador to Washington in the 1920s, predicted, "The United States will be alongside Britain and France on the day when the great decision must be made." *Le Temps,* almost certainly influenced by the Quai d'Orsay, was much more cautious: "It would be yielding to dangerous illusions to assume that at present the American people have rallied to a policy of active intervention in Europe." Bonnet himself, ambassador more recently, told the Chamber's foreign affairs committee, "I spent a long time in Washington, and I know how isolationist they all are at heart." How rapidly he changed his tone as August became September, for those days were hammer blows to what remained of France's preconceptions and confidence.[22]

Hitler began a tour of the Siegfried Line defensive works and on 29 August came to Kehl, where, with eight generals at his side, he stared malevolently across the Rhine River toward Strasbourg, only a bridge away. At almost the same moment Lord Runciman finally grasped that his arbitration was not between the Czech government and its Sudeten German minority but between Czechoslovakia and Germany, with Konrad Henlein, the Sudeten leader, only Hitler's straw man. After Henlein's sudden consultation with Hitler at Berchtesgaden on 1 September, the evidence was incontrovertible. Even Flandin denounced these maneuvers as destabilizing to the European equilibrium, but he continued to defend the Runciman negotiations as a means to détente. And the Marseille dock strike remained unsettled, Monzie each day revealing himself more hapless. Now editorial admonitions became more strident. Addressing Germany, first Romier, then Pertinax, insisted that France and Britain would not cede to bluff and intimidation. Addressing the strikers, Romier warned that continued social disorder might lead to British mistrust. And for Bonnet the imperative was demonstrating where France stood with the United States.[23]

On 4 September there was the dedication of a monument at the Pointe de Grave, near Bordeaux, where the first American troops had landed in 1917. Standing more than two hundred feet high, this concrete pyramid, the first stone of which was laid by Raymond Poincaré in 1920, faced out to the Atlantic, symbolically toward the Statue of Liberty, and was inscribed "To the glory of the Americans, to the soldiers of General Pershing, defenders of the same ideal of right and liberty which guided the volunteers of Lafayette." Francophile and fearful, Ambassador William Bullitt declared that "between the United States and France, there is today such a profound and confident friendship, such a mutual devotion to the ideals of liberty, democracy, and peace, such an accord on the essential principles of human life, that conversations between our governments are not debates between suspicious negotiators but intimate exchanges between old friends who seek in frankness and joint effort the solution to common problems. . . . World peace is essential to us because we know that a general war would destroy for a long time all the values of civilization accumulated with so much labor during the centuries." Bullitt then uttered a sentence that Roosevelt had personally approved: "If war breaks out in Europe once again, no man can say or predict whether or not the United States would be involved in such a war." To make certain what he meant he concluded: "The colors under which Lafayette fought are the colors of liberty. They are the colors of France and the United States and several other countries. They are the old, old colors of common sense and human decency, of Christian charity and tolerance. They are the colors of freedom and peace."

Bonnet had seen Bullitt's speech and answered in terms that were even stronger: "One is inclined to say that it is the fate of France's arms and America's arms to be assembled under the same banners whenever they are called upon to defend those principles which our two nations consider to be the most precious heritage of mankind. The one friend is irresistibly compelled to rush to the help of the other friend who is in danger. That is why there is no need between us for agreements, pacts, or alliances fashioned by chancelleries. We know that we have with us the public sentiment of America even as we know that we have justice with us. . . . We do not underestimate the gravity of the Czech problem, but we hope that thanks to the love of peace that must inspire all nations, thanks to the sense of grave responsibility that must be felt by the governments of Prague and Berlin, and thanks also to the loyal and close cooperation between Great Britain and France, the grave menace to European peace will be averted. In any case, France will remain faithful to the pacts and treaties she has concluded. No one in the world, and especially not in the United States, has ever doubted our wish for peace. I am moved but never surprised to hear your compatriots say that if France were attacked anew, they would come to defend her anew. But that is not what we expect from you. Our desire is not that you help us in war, for we do not want war. Our desire is that you help us safeguard and organize the peace to make the world better." [24]

What was Bonnet thinking? His words went far beyond anything Bullitt implied. For the hopeful with only a vague knowledge of the United States, he was hinting at salvation. Kérillis exulted that the American people "are capable at any moment of prodigious élan in the service of the greatest crusades." Romier predicted that they would "take fire all of a sudden if war breaks out over freedom of conscience or racial [anti-Semitic] persecution." Léon Boussard praised their willingness to shed blood defending "government of the people by the people for the people." But Bonnet had been in Washington when the Neutrality Act was debated and enacted. He was well aware that American public opinion, though disturbed by European developments and largely anti-Nazi, was profoundly isolationist. So much was it so that Roosevelt felt compelled on 9 September to say bluntly: "Ambassador Bullitt's speech does not constitute a moral engagement on the part of the United States toward the democracies. . . . To include the United States in an alliance France-Great Britain against Hitler is 100 percent false." [25]

Because Bonnet later embraced appeasement completely, his enemies were not unfair to allege that he deliberately provoked Roosevelt's denial of any American commitment. More likely, Bonnet spoke on 4 September in a manner carefully calculated to require clarification of American policy. Neutrality was the official position, but the mid-August speeches by Hull and Roosevelt and the hopes expressed by Bullitt introduced a certain doubt. Upon ambiguity cloud castles may safely be constructed but not a strategy for looming war. If the United States meant to back up the Western democracies, Great Britain and France could act with greater confidence and firmness toward Germany. If the United States meant only to offer moral suasion, France needed to know—and now did.

Bonnet was also testing Great Britain's resolve. On 31 August, when informed of French plans to reinforce the Maginot Line, Halifax replied

that Britain had made no commitment about assistance to Czechoslovakia. On 3 September Phipps complained to Bonnet that Reynaud,
Mandel, and Edouard Herriot, president of the Chamber, were "warmongers" for urging resistance to Hitler's claims. On 5 September
Phipps warned Bonnet against approaching the Soviet Union for support because it was "likely to infuriate Hitler." On 6 September, when
Emile Roche, a powerful Radical, argued in *La République* that Czechoslovakia cede Germany the Sudeten region to prevent war, the proposal
could be attributed to his close ally Caillaux. When an editorial the following day in the London *Times* endorsed the idea, British government
sources could be legitimately suspected of pushing it. Despite Simon's
speech on 27 August, all of these signals since then were against French
firmness, and that suited Bonnet's Maginot mentality. But on the afternoon of the *Times* editorial, 7 September, Halifax told Corbin that, although British public opinion opposed fighting for Czechoslovakia, it
would not "understand" failing to support France. Here was the mirror
of what Daladier faced, an inability to decide which he loathed more, the
idea of war or the disavowal of France's commitments. As if to stiffen his
own spine, Daladier called in Phipps on 8 September to tell him that a
German attack on Czechoslovakia required France to "march"—and
not for the Czechs alone, because "after a given time, Germany would,
with increased strength, turn against France." Afterward to Bullitt he declared that "however England might wobble or vacillate there would be
no vacillation on the part of France" and then with gallows humor joked,
as Bullitt recalled, about "our being blown simultaneously into the air
from both sides of the Seine." Then, having the report from Phipps of
Daladier's statement, Halifax insisted to Corbin that neither the British
government nor British public opinion would be "prepared" for hostilities over Czechoslovakia and that the French government "consult us
before embarking upon measures that might involve them in war." [26]

The context for these parries was the final stage of the Runciman
mission and the weeklong Nazi Party Rally at Nuremberg, which
opened on 5 September and was to culminate with a speech by Hitler.
In early August one of the first examples of French public opinion
polling found 78 percent of the nation convinced that "the Franco-
British entente will maintain peace in Europe." Whether this result was

more wish or more reality, it might well have withered during the next two weeks. On 6 September, under enormous pressure to strike a deal with the Sudeten German minority, Benes offered the fourth version of an autonomy plan that all but capitulated to Henlein's Karlsbad program. How could these concessions not be enough? *Le Petit Parisien* praised Benes for "having acted not only as a head of state conscious of his responsibilities but as a 'perfect European.'" These concessions would not be enough if Hitler did not want them to be enough. The following day a violent incident at Moravska-Ostrava between Czechs and Sudetens so inflamed passions that no agreement seemed possible. The responsibility of Hitler and Henlein could not be seriously questioned. In Paris *Le Figaro*'s Romier dared to warn openly that the entire European equilibrium was in question—meaning the threat of war.[27]

Now was the moment to display the colors of resolution or equivocation. Among the Radicals, who after all were governing the nation, the divide was public and deep and acrimonious. Under Caillaux's influence *La République* and a large segment of the party were ready to renounce the Czechs. Countering them were two other Radical legends, Herriot, who now rued having sponsored Daladier, and Jules Jeanneney, president of the Senate and once an undersecretary to Clemenceau. Another divide separated the Socialists. Blum and the party newspaper, *Le Populaire,* sounded like Romier: "The 'one-way extortion' has lasted long enough: what is at stake goes far beyond the Sudetens and Czechoslovakia to put at risk the future of Europe." But Paul Faure, party secretary-general, and Jean-Baptiste Séverac, his deputy, favored peace at any price. On the Left only the Communists were united, with Gabriel Péri asserting in *L'Humanité* that handing over Czechoslovakia would sacrifice the peace, not save it. The far Right of *L'Action Française, Candide, Je Suis Partout,* more or less pro-Mussolini, terrified of Communism, and semi-fascist, thought Hitler better than the Popular Front and Czechoslovakia rubbish to be rid of. Surprisingly, *Le Petit Journal* suddenly slipped from the resolute, with La Rocque himself claiming that the danger from Moscow equaled the danger from Berlin. As usual, Pertinax looked beyond the present crisis, arguing that for Hitler Central and Eastern Europe were only a means to the greater end of world domination. Kérillis sounded like a new Clemenceau: "Our statesmen fail to realize that each new retreat by Prague is a new defeat for London and Paris, and a new cause for German exultation. . . . But there will be no weakness in the France of 1938 just as there was no weakness in the Belgium of 1914." Of course, in 1914 highly public preparations for air raids and a dock strike that resisted settlement until 9 September were not sapping confidence.[28]

By now Bonnet had almost no confidence to sap. On 10 September he told Geneviève Tabouis, of the Herriot-Jeanneney camp, "If war comes, I will wind up in the Seine because there will be a revolution and that is where the people will throw me." Later in a panic, he asked Phipps "as an old friend" the tortured question once more, "We shall march on, will you come with us?"—to which Phipps gave the standard reply, "the question could not be answered in advance and without reference to the nature of the German aggression." That night at Nuremberg, Goering called Czechoslovakia "a nation of miserable pygmies" and proclaimed that Germany awaited "events that are inevitable," words unanimously interpreted to mean war. In almost derisory counterpoint at Geneva, the League of Nations, which had failed so abjectly to maintain the peace, was to hold its annual opening session the following day. Listless and discouraged, Bonnet traveled there to meet with Maxim Litvinov of the Soviet Union, who told him to gain passage rights for the Red Army, and with Nicolas Petrescu-Comnene of Romania, who refused. At the Quai d'Orsay, as dispirited as Bonnet, Léger suggested to Phipps that a conference of France, Britain, Germany, and Italy could impose a solution to the Sudeten question, but the proposal would have to originate with the British because French opinion would be shocked at the omission of Czechoslovakia and the Soviet Union. By contrast in London, Chamberlain warned Germany that "Great Britain could not remain aloof if there were a general conflict in which the integrity of France were threatened. . . . It is of the utmost importance that Germany should make no mistake about it: she cannot with impunity carry out a rapid and successful campaign against Czechoslovakia without the fear of intervention by France and even Great Britain," a statement that was published that evening by the Foreign Office as an "Authorized Declaration."[29]

Did Chamberlain mean what he said? After all he had heard for the preceding two weeks, Bonnet believed not and said so unofficially to the

Paris press soon after midnight on 12 September. Although *Le Petit Parisien* called the words "blinding clarity," *Le Figaro* and especially *Le Temps* reacted with circumspection. The general consensus by morning was that the British were bluffing—and too late in the game. For Hitler was to speak that evening, and he had surely already made up his mind. In early afternoon the French cabinet met to discuss "hypotheticals," emergency measures in the event of war. Afterward Daladier huddled with Bonnet, Chautemps, Monzie, and Pomaret, the men of choice if he meant to desert Czechoslovakia. Still later, he consulted with Gamelin and his principal field commanders, generals Joseph Georges and Gaston Billotte, about war strategy. They agreed that on land French forces could, within less than ten days of mobilization, begin an offensive between the Rhine and Moselle rivers which would be ultimately successful but not without long, difficult fighting and certainly not in time to save Czechoslovakia. In the air Paris and other French cities would be subject to devastating attack from the *Luftwaffe,* but German cities, especially in the Ruhr, would also suffer grievously from French and British bombing. For survivors of the Great War the prospects were dismaying: another Pyrrhic victory. The Manchester *Guardian*'s Werth watched Flandin, Caillaux, and their allies busily making certain that this truth sank in through predictions that "there will be only old men in France" and reassurances that "we will be safe behind the Maginot Line."[30]

Hitler's speech at the Nuremberg Rally on the evening of 12 September was intemperate even by his standards. He called the "oppression" of Sudeten Germans by Czechoslovakia intolerable. He claimed their right to self-determination—implying a transfer of territory through plebiscite. He threatened Germany's intervention no matter what the reaction of France and Great Britain. He warned that any further violent incidents such as those at Moravska-Ostrava could "lead to the gravest consequences" because the peace was "fragile." In the hours that followed, and obviously prearranged, there were just such disturbances throughout the Sudeten area. With every justification the Czechoslovak government declared a state of emergency. But, fearing war, the Quai d'Orsay deplored this reaction as eliminating further chances for negotiation, meaning, the Czechs realized, that the French were willing to push them beyond accepting the Karlsbad program. The mood in Paris could be measured from the press reaction to Hitler's tirade. Péri in *L'Humanité* wrote that "the end of it all will be a settling of accounts with France," and Kérillis in *L'Epoque* called this moment a "diplomatic Verdun" to be held at all cost. But otherwise Hitler was made to seem almost reasonable because he had used the word *settlement* but not the word *war*. La Rocque in *Le Petit Journal* urged against drawing hasty conclusions. D'Ormesson in *Le Figaro* even called the speech "an open door."[31]

On the morning after, Bonnet told Bullitt that Hitler's tone was less ominous than expected and took this opinion into the cabinet meeting that began before noon. The sole issue on 13 September was whether to resist or to yield, whether to back words with deeds, whether or not to order at least a partial mobilization to demonstrate French determination. Reynaud and Mandel argued that Hitler could be stared down if threatened with war by a coalition made up by France, Great Britain, Czechoslovakia, and the Soviet Union. If not stared down, his next move would be to demand the Sudeten region for Germany either outright or under the cover of a plebiscite: Czechoslovakia would be left a remnant; the Soviet Union would have to seek accommodation with Germany; and France's security position would be weakened beyond repair. Not as vehement but almost as firm were Campinchi, the minister for the navy, Auguste Champetier de Ribes, the minister of pensions, Jean Zay, the minister of education, and Henri Queuille, the minister of agriculture. They were opposed by Chautemps, the vice-premier, Bonnet, Monzie, and Pomaret, who put forward the argument of Caillaux and Flandin: France had no quarrel with Germany which could not be patched up; France could not be expected to commit suicide for the sake of Eastern Europeans or German Jews; France could not afford the cost in blood and treasure of another war; defeat would mean Nazi conquest; victory would mean Communist revolution. For good measure Bonnet served up a military assessment emphasizing all the danger to France and none of the dangers to Germany. Daladier began by declaring that he was prepared to sign the mobilization order, but as the meeting went on, the horns of a bull became the horns of a snail. He grew hesitant, then morose, and finally surly, lashing out at

Mandel for what he called Clemenceau's "criminal errors" at the Paris
Peace Conference. Daladier then carried a majority of the cabinet with
him to do nothing. During the Nuremberg Rally *Le Figaro*'s special correspondent, Maurice Noël, reported that the Germans did not expect
war because "they have become used to victories without battles." [32]

The decision to yield had been made, but the terms, the manner,
and, most important, the pretext remained to be decided. For this
diplomatic etiquette of plausibility Great Britain's participation was essential, with Ambassador Phipps the master of protocol throughout the
late afternoon and into the night. Having blocked mobilization, Bonnet
pressed almost frantically for a British initiative—a proposal by Runciman, a statement by Chamberlain, anything to restore calm. At one
point he insisted that "the whole question of peace or war may now be
only a matter of minutes instead of days." Finding Daladier calmer but
"gravely perturbed," Phipps asked him directly whether he was standing by his declaration on 8 September of support for Czechoslovakia.
"He replied, but with evident lack of enthusiasm, that if Germans used
force France would be obliged also." Phipps drew the correct conclusion that Daladier was as anxious as Bonnet for British intervention.
And what Daladier wanted was a meeting of France, Great Britain, and
Germany to impose some solution, Léger's idea of 11 September minus
Italy. First by telephone and then through Phipps, he proposed this
great-power conference to Chamberlain, but there was never a chance
that Hitler would consent without Mussolini to even up the table. Besides, Chamberlain had already decided on what his response, through
Phipps soon after midnight, referred to as "another possibility of direct
action in Berlin." While French leaders waited abjectly all day on
14 September for the meaning of this cryptic phrase, Phipps called them
"ready for peace at almost any price." In the early evening a dispatch
from Halifax revealed that Chamberlain would fly the following morning to Germany for negotiations with Hitler. France had been consulted
neither about the offer nor about the acceptance. France had all
but begged for a British initiative and now had to accept the result.
Chamberlain expected "that the French Government will trust him
never to lose sight of the common aims and policies of the two Governments, French and British, who have worked so closely during the

crisis." This profession was disingenuous: French policy had become abdication.[33]

The news so steadied Bonnet's nerves that he immediately promised Phipps his support for "any proposal regarding Czechoslovakia that Mr. Chamberlain might make, whether it were accepted by the Czechs or not." Roche, Caillaux's minion at *La République,* exulted that war was "henceforth impossible." Not that certain, Flandin argued in *Le Journal* that the cabinet had no right to order mobilization unless France were actually attacked. Then, showing off his excellent English in the London *Evening Standard,* he praised Chamberlain's "noble and courageous initiative." For *Paris-Soir* the prime minister was "daring, bold, and courageous." For Blum in *Le Populaire* he was showing "a noble audacity in his will for peace." *Le Figaro* and *Le Temps* especially rejected any accusation of capitulation: "In pushing the spirit of conciliation and negotiation to its extreme limit, Great Britain and France are in reality committing their strength to the service of peace." But the accusation was made: by Péri in *L'Humanité,* who condemned the "dealing in peoples," and by Kérillis in *L'Epoque,* who warned that a plebiscite meant the end of Czechoslovakia.[34]

Daladier remained glum—and petulant. Publicly, he asserted having had the idea to negotiate directly with Hitler. Privately to Phipps, he complained that his suggestion was for a meeting of *three* great powers. Reinforcing his mood was an analysis of the Sudeten crisis prepared by Emile Giraud of the Quai d'Orsay, whose views were close to Massigli's. France, Giraud insisted, had many advantages, above all the likelihood of facing Germany with Great Britain, Czechoslovakia, and the Soviet Union as allies, but public opinion failed to recognize them because it was divided between a pro-fascist Right and a thoroughly pacifist Left. He described his fellow citizens as "fearful, wedded to moderation, thirsting for tranquility and comfort, knowing nothing about the 'frenzied mentality' of totalitarian nations, believing they can cut their losses in the 'absurd' hope that the annexation of the Sudetens will mark the end of Hitler's demands." Instead, he concluded, it would be the prelude to a war in which France would end up "defeated, dismembered, and treated as a vassal." For Daladier reading this description, so similar to his own pessimism and hesitancy, must have cut close to the bone.[35]

On 15 September, flying for only the second time in his life, Chamberlain traveled the six hundred miles from London to Munich, where he boarded a special train that took him to Hitler's mountain retreat at Berchtesgaden. There after tea Hitler calmly threatened war unless Czechoslovakia rapidly ceded to the Third Reich the areas in which three and a half million Sudeten Germans lived. When Chamberlain protested, Hitler declared his willingness to accept the verdict of self-determination but demanded every territory where Germans were a majority, however small. Because the Runciman mission had already demonstrated that no agreement on the basis of autonomy was possible and with the French seemingly prepared to force Czechoslovakia beyond the Karlsbad program, Chamberlain considered Hitler's ultimatum just possible to accept—if it meant peace. France and Czechoslovakia would have to be convinced, and Chamberlain flew home the following day to apply whatever pressure was necessary.

In Paris police officials readied for war, sending the flying squad to arrest nearly three hundred "agitators" and distributing sand to use against fire from incendiary bombs, but the smart money drove up stock prices. Like investors, the building trades workers were betting on peace, threatening a general strike to protest the new workweek rules. On 18 September a five-member French delegation led by Daladier and Bonnet arrived in London to meet about the Sudeten crisis. Stopping at the French embassy to pick up Corbin, Daladier fumed before his diplomats: "Do you know what I did this morning before taking the plane? I met with the building workers. Yes, even when it's a question of peace or war, the building workers are on strike!" He became all the more exasperated when Chamberlain and Halifax described what they expected from Czechoslovakia as the only means of preventing war. After discussions that lasted late into the evening, Daladier did win two important concessions: Prague would hand over the Sudeten areas without recourse to plebiscites, the use of which would encourage demands by the Polish and Hungarian ethnic minorities; and Britain would guarantee the defense of this smaller, weaker Czechoslovakia. But he was under no illusions. During one of the breaks he addressed his delegation: "I am not proud. No, I am not proud. The Czechs are our allies, and we have obligations to them. What I have just done betrays them. . . . The truth is that France is in a serious state. I do not know whether you realize it, but that's the case. What can I do if I have no one behind me?" And he asked Bonnet directly, "Do you really approve of what we have just decided with the British? What a negotiation, a knife to the throat, eh?" Although Chamberlain wanted a commitment immediately, Daladier insisted on returning to Paris to present the proposal to his cabinet and promised an answer by noon the following day.[36]

After an early-morning flight from London, Daladier assembled his ministers at the Elysée Palace and explained to them the details of this "Anglo-French" plan. He called it the sole option to war and emphasized that Britain would not otherwise intervene to save Czechoslovakia. As for France, "we have two thousand aircraft, the Germans have four thousand that are faster, . . . and both the Germans and the British know it." La Chambre, the minister for the air force, cited Vuillemin's apprehensions, and Bonnet added Gamelin's. When Mandel asked that the plan not go into effect without the approval of the Czechoslovak government, Chautemps replied, "It is honorable and indispensable to warn Benes that if he refuses, he cannot count on us." Mandel and Campinchi protested this treatment of an ally, but Daladier insisted that even with these heavy sacrifices, "Czechoslovakia can live on, and Britain is ready to participate in a guarantee of its independence." Almost exactly at noon the cabinet approved the plan, the vote reported as unanimous, but if so, Mandel, Reynaud, Campinchi, and Champetier de Ribes clearly joined in reluctantly.[37]

A half-hour later Osusky heard from Bonnet that Prague could either accept the plan without modification or lose French support. Leaving the Quai d'Orsay, he said to reporters: "Here you see the condemned man. He has been sentenced without even being heard." This severe and despairing epiphany had several echoes. A Communist Party manifesto decried the "dismembering of Czechoslovakia, the integrity of which is inseparable from France's security and the peace of Europe." Blum confessed that while "war has probably been averted, it has been averted in such conditions . . . that I cannot feel any joy and am merely filled with mixed feelings of cowardly relief and shame." Kérillis refused to believe that the French people would not rise up "against those responsible for this evil, . . . against all those who have led them blindfolded to this abyss of shame." He was wrong. The reaction was not even the ambiguity felt by Blum. Newspapers like *Le Temps* and *Le Figaro* justified ceding the Sudeten areas as better than war and thus true support of an ally. *Le Petit Parisien* said that Czechoslovakia could become an East European Belgium. *La République* blamed the Czechs for all their troubles, while *Paris-Soir* merely referred to their "surprising blindness." The far Right press accused Prague and its supporters of seeking to draw France into a war that could only benefit the Communists; La Rocque's *Le Petit Journal*, which had only recently been in sometime agreement with Blum, now threatened to "open a dossier on Mandel." [38]

In the early evening of 20 September Benes and his cabinet replied that they could not accept the Anglo-French plan, which would "mutilate Czechoslovakia economically and militarily." Instead, they invoked the arbitration treaty signed by Prague and Berlin as part of the Locarno Pact. After rapid consultations British and French leaders bluntly demanded that Czechoslovakia capitulate or face Germany alone. There was no delay in alerting Benes, who was awakened after midnight by the French and British ambassadors, Lacroix and Basil Newton. Late that afternoon, 21 September, the deed was done: Czechoslovakia, "compelled by circumstances and pressing demands made repeatedly by the French and British governments," accepted the plan "with aggrieved feelings." Utterly hypocritical, *Le Temps* and *Le Figaro* now praised the Czech "nobility of soul." Mandel and Reynaud considered resigning from the cabinet in protest but were dissuaded after meeting in Paris on 20 September with Winston Churchill and former British military attaché General Spears, who had failed to alter British policy under Chamberlain but argued that Daladier might still be turned from appeasing Hitler. A resignation did take place in Prague. General Eugène Faucher, head of the French military mission to Czechoslovakia since 1926, requested relief from his post, returned all his decorations, offered his services to the Czech army, and when accepted, adopted Czech citizenship. [39]

In 1938 such a conception of honor was quixotic, more proof coming when Chamberlain made his second trip to Germany on 22 September, exactly a week after the first, this time flying to Bad Godesberg, on the Rhine just south of Bonn. Hitler rejected the Anglo-French plan as no longer sufficient. What he demanded now would compromise not just the military and economic security of Czechoslovakia but its very sovereignty. Insisting on the "language frontier," he told Chamberlain that the Czech security and administrative apparatus had to be withdrawn immediately from the entire Sudeten region, which would then be occupied by German troops. He also advanced claims for Polish and Hungarian minorities with the threat that he would not offer any promise of nonaggression until they were settled. Taken aback and believing that Hitler was bluffing, Chamberlain angrily broke off the meeting. Far from it: the following day Chamberlain received a memorandum detailing these demands. The Czech withdrawal was to begin on 26 September, with no property public or private to be removed. The German occupation would follow two days later, including even areas where Sudeten Germans were a minority. A plebiscite conducted according to Hitler's rules would set the final border between Germany and Czechoslovakia—if the Czech state survived. Chamberlain's protests gained a single concession, pushing the date for occupation back to 1 October. The change was entirely to Hitler's benefit: his military plans would be complete by then if there were to be war, and the four extra days allowed a greater chance to gain all he wanted without fighting.[40]

On the night of 22–23 September, as Chamberlain contemplated the new ultimatum, Sudeten paramilitary forces took control of Eger and Asch at the extreme western end of Czechoslovakia. France and Great Britain had asked the Czech government to refrain from any act likely to inflame Hitler during the negotiations—above all not to mobilize. With the news from Godesberg and from Prague, both London and Paris rescinded the request late in the afternoon of 23 September. That night Czechoslovakia announced a general mobilization. Indeed, the first report from Godesberg galvanized Daladier and Gamelin into ordering a partial mobilization of French forces. On 22 September the most fervently resolute of the cabinet, Mandel, Reynaud, and Champetier de Ribes, confronted Daladier with a threat to resign but agreed to stay on when he revealed the new military dispositions. On 23 September, as large-scale Communist Party demonstrations protested the cabinet's supine policy, Daladier told a delegation from his own Radical Party, "If Czechoslovakia is the victim of unprovoked aggression, France will immediately take the necessary measures for assistance." On 24 September the mobilization posters went up through-out France, recalling two categories of reservists and thus constituting an army of 1.2 million men, approximately equivalent to the current total in Germany. Further orders requisitioned some civilian automobiles, im-posed censorship on radio broadcasts, and announced plans to evacuate nonessential civilians from Paris. In a "noble gesture" the building trades workers abruptly ended their strike. Daladier issued the traditional, ex-pected, yet nonetheless stirring statement: "The vital measures for secu-rity taken this morning have been greeted and executed everywhere in France with the sangfroid and resolution that the government expects of the nation." Jean Verdier, cardinal-archbishop of Paris, promised, "God will not abandon the nation which is the eldest daughter of His Church." [41]

At the Gare de l'Est (East Station), from which the special trains were departing, mobilized reservists and their families were embodying Daladier's words. The *Guardian*'s Werth found almost no one singing "La Marseillaise" but almost no one singing "The Internationale" ei-ther. "There was no terrible gloom or depression . . . but only a feeling of bitter necessity." He "was impressed by the deep unity of the French people in a moment of danger." *Le Figaro*'s d'Ormesson was more poetic, intoning that "France eternal is a single family, composed and resolute, united around the homeland." This reaction was too much for the equivocators. Flandin wrote Daladier that he needed the consent of the legislature to act and that the Senate would surely refuse. Then he rushed to tell Phipps that "all [the] peasant class were against war." Caillaux was also stopping by the British embassy to accuse deputies who favored opposing Hitler of being in the pay of the Soviets and to predict "another Commune" after the first air raids. The far Right newspapers like *Le Matin* and *L'Action Française* were printing the same, while even an old nationalist like Louis Marin warned in *La Na-tion* as much against the "warmongering" of the Communists as against the threat from Germany. Nevertheless, Phipps was consciously and severely shading the truth when he reported to London that "His Majesty's Government should realize extreme danger of even appearing to encourage small, but noisy and corrupt, war group here. All that is best in France is against war, *almost* at any price." [42]

Chamberlain had flown back to London on 24 September and found his cabinet badly split over the Godesberg ultimatum. Some, notably including Halifax, were now convinced that Hitler was bent on European domination and mocked his promise that the Sudeten region was his "last territorial demand." Others still thought that the Czech government could be bullied further until its ambassador to London, Jan Masaryk, delivered a ringing and defiant rejection: "Against these new and cruel demands my Government feel bound to make their utmost resistance and we shall do so, God helping. The nation of St. Wenceslas, John Hus and Thomas Masaryk will not be a nation of slaves. We rely upon the two great Western democracies, whose wishes we have followed so much against our judgment, to stand by us in our hour of trial." With hostilities between Germany and Czechoslovakia seemingly inevitable, consultations with the French had to be considered war strategy.[43]

On 25 September, before leaving for London, Daladier gathered his cabinet and denounced Hitler's Godesberg memorandum as unacceptable. Bonnet demurred, arguing that a basis remained for negotiation, but this time he was badly outnumbered. Mandel and Reynaud led the resolute, and they had a new ally, Albert Sarraut, minister of the interior, who regretted deeply his failure to act when Hitler remilitarized the Rhineland. Given the state of crisis, Daladier again demanded and got a unanimous decision, although this time it was Bonnet, and Monzie as well, who looked decidedly unhappy. Bonnet would soon be all the more discontent because Daladier shunted him aside as soon as they flew to London early in the evening: Chamberlain's equivocations would be problem enough. As Roland de Margerie, secretary to Ambassador Corbin, recalled, the meeting was "a veritable corrida. The 'bull of Vaucluse' was literally bombarded with questions as if to plant the banderillas. . . . But he resisted these assaults while Bonnet remained silent from start to finish." Of course, Bonnet could remain mute because Chamberlain argued his position, portraying the Godesberg memorandum as not much worse than the Anglo-French proposal. Daladier then declared that his cabinet had unanimously rejected the Godesberg memorandum and offered his own idea: to create an international commission that would rapidly establish a revised German-Czech border and only then permit German occupation of the ceded regions. He added, "No honest man could object to such a procedure and retain his sincerity." When Chamberlain replied that Hitler surely would object, Daladier answered that, if so, "each of us would have to do his duty." And if that meant war "the French Government had always said . . . that, in the event of unprovoked aggression, France would fulfill her obligations."

And so came the great question: how? At a signal from Chamberlain, John Simon, a celebrated barrister before entering government, began cross-questioning. As minister of defense, Daladier certainly knew everything about French war planning and could give the British at least a broad outline. Offended by this hectoring, Daladier responded with sarcasm: "he would consider it ridiculous to mobilize French land forces only to leave them under arms doing nothing in their fortifications" and "equally ridiculous to do nothing in the air." He also protested the suggestion by Chamberlain, based on reports from Phipps, that the French were unwilling to fight, citing the resolve of the mobilized reservists and the self-possession of the general population. Reversing the accusation, he asked whether Great Britain preferred "that France do nothing." In a face-saving retreat Chamberlain agreed that Gamelin should be dispatched from Paris to provide a briefing the following day.[44]

The next morning, 26 September, Chamberlain answered Daladier's question and bowed to his suggestion by proposing that Sir Horace Wilson, his industrial advisor and chief confidant, bear a letter to Hitler offering the establishment of a German-Czech commission to implement the Anglo-French plan for the Sudeten region. Upon Hitler's likely refusal Wilson was to declare that if Germany attacked Czechoslovakia and France came to Czechoslovakia's aid, Great Britain would support France. Here was the guarantee that France had sought since the Paris Peace Conference in 1919 but a guarantee that eliminated any excuse for not honoring the pact with Czechoslovakia. When Gamelin was called in, uniformed and booted, he presented an optimistic assessment if war came. By mobilizing five million men, France could put one hundred infantry divisions into battle and could mount an offensive within five days. Its fortification system was impregnable, while the German Siegfried Line was improvised. Its air force, although inferior to the *Luftwaffe,* could provide tactical support to the army and impose unacceptable losses on German industry in the Ruhr. Through an attack between the Rhine and the Moselle rivers France would draw off German troops from Czechoslovakia. He called the Czech military worthy, the Italian not. Although uncertain about the Soviet Union's army, he was confident that its air force would present Germany with many problems. But, having begun with such panache, he suddenly became cautious, revealing that the offensive would continue only until there was serious resistance, upon which the French army would retreat to the Maginot Line and await reinforcements from Great Britain and perhaps other nations. This admission worried British leaders, who wondered which version of French strategy to believe. They also had their own problems, embarrassed to admit that they had only two divisions—the French were asking for twelve—available for rapid deployment to France and that the Royal Air Force would be reserved for home defense and not committed to Continental action.[45]

On 26 September the French mood was as ambiguous as Gamelin's briefing. Godesberg had finally torn the veil from Hitler, and even Phipps wrote of a calm resolve to confront the German threat. Prices were firm on the stock and bond markets as investors judged the lack of disruption to mobilization as proof of the government's strength. Yet in the cities great trepidation about the threat of air raids created an exodus to the countryside. Children especially were sent to stay with rural relatives. So often hesitant, Daladier had suddenly become as firm as sullen, telling Bullitt: "Hitler's last memorandum is not only the means for Germany to finish off Czechoslovakia but the expression of his determination to humiliate France and Great Britain. *Better to fight and die than to accept such an abasement.* The war risks being long and painful, but whatever the final cost, France will triumph." To reporters he told a brave lie, "I am always optimistic because we are on the side of truth." But Daladier's new tenacity and Herriot's prediction of a majority in the Chamber of Deputies for supporting Czechoslovakia appalled Caillaux and Flandin. Their pessimism and conviction that France was about to commit a suicidal error were widely shared among the middle classes, who feared war would benefit only the Communists. General Vuillemin repeated to anyone who would listen that the American aviator hero Charles A. Lindbergh believed the *Luftwaffe* invincible. Bonnet, silenced in London, frantically dunned Phipps with requests for Britain to order mobilization and conscription because he believed such announcements would shake British nerve.[46]

Everyone was waiting for Hitler's reaction, and it came the evening of 26 September in his speech at the Berlin *Sportspalast* (Sports Palace). William L. Shirer described it a "mad outburst before a delirious crowd," F. A. Voigt of the Manchester *Guardian*, "a passion of fury," and Péri of *L'Humanité*, "a program of annihilation." Kérillis wrote in *L'Epoque* that these "words of a fanatical madman" were the final proof that for France and Great Britain "much more than their honor, their prestige, their immediate security, and their supreme interests were at stake." But despite the paroxysm of rage, Hitler left just enough room for hope among the equivocators, the proponents of negotiation to "appease" him. *Le Temps,* arguably speaking for Bonnet, heard "also finesse," and Romier in *Le Figaro* pronounced, "Nothing irreparable." This utter divergence in Paris was replicated by official British reaction. Just before the speech Wilson delivered Chamberlain's letter, but Hitler's reaction was so fulminating that he dared not add the oral declaration of Britain's promise to support France in a war over Czechoslovakia. After the speech Halifax authorized the release of a communiqué to the London office of Havas, the semiofficial French news agency, publicly avowing that support. Yet Chamberlain issued his own statement, offering further compromise over cession of the Sudeten regions, "providing the German government agreed to implement the terms and the conditions for transfer through persuasion, not through force." Because his own position was so much closer to Chamberlain's words, Bonnet used the power of the Quai d'Orsay to cast doubt on the authenticity of the Halifax communiqué, exploiting its unorthodox arrival through Havas rather than through diplomatic channels. The far Right press derided *fausse nouvelles* (false news), many papers omitted any reference, but *Le Figaro,* wavering over what line to follow, reported it as official British policy.[47]

On 27 September French resolution reached its zenith and began to decline. Early in the morning Daladier met with Gamelin, who warned that permitting Hitler to crush Czechoslovakia would give Germany command of all Eastern Europe and within ten years the strength to humble France. Armed with this sobering prediction, Daladier called together his cabinet an hour later. He began boldly by insisting, "If France upholds her commitments, Great Britain will be obliged to follow her," by rejecting the need to convene the legislature, and by asking approval for general mobilization. Bonnet immediately argued the opposite: that France owed Czechoslovakia only indirect assistance, that the Chamber (meaning Flandin) and the Senate (meaning Caillaux) should be consulted, and that general mobilization had to be avoided "because it would mean war. . . . At any price, we must find an accommodation." Campinchi then deplored this tenor at a time when France finally had firm British support, and Reynaud exclaimed that if Bonnet's words became public, "It would be a catastrophe for France." Sensing his isolation, Bonnet stalked out, but when President Lebrun also urged a delay in ordering the general mobilization, Daladier settled for calling up a few more reserves. His tendency to vacillate, the essential trait of his personality and his career, was reviving. That afternoon Daladier made up with Bonnet, who rightly regarded this reconciliation as an encouragement to pursue the accommodation he had urged. And so he did, complaining loudly that France was isolated and without defense against German air raids. He could count on the usual sources, and with the threat of war so clear he had new support from the once-resolute, now-equivocal, like the Catholic leader Marin. Herriot's contention that a majority of the deputies favored defending Czechoslovakia was becoming dubious. Phipps, long in Bonnet's camp, made the most of evidence for appeasement.[48]

And of this sentiment and mood there was much to be made. Some hoped to exploit the appeal for peace issued the day before by President Roosevelt: "I earnestly repeat that so long as negotiations continue differences may be reconciled. Once they are broken off reason is banished and force asserts itself." They noted that Blum gave Roosevelt the blessing of the Socialist Party for "having spoken in the name of universal conscience." More pointed at a poster bearing Flandin's signature which suddenly appeared all over Paris. Bold letters proclaimed, "ON VOUS TROMPE!" (You are being deceived!), and smaller print denounced mobilization as the prelude to a war massacring millions of Frenchmen. As minister of the interior, Sarraut ordered the police to tear them down.

Mandel would likely have charged Flandin with treason. Of course, Charles Maurras in *L'Action Française* was calling the partisans of firmness "criminals," and his henchman, Maurice Pujo, had long ago labeled Mandel a "clumsy impersonation" of Clemenceau. More than a half-million Parisians took advantage of extra trains to flee the city. Others prepared to go by purchasing trunks and withdrawing their savings. Custodians packed up artworks at the Louvre, painters gave train stations and factories a coat of camouflage, construction workers dug air raid trenches in the Montsouris park. That evening Daladier told reporters: "At the end of this new day of crisis, I would make two observations. On the domestic plane, I underline again the perfect order that reigns in the country, the nation's calm, the equability with which the security dispositions we have had to impose have been applied. On the international plane, the struggle for peace is not over. Negotiations continue. Do not believe that our diplomacy has been ineffective. It has been active today in numerous capitals. As a veteran of the Great War, I need hardly say that the government over which I preside will neglect not a single possibility to maintain peace with honor."[49]

Great Britain appeared at least as unsteady. On the morning of 27 September, during a second meeting with Hitler, Wilson was able to deliver Chamberlain's pledge to back France over Czechoslovakia. Hitler turned furiously on him, shouting: "In the event of a rejection of the memorandum, I will smash Czechoslovakia! In six days we will all be at war with one another, and only because the Czechs refuse a proposal for the execution of obligations they have already undertaken." After the trembling Wilson left, Hitler dictated a letter to Chamberlain repeating the same argument: his demands at Godesberg were only a procedural change from the Anglo-French plan Czechoslovakia had already accepted, but Czech leaders were distorting them to generate a "warlike conflagration." In London deep gloom accompanied preparations similar to those in Paris. The cabinet authorized ordering the fleet to war status. That evening Chamberlain, clearly more discouraged than Daladier, addressed the nation by radio: "How horrible, fantastic, incredible it is that we should be digging trenches and trying on gas masks here because of a quarrel in a far-away country between people of whom we know nothing. It seems still more impossible that a

quarrel which has already been settled in principle should be the subject of war." [50]

Despite the fury, despite the despondency, Hitler in his letter
and Chamberlain in his radio address were both suggesting the same
means to resolve the crisis—at the expense of Czechoslovakia. Czech
leaders had, under duress, accepted the Anglo-French proposal, meaning the loss of the Sudeten regions to Germany. If Hitler were willing to
soften the appearance of the Godesberg terms—never mind their reality—and thereby make them seem merely a "procedural change" to a
"quarrel which has already been settled in principle," and if this "concession" were arranged at a conference of great powers, Czechoslovakia
could be made to agree. Appeasers clung to this pernicious hope. On
27 September Halifax, no longer resolute, prepared a "time-table" by
which Germany would occupy the Sudeten region in stages beginning
on 1 October, with an "International Boundary Commission" providing
a specious legitimacy. Like witches three, the ambassadors had their instructions to throw principle into the cauldron of expediency: at Berlin
Henderson was to present the time-table to Hitler as soon as possible; at
Prague Newton was to tell Benes that it was the "only alternative"; at
Paris Phipps was to tell Daladier not to undertake any offensive action
before consulting with the British. However ignominious this British
plan, Bonnet thought it insufficient to deter Hitler from war and early
on 28 September sent his own through François-Poncet. He offered
Hitler immediate occupation of the Sudeten regions, disputed or not—
in essence, the Godesberg memorandum—with the Czechs to be informed coldly that acceptance or fighting alone was their choice. France
needed no lesson in perfidy from Britain. Both Chamberlain and
Bonnet accompanied their abasements before Hitler with desperate
pleas to Mussolini that he intervene with his ally by proposing a great-
power conference. And Mussolini, well aware of Italy's military deficien-
cies, eagerly played his role. Recognizing that he could have all he wanted
without war, Hitler agreed.

On the afternoon on 28 September the German, Italian, French,
and British governments announced that they would meet the following day at Munich to resolve the crisis over the Sudeten region of
Czechoslovakia, by which they meant deciding how rapidly Germany

was to take their possession. Daladier had called for such a conference, although without Italy, before Chamberlain's Berchtesgaden trip and could hardly refuse one now. As the sacrifice for the cause of peace, Czechoslovakia had no place at the conference, no more than the goose at the planning for a feast. Neither did the Soviet Union, whose exclusion was easily justified by arguing that Communists hoped to profit from war and because its alliances with France and Czechoslovakia were an embarrassing reminder of erstwhile French commitments. When the news reached Paris in the evening papers, families awaiting trains to evacuate surged back to their homes shouting happily, "Pas de guerre!" (No war!). But Alexander Werth overheard this conversation between two men at the Café des Capucines: "All the same, what a relief!" "Well, maybe the relief you have after wetting your pants." Daladier's own reaction was as ambiguous, but a few hours later in his radio speech he put up a brave front: "Before my departure, I want to thank the French people for their courageous and dignified bearing, for their new proof of sangfroid and resolution. My task is difficult. . . . I have never ceased to work with all my strength for the safeguard of peace and for the vital interests of France. I shall continue this effort tomorrow, with the thought that I am in complete agreement with the whole nation." [51]

One window into the sentiment and mood of the French during the last week of September 1938 is Jean-Paul Sartre's novel *The Reprieve*, which he wrote between 1941 and 1944 with constant reference to the newspapers for those days and his own memory of living through them. All of the characters from *The Age of Reason* return—after all, only three months have passed—and added to them are many new ones to create a kaleidoscope of French reactions. Maurice Gounod, a Communist, tells his girlfriend, Zézette, that if war comes, "We guys'll do the job. But when we come back, we'll keep our rifles. . . . The bourgeoisie doesn't want war. . . . They are afraid of victory because it would mean the victory of the proletariat." As he contemplates his class enemies, Maurice concludes, "They must be bled; it would be a nastier process than squashing snails, but it couldn't be helped." Relaxing on the Riviera at Juan-les-Pins, Jacques Delarue, a wealthy solicitor, agrees, arguing to his brother, Mathieu, a lycée professor, "And even if we win this infernal war, do you know who will profit by it? Stalin." When Mathieu replies, "And if we do nothing, Hitler will," Jacques says resignedly, "Well, and what then? Hitler—Stalin, it's all the same. Except that an understanding with Hitler will save us two million men and spare us a revolution." Mathieu explains to Jacques's wife, Odette, that he must write Ivich Serguine, the young émigré Russian student with whom he is infatuated: "She has taken to reading the newspapers and she doesn't understand what's going on; she wants me to explain. It's going to be an awkward business. She mixes up the Czechs and the Albanians, and she thinks that Prague is by the sea." At her parent's house in Laon, where she is staying after failing her qualifying examination for medical training, Ivich listens to Hitler's *Sportspalast* speech with her father. "What would happen if there was a war?" she asks him. He answers, "The French would be beaten." She cries, "Pfui! Would the Germans invade France? . . . They would get to Laon?" Without hesitation he says: "I imagine so. I imagine they would head for Paris." "She was sorry she had asked the question. Since the Bolsheviks had burned his country houses, her father rather enjoyed catastrophes." [52]

In Paris the wildest stories pass for truth: a customer warns her butcher, "You've heard what they've invented? . . . The Germans. Kills people like flies, in great agony. . . . A kind of gas, I believe, or ray, if you like—I have had it explained to me." Traveling from Marrakech to Marseille, Pierre stares at a book on facial wounds suffered in the Great War: "I want to know what I shall look like next year. . . . Those men . . . live in an institution on the Val-de-Grâce. They go out at night only, and always masked." Boris Serguine, Ivich's brother and Mathieu's student, passes time computing the number of meals he will have eaten, the number of trips to a café, the number of women to whom he will have made love, before he is killed in the war: "One woman only. It was quite a small life; indeed, it had an air of already being concluded, since he knew in advance all that it would not contain." At Saint-Flour pharmacist François Hennequin seeks the comfort of the familiar as he prepares for mobilization: "Ah, yes, coffee, I shall need something hot to settle my stomach; it will be the first time since I married that I shall dine without soup. . . . I'll take my musette bag." Jacques Delarue insists, "it's none of our business." But Gomez, back from the Spanish Civil War now that the Republican cause is lost, presents his son, Pablo, with a soldier's outfit and tells his wife, Sarah, "He must learn to fight. . . . Otherwise he'll become a mouse, like the French. . . . There are moments when one ought to want to fight."[53]

Despite the more than thirty characters, the essence of *The Reprieve* lies in the accounts of Mathieu, Sartre's alter ego, and Ivich, who is based on Olga Kosakiewicz, for whom he had his own ill-fated infatuation. Mathieu defines the ambiguity of the French response, recognizing the threat, seeing war as a bitter necessity, hoping for a way out. Returned to Paris to put his affairs in order before joining his unit, Mathieu contemplates his life: "There had once been a kindly, rather diffident man who was fond of Paris and enjoyed walking in its streets. . . . This man had shaped a future to his measure, a decorous, arid, uncomplaining future, rather overburdened with human contacts and schemes. A historic and mortal little future: the war had thundered down upon it and crushed it to powder." How like France and the French since the Great War. Halfway across the Pont-Neuf bridge he begins to laugh: "Liberty—I sought it far away; it was so near that I couldn't touch it, that I can't touch it; it is, in fact, myself. I am my own freedom. . . . What shall I do with all this freedom? What shall I do with myself? His future lay marked out by definite tasks: the railway station, the Nancy train, the barracks, the manual of arms. Nothing was any longer his: war seamed the earth, but it was not *his* war. He was alone on the bridge, alone in the world, accountable to no man. 'I am free *for nothing*,' he reflected wearily." Not quite—he wants someone to remember him and picks up Irène, "a plump girl with a sallow skin, a little too forthcoming, rather moist and faintly unclean; . . . I shall leave her in an hour or two and yet I shall remain in her forever. In her, in this nameless night."[54]

After Hitler's speech Ivich goes to bed obsessed by war. "It's too unfair, . . . at the best, it will last six years, even ten years, all the women will be dressed as nurses, and when it's over I shall be old . . . they'll probably violate all the women, I dare say they'll cut off one of my legs." With such a future all too much to bear she abruptly decides to sneak out and catch the early morning train. In Paris, she says, "I shall rediscover myself; . . . And someone will show me Czechoslovakia on a map. Ah, . . . let them bomb the city if they will, we shall die together." She takes a taxi to

Mathieu's apartment on the rue Huyghens, for he always promised to take care of her. When she appears at his door, he has barely returned from spending the night with Irène and is hastily packing his suitcase to leave for mobilization at Nancy. He immediately assumes that she will live in the apartment while he is gone and begins explaining what she must do about housekeeping, bills, taxes, and utilities. She was hoping for a declaration of love but settles for asking where Czechoslovakia is. All Mathieu has is an atlas published before 1914, and so he draws it freehand with his fountain pen over the map of Central Europe. When she offers to go with him to the station, he tells her she should rest and promises to write. He has, in fact, arranged for Irène to bid him farewell. Ivich waits only moments before leaving to seek out Georges Sturel, who tried to seduce her the day she learned she failed the qualifying examination. He is in his pajamas as she bursts in exclaiming: "I want to enjoy myself! . . . You wanted to take me to your room; you were waiting for a chance. . . . And here I am . . . in your room." As he reaches for her, she says to herself: "At Berlin the bombers had perhaps already taken off . . . this is where I shall die . . . anyway, I shan't die a virgin." [55]

After Daladier's radio speech late on 28 September, Jacques Delarue "waltzed Odette round the drawing room, . . . he was in an ecstasy." So too were the Paris newspapers that appeared the following morning, their unanimity in proclaiming peace saved producing strange pairings. There was simple rejoicing: Blum in *Le Populaire* that "an armful of wood [had been] thrown on the sacred hearth at the moment when the flame fell and was about to die out"; and Kérillis in *L'Epoque* that "a great hope has taken hold since yesterday." There was inevitability: *Le Temps* insisting that earlier negotiations had already delineated the form of an agreement; and La Rocque in *Le Petit Journal* emphasizing "the good sense that rejects with horror the idea of a war over a question of procedure." There was moralizing: Péri in *L'Humanité* calling "for the solemn affirmation of solidarity by the peace-loving powers against others who wish to incinerate the world"; and d'Ormesson in *Le Figaro* boasting that Daladier had behind him a France "conscious of its European responsibilities." [56]

Daladier shared neither the ecstasy nor the confidence. From mid-afternoon until late in the night of 28 September he telephoned London seeking to coordinate strategy, only to be told every time that Chamberlain was "in conference." Without a common brief the preparation of dossiers for the French delegation was all the more critical. From Gamelin and the Deuxième Bureau came the warning that the preservation of Czechoslovakia depended upon retaining as much as possible of its defensive fortifications and securing an international guarantee of its new boundaries. From Bonnet and the Quai d'Orsay came nothing. Partly because Hitler preferred to deal without foreign ministers and more so because Bonnet had acted too independently during the preceding days, Daladier decided to leave him behind in Paris. Léger agreed to be his chief diplomatic aide but only if Bonnet would provide precise instructions. For reasons never properly explained, but most likely for fear of committing to paper his willingness to accept peace at any price, Bonnet did not meet with Léger until the last moment. Then, as the delegation was leaving for the airport, he passed him an envelope of documents and the injunction, "Do not accept what would be unacceptable for Czechoslovakia."[57]

That morning, 29 September, the weather was overcast and dismal at Le Bourget airport when Daladier, Marcel Clapier, his principal secretary, Léger, and Charles Rochat, head of the foreign ministry's European section, boarded a small twin-engined plane. Nearly two and a half hours later they landed in Munich, meeting up with François-Poncet and air force attaché Paul Stehlin, who took the train from Berlin. Daladier was visibly unhappy, unimpressed by the fulsome welcome from Hitler's foreign minister, Joachim von Ribbentrop, and revulsed by the well-organized crowd of women and children who saluted him, arms extended, with the cry "Heil!" To his own colleagues Daladier confessed, "Everything depends on the English . . . we can do nothing but follow them." Yet for their part the British continued rebuffing his request to concert tactics even though the two delegations were staying only floors apart in the venerable Vier Jahreszeiten (Four Seasons) Hotel. Daladier did not see Chamberlain until the conference formally assembled shortly after noon at the *Führerbau* (national headquarters of the Nazi Party) and received not a greeting but a glacial stare. His isolation—France's isolation—was brutally confirmed. Later he would say, "I had the impression of having fallen into a trap."[58]

Hitler began with a diatribe against Czechoslovakia's treatment of its German minority since 1918 and demanded an immediate remedy: the Czechs were to withdraw their governmental apparatus from the Sudeten region, which Germany would then occupy, the process to begin on 1 October and to take no more than ten days. Here were the Godesberg terms with a slightly extended schedule. When Chamberlain made no objection, Daladier asked whether the real objective was not to destroy Czechoslovakia, and, if so, he would take no part in such a "crime" and instead "return to France." As often, Daladier began by playing the bull but a bull with shrinking horns. Mussolini then offered a memorandum, actually drafted for him by the German foreign ministry, which embodied exactly Hitler's demands while calling for them to be carried out under the auspices of an international commission made up of Germany, Italy, France, Great Britain, and Czechoslovakia. Both Daladier and Chamberlain quickly accepted it as the basis for discussion. They did request that a representative from the Czech government enter the negotiations, but when Hitler objected they backed down. As they had at London on 18 September, the leaders of France and Great Britain were willing to deal in the territory, the sovereignty, and even the survival of a friendly nation, for France, an ally.[59]

During a mid-afternoon adjournment to convert the "Mussolini memorandum" into a more formal draft, Daladier sulked in his hotel suite but without any plan, without even the intention, of altering what he called Hitler's "unacceptable" exactions. When discussions resumed, Daladier, as if he had suddenly recalled Gamelin's warning, attempted to prevent some of the Czech defensive line from falling to the Germans. Losing fortifications south of Breslau and north of Brno would cut Czechoslovakia almost in half. To save them he had to argue that the linguistic line, so sacred in Nazi ideology, bend to geographical and economic factors. When Hitler did agree, as a meaningless gesture, that the international commission could recommend slight modifications to the "ethnological determination," Daladier gushed that this concession "would considerably ease the position [meaning his own] in France." Assigning the details of evacuation, occupation, plebiscites, and the final frontier to the commission and resolving the terms of a guarantee to the much-diminished Czechoslovakia—France and Great Britain pledging immediately, Germany and Italy only after Polish and Hungarian demands had been resolved—took up several more hours. During them Daladier made almost no contribution, sometimes leaving the room to smoke or "ask for a Munich beer." Careless from frustration, fatigue, or drink, he offhandedly criticized Benes for refusing to grant the Sudeten Germans autonomy long ago and denounced the "French warmongers who would have liked to push the country into an absurd and impossible war."[60]

Eventually, rather than wait during the preparation and translation of the final documents, Daladier returned to the Four Seasons, where he could brood in private, "miserable and overwhelmed." Shortly after midnight on 30 September he joined Chamberlain, Hitler, and Mussolini in signing the Munich "Agreement." He murmured that while the French would appreciate his preserving the peace, they would also reckon the cost. François-Poncet was more blunt, declaring, "See how France treats the only allies who remained faithful to her." Within the hour Czechoslovakia would have an object lesson in that treatment. Vojtech Mastny, the Czech minister to Germany, and Hubert Masarik, from the Czech foreign ministry, were waiting to hear their nation's fate. While Chamberlain yawned and Daladier stood silently embarrassed, Léger had to admit that a reply from them was unnecessary because the Agreement was not subject to further negotiation. Through Bonnet, who exalted, "Peace is assured. . . . That is the main thing. Everybody will be happy"—so much for his injunction to Léger—Daladier lied to Benes that the Agreement enabled Czechoslovakia to "retain faith in the future" and that "it had not been in his power to ensure that a Czech representative attend" the conference. Abandoned and betrayed, Czechoslovakia coupled its submission with a "protest against the decisions which were taken unilaterally and without our participation." Kamil Krofta, the foreign minister, told Lacroix: "I know for certain that we shall not be the last. After us, it will be the turn of others."[61]

In Paris the morning newspapers had only spare details of the Agreement but bannered deliverance in large type: Le Figaro's headline "LA PAIX EST SAUVEE" (Peace Is Saved) was typical. Even when more was known by afternoon, Paris-Soir's Jean Prouvost wrote that Daladier and Bonnet had preserved "peace in honor and dignity." At Munich that was not the impression of the French delegation and especially Daladier himself. His mood was black and would have been blacker had he known that immediately after breakfast Chamberlain sought a meeting with Hitler. Together they signed a statement declaring that "the question of Anglo-German relations is of the first importance for the two countries and for Europe. We regard the agreement signed last night . . . as symbolic of the desire of our two peoples never to go to war with one another again." Quite deliberately, Chamberlain told an aide that he "saw no reason whatever for saying anything to the French." When Daladier learned of this deceit a half-day later, he hardly exaggerated in exclaiming that the "Franco-British entente was called into serious question." [62]

But first came the return to Paris. The French delegation left for the Munich airport almost exactly twenty-four hours after arriving. Once again, a well-programmed crowd offered cheers, and Ribbentrop provided the escort. During the flight Daladier sat silent and morose, worried about the reception he would receive at Le Bourget, about how the French would react to his having betrayed Czechoslovakia and France's promises. As the plane circled for landing, he and the others saw a massive crowd awaiting them. Expecting jeers, hissing, rotten fruit, and maybe worse, Daladier declared stolidly: "They are going to mob me, I suppose. . . . I appreciate their feelings," and insisted on absorbing their wrath by being the first off the plane. But as he stood dumbfounded on the gangplank, thousands surged forward carrying flags and flowers, shouting: "Hurrah for France! Hurrah for England! Hurrah for peace!" Daladier turned back to Léger and cursed, "The God-damned fools!" Quickly, the police cleared a path for Bonnet, who had brought a chauffeured convertible for the return in glory. And triumphant the ride was back to Paris, Bonnet having broadcast the route on radio and the dense crowds along the way cheering and showering the car with wreaths and bouquets. In the backseat Bonnet, radiant and beaming, waved excitedly. Beside him Daladier, his eyes lowered, hunched down almost prostrate. Their posture was the very definition of *écroulement morale,* the "moral collapse" that had come to the Third Republic.[63]

4 Fall

October to December

In Moscow, thirteen hundred miles from the triumphal entry into Paris, Ambassador Robert Coulondre meditated on the meaning of 30 September. "Munich," he concluded, "tolled the bell for a certain France, the greatness of former times and even of 1914.... The sound of the bells does not kill a sick man; it announces his death." But a different and diminished France did survive and had to carry on. In Jean-Paul Sartre's novel *The Reprieve* Ivich Serguine looks up from the bed at Georges Sturel, who has gone out for the morning newspaper. When he tells her, "It's all right, they signed last night," she is distraught as she realizes, "no war; no planes over Paris; no bomb-shattered ceilings: life must now be lived."[1]

And blows passed down—as they were in the trial of "La Plevitzkaïa." France was the adopted land of many White Russian émigrés and Paris the headquarters for their fantastical plots spun out amid samovars and teacups to overthrow the Bolsheviks. The Soviet Union's secret police, the OGPU, made certain that these impractical counter-revolutionaries could never become a serious threat by periodically decapitating their principal organization, the Rossiiskii Obshchevoennyi

Soiuz (ROVS). On 26 January 1930 OGPU operatives forced its leader, General Alexandr Kutepov, into an automobile only a quarter-mile from Napoléon's tomb at Les Invalides and vanished without a trace. They duplicated the trick against his successor, General Eugene Miller, on 22 September 1937, but this time there were loose ends.

Several months earlier Miller began to suspect that his intelligence chief, General Nicolas Skoblin, was a double agent. On the day he disappeared and certainly was killed, he was to meet Skoblin shortly after noon about two potential sources in the German army. Apprehensive, he committed the details of this rendezvous to a sealed note, which he gave to his principal assistant, Colonel Pavel Kusonskii, with the injunction to open it if he did not return within a few hours. Miller then proceeded to the corner of rues Jasmin and Raffet at the western edge of Paris, where OGPU agents abducted him. They did the killing in an apartment on the nearby boulevard Montmorency, placed his body in a large trunk, and loaded it into a van bearing the diplomatic license plate CD 235 X. Driving at a high speed, they got to Le Havre about 4 P.M. and brought the trunk aboard the freighter *Maria Ulyanova,* which made a rapid and unscheduled departure at 8 P.M. Kusonskii did not open the note Miller left behind until 11 P.M.—unpardonable laxity. Then, thoroughly alarmed, he rushed to Skoblin's residence with three other White Russian leaders. When Skoblin denied all, they stepped aside to confer, and in that moment Skoblin made his escape—further unpardonable laxity. The only person left to hold accountable was his wife, allegedly the real spymaster in the household.

Mme Skoblin was La Plevitzkaïa, her life already legend: a peasant child who ran away from her novitiate to join the circus, whose unforgettably haunting voice led her from singing in the street for coins, to singing at the Winter Palace for the czar, to singing for armies—successively the Imperial, the Red, and the White—to singing for sold-out audiences all over Europe and the United States. Along the way she married a dancer, Plevitzkii, thus her stage name, then a Bolshevik, and finally Skoblin. When interrogated about Miller's disappearance, she gave a series of false alibis for her husband and tried to destroy a daybook in which he had foolishly recorded his plans. When arrested for attempting to frustrate the course of justice, she made a critical mistake in requesting the Bible bound in green leather from her bedroom. For the course of justice was indeed proceeding apace through the investigation by the State Security Police. The involvement of the Soviet embassy was irrefutable: renting the apartment on the boulevard Montmorency and holding the diplomatic license for the van. The actions of the Soviet-registered freighter, the *Maria Ulyanova,* were open to grave interpretation: never previously docking in France, leaving Le Havre without proper authorization after a shortwave radio transmission from the Soviet Union, and on the course to Leningrad avoiding the Kiel Canal, where it might have been stopped. The role of the OGPU in the operation was confirmed through the deciphering of secret messages: the key to the code discovered in the Gospel of St. John. For La Plevitzkaïa her Bible was not about her salvation.

And her trial was not about her guilt. As sold-out as those long-ago concerts, the proceedings covered eight days in early December 1938. Fifty-two years old, her imperious manner withered by more than a year in prison, she put up remarkably little defense to the charge of complicity in kidnapping and murder. Her conviction was expected, but her sentence, twenty years of hard labor, astonished—and indicated what this trial was truly about. La Plevitzkaïa had to pay because the prosecution could not place the Soviet Union and the Popular Front in the defendant's dock with her. Not for want of trying. For the Soviet Union there were all the hoary tales of OGPU brutality to enumerate. For the Popular Front there were allegations of misconduct at the highest level of the State Security Police. Diplomatic immunity barred the prosecution from doing more than declaim about the Soviet Union. Was there similar political immunity for the Popular Front?

Among the vexing questions about the Miller case one of the most important was why French officials, having been alerted to the suspicious activity involving the *Maria Ulyanova,* did not intervene either by searching the ship before it departed or afterward by sending a naval vessel in pursuit. A decision apparently was made to do nothing. When the loose ends dangling from Kusonskii and La Plevitzkaïa ensured that the case received maximum publicity, the ministry of the interior excused its inaction by alleging that the van arrived in Le Havre at 2 P.M. If so, it had to have left Paris before Miller could have been killed. Thus, the report telephoned to the ministry late in the afternoon by the State Security Police superintendent in Le Havre placing the van's dockside arrival at approximately 4 P.M. was an acute embarrassment. The superintendent suddenly found himself under investigation and forced into retirement, but he triumphantly recounted his story before the court. Called to explain these matters, high-ranking police officials professed to be disgusted by the allegation that they could ever be influenced by "political considerations."

Ultimately, the decision not to intervene with the *Maria Ulyanova* and to alter an official report lay with the minister of the interior, who was then Marx Dormoy. In September 1937 the Popular Front was still governing France, and a political consideration important to the Léon Blum cabinet was a good relationship with the Communists and the Soviet Union. What had Dormoy to say about these issues? Nine months earlier he had avoided testifying in the Cusinberche murder case by evading a subpoena. This time, with his integrity directly questioned and under national scrutiny, he found a new means to evade such difficult questions. In answer to an order from the presiding judge he delivered a letter citing jurisprudence that a cabinet minister is responsible for his acts of government only before the legislature and universal suffrage. The prosecution considered that this evasion was humiliation enough and would be regarded by public opinion as an admission to the allegations. Dormoy considered that any inference was preferable to testifying under oath about the Miller case.[2]

Coming after the suppression of an attempted general strike on 30 November and the conclusion of a friendship pact with Germany on 6 December, the examples made during La Plevitzkaïa's trial were the third symbol in only two weeks of how thoroughly Edouard Daladier's government had embraced the implications of its Munich policy. The process began with defending the abandonment of Czechoslovakia, for the exultation at peace saved risked turning to second thoughts, soul-searching, and bitter recrimination at the cost.

Photographs of Germans marching into the Sudeten region, news that Czechoslovakia bowed to Polish demands for Teschen, and confirmation that Duff Cooper, first lord of the admiralty, resigned from the British cabinet to protest Neville Chamberlain's diplomacy undermined the sense that the Munich Agreement was honorable. On 1 October *Le Figaro's* Wladimir d'Ormesson called it the "Rainbow in the Sky," but the following day he asked, "Is Central Europe henceforth a German fief?" In *The Reprieve* Sartre has a successful Jewish businessman put down his paper—it could well have been *Le Figaro*—and say: "I was in favor of peace. . . . I feel ashamed." Far harsher words came, predictably, from Henri de Kérillis in *L'Epoque*, "the immense moral and material disaster," and from Gabriel Péri in *L'Humanité*, "the dismembering of a free people." The Communist Party published a manifesto of sympathy for Czechoslovakia that concluded, "This submission to fascism was not by the Popular Front." Dark British humor filtered across the Channel. Even before Munich the pseudonymous "Sagittarius" had rhymed:

> Meine Herren and Signori, clients of the British Tory,
> Kindly note that Number 10 requests your patronage again,
> Opening from today as Chamberlain and Daladier,
> Messieurs Hoare, Laval successors for doing business with aggressors.
> Frontiers promptly liquidated. Coups d'état consolidated.
> Loans on fascist risk advanced. Nazi enterprise financed.
> Have you problems of partition? Let us send a British mission.
> Breaking with Geneva's firms, we offer Nazis' favorite terms.
> For dirty deeds both great and small, our representative will call.
> Orders carried out with speed. Satisfaction guaranteed.
> We obsequiously remain, Daladier and Chamberlain.

Now the ridicule took a razor edge: that Chamberlain had "turned all four cheeks" to Hitler and of his three flights to Germany, "If at first you can't concede, fly, fly again."[3]

The government countered with drama. On the evening of 2 October Daladier led the Paris Association of Veterans to rekindle the flame at the Tomb of the Unknown Soldier beneath the Arc de Triomphe. An immense crowd filed past almost in silence while spotlights illuminated tricolor banners fluttering in the cold autumn wind. The next afternoon before a smaller but still impressive congregation at the cathedral of Notre Dame, Jean Cardinal Verdier presided over a service of thanksgiving for peace. And one more day later, because Daladier wanted approval from the representatives of popular sovereignty as the ultimate spectacular, the Chamber of Deputies would meet to consider the Munich Agreement.[4]

Almost reluctantly, the cabinet had assembled late in the afternoon of 30 September to hear Daladier claim that the alternative to the Agreement was to have seen Czechoslovakia overrun in a week and France confronted by a fait accompli. Without elaborating, he declared that he would recall the Chamber and Senate from their summer adjournment for a brief session. However much any ministers might take exception, there was no question of rejecting or altering what Daladier had done at Munich. Further discussion was pointless, and they unanimously endorsed President Albert Lebrun's proposal to praise "his decisive effort in favor of France and peace." Georges Mandel, Paul Reynaud, and Auguste Champetier de Ribes again considered resignation and again decided they might accomplish more by remaining. Four days later, when Daladier convened the cabinet before the debate in the Chamber, he revealed his plans. He called the September crisis proof that France was running out of time to redress weaknesses. The economy was recovering but not enough for a rapid and thoroughgoing rearmament. The stern measures necessary for this girding were certain to be unpopular, and compromise would take too long. The nation required, he insisted, the psychological shock of authority, and for that he was requesting that the legislature grant him new decree powers lasting until 15 November.[5]

A few hours later, when the Chamber met for the first time since mid-July, the deputies were well aware of how crisis had diminished their role. No constitutional provision required that Daladier submit the Munich Agreement to them, and he did not provide a *Livre jaune* (official report, "yellow book" from the binding) of the diplomacy, for Georges Bonnet had no intention of revealing the craven proposals that had led to the conference. The deputies were in session because Daladier was confident that they would approve the Agreement and the request for decree powers and afterward adjourn until he needed their presence again. Before them he disdained candor for a specious accounting worthy of Bonnet: "What the French people wanted was to avoid the irreparable. The irreparable was German aggression, which under the terms of the treaty would have triggered French assistance. . . . But France and Great Britain were agreed in our common will for peace just as in our common will to oppose aggression. . . . I accepted the invitation to Munich. It was not a question of discussing procedure or of submitting counterproposals. It was a question of saving peace when many considered it lost. I said 'yes,' and I regret nothing. . . . The Munich Agreement was an effective victory for peace and a moral victory for peace. . . . Certainly, the Agreement reduces the territory of Czechoslovakia, but the Czechoslovak Republic can live on as a free country, and we shall do all we can to help."

What Daladier wanted from the debate to follow was the correct combination of praise and reproach by which to define a new majority for post-Munich France, and to a great extent he was pleased. The testimonials were many and fulsome from Center-Left to Center-Right. One exception was Louis Marin, leader of the Catholic conservatives, who had made mistrust of Germany the basis of his long political career and who was now regretting his recent lack of resolution. After complaining about the absence of a *Livre jaune*, he warned that French diplomacy could not "perpetually choose between avoiding war and abandoning everything to the enemy." Because Daladier hoped to jettison Socialist support entirely, Léon Blum's only moderate reproof was another disappointment. With the indecision and idealism that were always his manner, he described being torn between "a profound joy . . . that the people of our country were delivered from a catastrophe beyond horror and a profound grief . . . that the people of Czechoslovakia have had to sacrifice their independence" and then imagined "reconstructing a Europe of equity, concord, and solidarity . . . through general disarmament."

The only true rebukes came from Péri and Kérillis. They had already been writing these home truths in their newspapers, but now at this moment of national self-deception they transcended anything they had done before or would again by laying the double-headed axe of strategy and morality to the Munich Agreement. Peace, Péri insisted, had been bought at the cost of "a people mutilated, . . . sacrificed because they were the friend of France and had believed in the word of France." By barring Germany's way to the Danube basin, the Balkans, and Asia, the Czechoslovak army had once "protected not only the Czechs but the French." But no more, for France has "killed that element of strength for a democracy, the confidence of peoples, demonstrating to the world how imprudent and dangerous it is to be her friend." He blamed the "ruling class" for the "inexpiable mistake" of bowing to "the designs of international fascism" and threatened, "It is against you that we will win the battle for peace." The more strident Péri's indictment, the better for Daladier, because he intended to portray the Communists as the domestic enemy.

That calculus was not so true of Kérillis, who represented the tony northwest Paris suburb of Neuilly. The proof came from an interruption, but by then Kérillis had applied the lash. Like Péri, he emphasized how France had betrayed obligations "declared ineluctable and sacred." "With Czechoslovakia, we have lost our only card in central Europe. How can anyone imagine that weakness will make us attractive to Great Britain or Italy or the United States? . . . When the people realize how they have been deceived, they will require a settling of scores, and then the dreadful specter of social revolution will loom." At this moment, because the prediction sounded uncomfortably close to what Péri threatened, Pierre-Etienne Flandin protested. With his conclusion Kérillis made clear how far he stood from Daladier. Condemning France's leaders for not having the "guts" to face down Germany, he proclaimed his vote against the Munich Agreement, "which will consecrate through Hitler's triumph the victory of international fascism. If any one or more, from the Right or the Left, wants to renounce partisan struggles and unite to remake France, I am with them!" And that vow placed Kérillis even farther from Flandin, who, rumor had it accurately, on 30 September sent telegrams of congratulation to Hitler, Mussolini, and Chamberlain and received in return a telegram from Hitler praising his "activity during the past year."

The farther Kérillis stood from Daladier and from Flandin, the farther he stood from almost everyone except the Communists, meaning that though his words and Péri's stung, they could not inflict serious wounds. The proof came in the vote on the Munich Agreement: 535 in favor, 75 opposed (Kérillis, Jean Bouhey, a Socialist, and the Communists). With the Chamber's stamp on the past Daladier needed it for the future, through the decree powers, saying "the interest and the very life of the nation are at stake. . . . The primary duty for everyone is to work as hard as possible. We can maintain the peace only if our national production enables us to speak as equals to the people around us. We can maintain peace only if we have sound finances and a balanced budget, only if we can count on the total resources of the nation. This country must have a moral transformation." Again, Daladier got the approval he sought: 331 in favor (the Right, the Center-Right, and the Center-Left), 78 opposed (the Communists and three maverick Radicals), 203 abstaining (the Socialists). And while the margin was not overwhelming, he had exactly the majority he wanted: no deputy left of the Radicals. In the Chamber of Deputies the Popular Front was a memory. In the Senate, where the Popular Front had never even existed, Daladier received decree powers on the following day by a margin that was simply overwhelming: 280 in favor, 2 opposed (the Communists), 21 abstaining (the Socialists).[6]

The Daladier who made his career in the Radical Party seeking alliances with the Left, who championed the Popular Front, and who served in every Popular Front cabinet destroyed it utterly in six months as premier. He adopted the argument of the Right and Center-Right that the Socialists and the Communists were willing to push France into war but unwilling to accept the economic regimentation necessary for rearmament. The obvious conclusion was that any cabinet relying on their votes would be hostage to their foreign and economic policies. Because Daladier believed France was unready for war, he went to Munich. Because he believed France could no longer afford the Matignon labor policies, he was preparing to overrule them by decree. Because he knew the Communists would not follow him and doubted the Socialists would, he made provision to govern without them. But every instinct from his past rebelled against leading the Radicals to side with the likes of Flandin or the promoters of riot on 6 February 1934. Daladier was not Bonnet, however much he sounded like him in addressing the Chamber of Deputies. Their postures in the convertible riding back from Le Bourget — disconsolate and radiant, respectively — continued to define the difference between them. On 3 October Daladier confessed to William Bullitt that Munich was an immense "diplomatic defeat" for France and Great Britain. On 8 October Bonnet insisted to ten thousand cheering constituents at Périgueux: "France's signature is sacred. Czechoslovakia was not invaded, was it?"[7]

Bonnet prepared for Périgueux with appearances before the two foreign affairs committees of the legislature. The scale of deceit runs in severity from equivocations to prevarications to lies to damn lies, and Bonnet danced along it as if to deception born. He needed that talent on 6 October before the Chamber's committee, where bad luck had concentrated some of the cabinet's vocal antagonists, the merely suspicious Marin, the openly critical Ernest Pezet, whose scorn during the long-ago *Anschluss* debate had left Foreign Minister Yvon Delbos shaking, and the deadly acid Péri. Bonnet tried to explain away French obligations to the Czechs by arguing that they were taken on when France had the sole large army in Europe and when the League of Nations was respected—and besides, the Paris Peace Conference should never have awarded the Sudeten region to Czechoslovakia. Less than a decade had altered the original conditions completely, and France was now essentially alone—from Britain there would have been only meager support, from the United States "not a man, not a sou," from the Soviet Union promises to be broken when Poland and Romania refused passage rights. The Munich Agreement, he insisted, was an improvement over the Godesberg ultimatum and had been accepted by the Czechs. Peace was preserved and a war avoided which "would have swallowed up all Europe." For the future "our foreign policy will be dependent on the political, moral, and material strength" of the nation, which "must summon up all its energies." Bonnet rejected every challenge to this duplicitous rendition with lies and damn lies, which were accepted as truth by the majority of the committee. The critics scored only a single direct hit, and that not against Bonnet or Daladier. Through a contact in the telegraph service Salomon Grumbach of the Socialists had obtained a copy of the message Hitler sent in reply to Flandin's congratulations and read it aloud. The rumor was correct: "I assure you of my gratitude for your energetic efforts in favor of an entente and a complete collaboration between France and Germany." Furious, Flandin managed to say only that he would respond "in another place to this personal attack."[8]

Before the Senate's committee on 7 October Bonnet did not even need to deceive. The senators had no qualms about the Munich Agreement or where it left France. Pierre Laval, who had reluctantly signed the mutual assistance pact with the Soviet Union in 1935, spoke for almost all of them in urging Bonnet to act as if that arrangement "no longer existed." France, he argued, should put aside ideological prejudices against fascism and make up to Mussolini, as he had tried to do until the Ethiopian crisis. The committee chairman, Henry Bérenger, who had been wrong about the Americans in late August, was as eager for accommodation with Germany as Flandin or Joseph Caillaux. He proposed that Bonnet initiate direct talks with Hitler to match the statement of amity signed by Chamberlain—calling this approach "a revival of realistic diplomacy." And as a warning to anyone who might object, Bérenger concluded with the reminder that the Senate rendered judgment when politicians were charged with high crimes and misdemeanors: "We are not at this moment the High Court, but perhaps one day we shall be."[9]

Bérenger's threat had been made more crudely, more nakedly, by *L'Action Française* on 29 September in its parody of "The Internationale": "If these cannibals insist on making us heroes, let the first bullets be for Mandel, Blum and Reynaud." Such far Right claptrap had limited appeal, but, with the new political tide and public opinion both running strongly for Munich, the moderate newspapers sensed that they should follow the current—sometimes farther than expected. The easiest course to navigate was calling for rearmament. During the September crisis no one, especially not its commander, General Joseph Vuillemin, believed that the French air force could stand against the *Luftwaffe*. The newspapers now called for 5,000 new planes—more than doubling the current total of 3,500—"somehow and at any price." Of course, the calling was vastly simpler than the doing. Because French factories could produce only 250 planes a month, as much as half of the new aircraft would have to come from abroad, most likely from the United States. Their cost would be an enormous charge to the balance of payments, and the American Neutrality Act could prevent their delivery if war broke out.[10]

A second course in the post-Munich flow, more dangerous, was adopting the principles of the Bonnet-Flandin-Caillaux foreign policy. Flandin himself set the tone in *Paris-Soir* by warning that France could not count on British support for "Continental complications" and thus should concentrate on its empire and concede control of Eastern

Europe to Germany. Newspapers such as *Le Temps, Le Figaro, Le Journal,* and *L'Epoque* adopted Bérenger's term *realism* to describe such surrender and its accompanying corollaries. By this reasoning Munich initiated a "new European equilibrium" in which cooperation between democracies and dictatorships would be unhindered by ideological reservations. France should join with Great Britain in accepting the Nationalist victory in Spain. France should reconcile with Mussolini by restoring an ambassador to Rome and then with Italy maintain peace in the Mediterranean. France should seek an accommodation with Germany by acquiescing in the German "drive to the east." France should recognize the impotence of the Soviet Union as a military power but its danger as an instigator of domestic dissent. France should, in sum, recognize that the Europe of Versailles was dead and that a new Europe was in creation, that Munich was not an abdication but an opportunity.[11]

The course into much deeper and darker waters led to proposals that risked the traditions of the Third Republic. For Kérillis "remaking France" required establishing an "authoritarian Republic" with laws limiting the rights of labor unions and the press. Appalled by the welcome given Daladier after Munich, Pertinax compared France's "institutions and public morality" unfavorably to Germany's. On 11 October the Union Fédérale des Anciens Combattants (Federal Union of Veterans), which was politically more Left than Right, had a membership of two million, claimed to speak for six million, and for these reasons could not be ignored, declared through its leader, Henri Pichot: "The country needs a Government of Public Safety. The time has come for men of action—men who are honest, intelligent, and with character, who are Republicans but without party labels. The day of party combinations is over. To give such a government time to work, it must have plenary powers until the 1940 legislative elections. If the Chamber refuses, it shall be dissolved." Six days later *Le Temps,* bastion of Republican values, dared editorialize that Daladier's need to ask for decree powers and their successful use argued for a permanent strengthening of the premier at the expense of the legislature. Farther Right the reaction was faster and not nearly so tentative. Gustave Hervé in *La Victoire* demanded a constitutional revision that smacked strongly of Italian Fascism: a president elected by universal manhood suffrage would wield the "authority of the state," while a single assembly, made up of representatives from professional corporations, would be merely consultative. Hervé proclaimed Marshall Philippe Pétain the obvious choice for dictator of France. Although *L'Action Française* preferred restoring the monarchy, Maurras was willing to take Pétain as a stopgap.[12]

But just as disgust with the Third Republic could be based on disgust with Munich, demanding more combat aircraft or supporting some aspect of the Bonnet foreign policy did not always mean staying in the pro-Munich channel. Some of the moderate newspapers some of the time gloried in fighting the current of the new majority and public opinion. Categorizing anyone was difficult—even in the far Right *L'Action Française*. Maurras would not fight for Czechoslovakia and detested liberal democracy, but he saw that the Munich Agreement was the emperor's new clothes. Of Flandin's telegram to Hitler he wrote: "Is the man an imbecile? Has he understood nothing of Munich's implications?" Pertinax condemned the duplicity and corruption of French leaders, but he judged even more harshly the nation's economic elites for their obsession with the peril of social change and their attitude of "Better Hitler than Blum." Kérillis did argue that France should seek a strategic and cynical bargain with Mussolini, but he also insisted that the Soviet Union would have joined in fighting for Czechoslovakia and that its alliance was vital to control Germany by threatening a war on two fronts. In the Chamber on 4 October his excoriation of Munich was matched only by Péri's. Ten days later they could almost have written each others' editorials in *L'Epoque* and *L'Humanité* demanding the resignation of the appeasers in the cabinet and the arrest of Flandin.[13]

Of course, the Communists soon went much farther by calling for a broad purge of the government, the bureaucracy, and the press—providing abundant evidence for the accusation that they planned Stalinist terror for France. They might better have stuck to the tendentious but acute analysis of Munich that Party secretary-general Maurice Thorez presented before a mass meeting at the Vélodrome d'Hiver on 7 October: the national interests of France were betrayed by men who feared the "French people in arms" more than Hitler; the partial mobilization was meant less to deter Hitler than to evoke the hecatombs of war and thus make capitulation acceptable; Munich was, therefore, "the greatest treason perpetrated against France, against peace, and against democracy." The only remedy was a "union of the French people" to create a "government worthy of France." Two days later *L'Humanité* published an appeal by the Communist parties of France, Great Britain, Spain, Czechoslovakia, the United States, Germany, and Italy under the title "Against the Treason of Munich."[14]

Compared to the Communists, the Socialists were meek because Blum was weak. After offering only hesitant, fence-straddling comments during the Munich debate, he led the Socialist deputies (minus Jean Bouhey) to vote for what he—as former premier— knew were lies. On the issue of decree powers, which he himself had twice requested and been twice denied, he led the Socialists to abstain. Moments of crisis demand courageous choice. Kérillis stood utterly alone among deputies of the Center and Right in opposing the Munich Agreement but rejoined them in supporting the decree laws, each time voting his conscience. Beside Kérillis, Blum was a moral pygmy. As a result, the Socialists, who were the great winners of the 1936 legislative elections and so the largest party in the Chamber, were rendered political ciphers, deserted by the Radicals, despised by the Communists, scorned by the Right. During the next month Blum never once avowed in print whether Munich was a blessing or a curse, never once said what he would have done in September 1938. But he did manage to write, almost as if he were detached from reality, that the doctrine of socialism did not require unconditional pacifism and that the treaties imposed after the Great War were "imperialistic" but "less imperialistic than Europe had generally known."[15]

In the fall of 1938 Blum failed his nation, his party, and himself because he could not decide which was worse, war or humiliation. Whatever his failings, Daladier made a choice and defended it. The only serious effort to assess the moral consequences of choosing and abstaining came from Georges Duhamel, writing in *Le Figaro* at the beginning of November. The newspaper of the educated bourgeoisie had mostly adopted the Daladier-Bonnet line on Munich for its editorials and was celebrating peace for now as reason enough to spend for the *rentrée* (beginning of the social season and the return to school). Department stores Au Louvre, Galeries Lafayette, and Au Bon Marché enticed through the "*rentrée* silhouette," the necessity of fur (preference for fox or beaver), the importance of accessories (the more the better), and all the latest winter fashions (from the bolero jacket to the long manteau). The thirty-second annual Automobile Exposition at the Grand Palais generated half-page advertisements and then huge crowds for new models from Matford, Berliet, Renault, and Hotchkiss. Although this bounty reassured that all would be well, *Le Figaro*'s editor, Lucien Romier, had sufficient doubts to ask whether France was being lulled to sleep while Germany spread its domination across the Danubian basin. These same doubts led him to commission Duhamel's essay "Europe after the Crisis."[16]

Fifty-one months as a frontline surgeon during the Great War led this physician turned litterateur to hate war, to fear technology, and to exalt individualism as their counter. In Hitler, Duhamel recognized the antithesis to his values and thus, in Munich, France's capitulation to modern barbarism. He feared its spread: "If the success of violence involved only political and economic results, the moral observer would already have good reason to be distressed, for these results are going to place in the balance all breathing, and suffering, beings on this earth. But the success of violence appears as well to exert a vertiginous attraction on weak and easily influenced minds, and that is a calamity for the present and for the future." To all who would seek an accommodation with Germany, he recalled that "the first act of the Nazi Party was to burn books in public squares. A regime which burns books has sinned against the mind and spirit." France had to recognize, he contended, that in seeking fearful refuge behind the Maginot Line, she had abandoned the "Descartes line," by which he meant the defense of certain ideals, liberty and truth above all. A principal symbol of this spiritual leadership was the Alliance Française (French Institute), which at the beginning of 1938 included seven hundred local committees and six hundred schools, teaching "not only to speak French but to think French." Now they were winking out, closed down by enemies and by friends betrayed. From Czechoslovakia came massive resignations, diplomas returned, sometimes torn in pieces. "This redoubt of the French mind in Europe is in peril," Duhamel lamented, but not lost: "France retains the power to save these values for which she has been the guardian and guarantor."[17]

One defense of the Descartes line would have been to admit that Munich was a grievous failing and then to pledge against a recurrence. Was Duhamel's censure so powerful because he wrote the truth or because truth was the first casualty of the powerful Munich current? Late fall is the season for party congresses in France, and their proceedings cast Duhamel as Cassandra.

The Radicals met in Marseille at the end of October. They were interrupted by a terrible fire that spread through the sixteenth-century Canebière district, leaving at least seventy-five dead. A cynic might remark that the cause of the devastation—the first alarm coming only thirty minutes after the flames were noticed—was an appropriate analogy to the government. Of course, Daladier vaunted how he had "maintained the peace and dignity of France" at Munich and then bitterly criticized the Communists for daring to disagree. They were, he claimed, "agents of a foreign power pretending to instruct us French in our duty." Bonnet was equally facile. He called the relationship with Great Britain the "cornerstone of our security" but passed over completely the many times that London warned Paris not to act without its consent. He distorted the sequence of events in late September to magnify his own role and insisted, as at Périgueux, that France had upheld her commitment to Czechoslovakia because Germany had not used "military measures" to annex the Sudeten region. In a single sentence Paul Marchandeau, the minister of finance, illustrated the Radical Party's scorn for the forty-hour week: "we must substitute the spirit of work for the spirit of play." Pierre Cot, once minister of the air force, and Albert Bayet protested this swing to the Right, but they were hooted down. Even Edouard Herriot, president of the Chamber and Radical doyen, had to begin by lauding the "sangfroid and intelligent vigilance" shown by Daladier when he spoke to urge retaining the alliance with the Soviet Union, for which he had been a great sponsor. The final resolution of the congress ignored him, calling Munich the "beginning of more extended diplomacy to improve the relations of Paris with Berlin and Rome."[18]

Flandin's Democratic Alliance and Marin's Republican Federation would meet about two weeks later in mid-November, but beforehand Berlin demonstrated the cost of improved relations. On 7 November

Herschel Grynszpan, seventeen years old, a refugee from Poland, and a Jew, entered the German embassy in Paris. He was hoping to shoot the ambassador but settled for the third secretary, Ernst vom Rath, who died three days later despite the ministrations of Hitler's personal physician. In Germany the Nazis took terrifying revenge, arresting and sending to concentration camps more than 30,000 Jews and destroying 267 synagogues, 177 private homes, and approximately 7,500 shops. They struck in the dark of 9–10 November and left so many shattered display windows that these hours were called *Kristallnacht* (the night of broken glass). Hitler's partner Mussolini took advantage of the moment to promulgate new anti-Semitic laws, closing a great number of jobs and professions to Jews and banning their intermarriage with Aryans. But in the United States President Franklin D. Roosevelt declared the American people profoundly shocked and recalled his ambassador from Berlin. In Great Britain, where the archbishop of Canterbury condemned these atrocities, there was enormous public indignation.[19]

And in France there was also indignation, but more so at Grynszpan, who was living in France without authorization, had illegally obtained a pistol, had committed murder with it, and had thereby dragged France into his personal vengeance against the Nazi persecution of his family. The cardinal-archbishop of Paris had time to denounce sterilization and euthanasia but not pogroms. Afraid of upsetting negotiations in progress for a friendship pact, the government failed to protest and even encouraged the press to play down the horrifying stories from their correspondents in Germany. Some, but not many, newspapers flouted this guidance, prominently *Le Figaro*, which ran a graphic front-page account of *Kristallnacht* on 11 November. To his credit the relatively pro-Munich d'Ormesson deplored "this return to the most fanatical excesses of the middle ages" and recalled that Germany had praised the murder of Austrian chancellor Engelbert Dollfuss in July 1934: "When you have so glorified political assassination, you have no right to make thousands of innocent people expiate the crime of another assassin."[20]

D'Ormesson wrote on 14 November, the very day that the congress of the Democratic Alliance urged the French government to seek a "policy of collaboration" with Italy and Germany. By a vote of 1,626 to 25 the delegates reelected Flandin as their leader. In his acceptance speech he defined "true patriotism" as refusing to lead France into danger, for behind the shelter of the Maginot Line, supported by a strengthened air force, the country would be invulnerable. However restive, Paul Reynaud had remained a vice president of the Democratic Alliance, but now he resigned in protest and disgust—better late than never. Two days later the congress of the Republican Federation called for an "effective collaboration" with Great Britain, Italy, and the countries of Central and Eastern Europe, apparently considering that not naming Germany specifically was criticism enough for *Kristallnacht*. In their final resolution these Catholic conservatives condemned two decades of history by praising Marin for having voted in 1919 against ratification of the Versailles treaty, from which derived the "miserable" Locarno Pact and the "imprudently concluded" alliance with Czechoslovakia.[21]

The policy of collaboration was already proceeding apace—with attendant humiliations. In requesting details of the Anglo-German friendship agreement, Bonnet plaintively noted that it had been "drafted without France's participation." On 3 October Coulondre had the even more "disagreeable mission" of "explaining" the Munich Agreement at the Soviet foreign ministry. Vladimir Potemkim, the assistant commissar, replied: "I take note that the Western Powers deliberately kept Russia out of the negotiations.... My poor friend, what have you done? For us, I see no other way out than a fourth partition of Poland." Coulondre knew his history: on three occasions from 1772 to 1795 Germans and Russians had divided the Poles between them, and a fourth could take place only if they came to a new understanding that would leave out France. He cabled the Quai d'Orsay that every relationship with the Soviet Union was in jeopardy. A similar warning came from Louis H. Aubert, the jurisconsult for the French delegation to the League of Nations. Citing *Mein Kampf,* he insisted that Hitler's dream of European hegemony eliminated any basis for a "lasting agreement" between Germany and France. Faced with the prospect of general war, French leaders should hold fast to all possible alliances in Eastern Europe, especially that with the Soviet Union, and exploit the antagonism between Germans and Slavs implicit in Hitler's ethnic and racial theories. To seek safety by concluding a bilateral pact with Germany, Aubert argued, would symbolize French abdication and would "add legal isolation to our physical isolation."[22]

Bonnet rejected these analyses. He feared and mistrusted both Germany and the Soviet Union, but he knew that the ruling Conservative Party in Great Britain feared and mistrusted the Soviet Union more. To have and hold the promise of British military support in case of war, France had all but subordinated its diplomacy to the Foreign Office in London. Great Britain had signed a bilateral pact with Germany—never mind the duplicity at Munich—and so France should as well. Great Britain wanted no obligations in Eastern Europe, so France should put aside its obligations. The Soviet Union might well posture. Its control of national Communist parties could provoke domestic disorder throughout Europe. Its proclivity for brutal intelligence operations engendered a wary respect. But the public purge trials of the Red Army high command left dubious its military capacity, especially to mount an offensive. And because Bonnet could quote *Mein Kampf* as well, Hitler's loathing of Slavs and Communists made any reconciliation between Berlin and Moscow unlikely, whatever the historical precedent. So Bonnet concluded, and Daladier concurred.

The Quai d'Orsay drew up a statement of Franco-German amity, taking the Chamberlain-Hitler declaration at Munich as a model. After a preliminary discussion on 13 October with Ernst von Weizsächer, state secretary at the foreign ministry, Ambassador André François-Poncet received the ultimate mark of German interest, an invitation to Berchtesgaden. There five days later Hitler proposed a mutual recognition of boundaries—meaning no claim by Germany to Alsace and Lorraine—and a pledge to consult on all issues of European importance. François-Poncet had once found Nazi Germany fascinating but no more, and the analysis he sent back to Paris of this interview was chilling: "I certainly have no illusions about the character of Adolf Hitler. I know him to be fickle, secretive, contradictory, hesitant. The same easy-going man who appreciates the beauties of nature and who has put forward over cups of tea the most reasonable ideas about European politics is capable of the worst frenzies, the wildest exaltations, the most delirious ambitions. . . . The overtures he is disposed to make toward France are dictated by a sentiment that he shares at least intermittently with the majority of

Germans: the desire to end a wearisome and age-old duel. . . . But you can be certain that he remains determined to split the Franco-British bloc and to offer peace in the West for a free hand in the East."[23]

The measure of how thoroughly Bonnet embraced appeasement is that he judged François-Poncet's account "hopeful" and that he had already quashed dissenting opinion. He was tired of hearing from René Massigli, the political director at the Quai d'Orsay, that France should make its stand against Germany with Czechoslovakia and the Soviet Union. Massigli could henceforth contemplate Eastern Europe from the embassy at Ankara. He detested the Popular Front politics of Pierre Comert, the press officer, whom he now dismissed from the diplomatic service altogether. To succeed Massigli he chose Emile Charvériat from the League of Nations delegation. To replace Comert he took Jean Bressy from the Warsaw embassy. Both were notable above all for their unswerving attachment to Bonnet and to accommodation with Germany. Alexis Léger, the secretary-general, he could leave in place, knowing his reluctance to object and his preference for compromise. But not François-Poncet, the dean of the ambassadors: because his experience at Munich had turned him decisively against appeasement, he had to be moved from Berlin. Bonnet's elegant solution was to flatter Mussolini by making France's ambassador to Germany France's ambassador to Italy—as if a promotion. This move necessitated a further exchange of dictators, Coulondre leaving Stalin for Hitler, because he was the only other ambassador prominent enough for Berlin, and Emile Naggiar taking over in Moscow after leaving Chiang Kai-shek in Peking.[24]

Mussolini learned his own lesson from Munich: that the French were weak and perhaps vulnerable, and the François-Poncet nomination seemed further evidence. France was finally sending an ambassador bearing the vital accreditation not merely to the king of Italy but to the emperor of Ethiopia. Scornfully, Mussolini delayed agreeing to the appointment until late October and, after François-Poncet's arrival in Rome on 7 November, made him wait twelve days before arranging his formal acceptance by King Victor Emmanuel III. Afterward came a welcoming gift: Galeazzo Ciano, the foreign minister, handed him an end to the ban on travel by Italians to France. Then came the tease that better relations were in the offing: the arrangements negotiated between

Italy and Great Britain in April were now taking effect, and Ciano was to celebrate this recognition of Italian status with a speech before the legislature on 30 November. He invited François-Poncet's presence in the diplomatic box. Dear to the hearts of all the French who dreamed of weaning Mussolini from Hitler was negotiating something similar between Italy and France. Finally came the sucker punch: Ciano declared that "the agreement takes into account the new realities of the European, Mediterranean, and African situation. . . . This is to be the prime object of our policy, which we will pursue with tenacity and realism but also with that circumspection which is indispensable when it is our intention to safeguard with unshakeable firmness the interests and natural aspirations of the Italian people." At those last words, and with a unanimity that signified prearrangement, the legislators stood up to shout: "Tunisia! Corsica! Nice!" Rather than walk out in protest, François-Poncet decided that the better part of wisdom lay in remaining seated and unruffled.[25]

France had imposed a protectorate on Tunisia in 1881 despite Italian ambitions, had purchased Corsica from the city-state of Genoa in 1768, and had annexed Nice and Savoy in 1860 as the price for assisting Italian unification. Fascist Italy now claimed the right to reverse history. Appeasing Hitler had emboldened Mussolini. The dismay in Paris at this diplomatic affront was widespread, with the blame affixed by the Left for the failure to support the League of Nations and defend the Spanish Republicans, by the Center and Right for the illusions of the Popular Front and the failure to embrace the Spanish Nationalists. The Daladier cabinet was especially unhappy that Italy set upon the "colonial" issue because Hitler had already raised it on 8 November. Nothing in his speech encouraged believing that accommodation with him could be more than temporary. He made his—latest—last territorial demand, for colonies and not just the ones taken from Germany after the Great War. He insisted that the Third Reich was now so powerful that the arms of other nations no longer impressed him. He warned that British and French warmongers might get what they wanted.[26]

On 16 November Daladier answered Hitler's hectoring with a brief statement: "No colonial cession has ever been nor will be considered. Thus, no negotiation on this subject is contemplated." He could be blunt because the public revulsion in the democracies to *Kristallnacht* had weakened the German position. New threats now might stiffen spines against appeasement. At the moment Germany needed to beat a few swords into plowshares. For however long it lasted, France wanted a friendship pact with Germany. The synergy yielded rapid diplomatic results. On 19 November Joachim von Ribbentrop, the foreign minister, and the newly arrived Coulondre agreed on a draft similar to what Hitler and François-Poncet had discussed a month earlier. To demonstrate pacific intentions and amicable relations, a statement of goodwill, a recognition of boundaries, and a promise to consult were sufficient. On 23 November the French cabinet considered and approved these provisions but balked at an additional cost Germany insisted upon adding, Ribbentrop's presence in Paris for the signing. France would be rehabilitating Germany after *Kristallnacht,* in effect declaring that the horrors just weeks past could be wiped clean if the price were right. Daladier and President Lebrun argued that the moment was inopportune for a high-ranking Nazi to visit France. Reynaud and Jean Zay agreed that a postponement was necessary. But Bonnet, Camille Chautemps, and Guy La Chambre eventually won by warning that Ribbentrop might turn the snub into a serious incident and undermine the whole purpose of the accord.[27]

And so the former champagne salesman posing as a diplomat came to Paris on 6 December for a welcome that ranks as the single most shameful act by France in 1938. Abdication before the *Anschluss* and betrayal of Czechoslovakia were—merely—cowardice at the risk of war. Feting Ribbentrop was supine debasement. To ward off any hostile demonstrations, more than two hundred police surrounded the Invalides station, where he arrived with his wife by special train in late morning. Bonnet, his best smile in place and his own wife, Odette— *la soutien-Georges*—at his side, waited on the platform with his new loyal subordinates from the Quai d'Orsay. Outnumbering them were officials from the German embassy and Germans resident in Paris. To each Ribbentrop gave the Nazi salute. Following a brief stop at the Hotel Crillon in the Place de la Concorde, where the entire second floor was set aside for him, he had a brief and perfunctory meeting with Lebrun and then an informal luncheon organized by Daladier at the

Matignon Palace. The guest list was a problem. The German ambassador, Johannes von Welczeck, expressly asked that no "non-Aryans" be present. Mandel and Zay were Jews. If Daladier invited his ministers, he had to exclude these two or risk German ire. He resolved the difficulty by asking only Bonnet and Chautemps, the vice premier, from the cabinet, along with the chairmen of the Chamber and Senate committees for foreign affairs, Jean Mistler and Henry Bérenger—all of them proven appeasers.

During the afternoon Bonnet and Ribbentrop, joined by Léger and Welczeck, met for one of those "consultations" their new accord promised. The Bonnet smile crimped at Ribbentrop's blunt assertion that Eastern Europe was henceforth a German sphere of influence, that France's treaties with the Soviet Union and Poland were "remnants" of a time long past, and that Germany would dismantle them either through negotiation or through other means. Hitler's friendship did indeed come at a price, but Bonnet could hardly refuse now. He and Ribbentrop then signed the Franco-German declaration with a golden pen on a Louis XVI desk in the Quai d'Orsay's storied Clock Room. Later that evening in the same reception hall used for the British monarchs, Bonnet was the host for a banquet celebrating the amity between French and Germans. Lacking even Daladier's scruples, he invited all the "Aryan" cabinet ministers, Joseph Caillaux and his infamous wife, important members of the French foreign ministry and the German embassy, as well as the reliably pro-German social elite of Paris, including Daladier's mistress, the Marquise Jeanne de Crussol, a great friend of Odette Bonnet. Reynaud and Campinchi refused to attend because of the insult to Mandel and Zay. They would hardly have appreciated the atmosphere Anatole de Monzie described as a "dinner of diplomatic euphoria," where Caillaux "spoke admirably of Franco-German collaboration." *Le Populaire* asked when Nazi racial legislation had been passed by the French legislature. *Le Figaro*, which had never forgiven Caillaux for anything and had just published Duhamel's moral imperatives, printed the guest list prominently without comment.[28]

The second day of the visit was almost as appalling. In full-dress uniform Ribbentrop laid a swastika-laden wreath on the Tomb of the Unknown Soldier. Back in his suit, he vaunted German Kultur at the

"Goethe house" on the avenue d'Iéna and Nazi ideals at the "Brown house" on the rue Roquépine. Admirers of Hitler, organized in the Comité France Allemagne (French-German Committee) honored him with a luncheon at the Crillon. That evening he was the host for a grand reception and dinner at the German embassy. Many of the guests were obvious choices: Daladier, Bonnet, Chautemps, Monzie, Caillaux, Flandin, Bérenger, Mistler, Léger, and Charvériat. Of course, he did not include Mandel or Zay, but otherwise he was confident enough to invite opponents such as Reynaud, who came this time, and Herriot, who looked sullen throughout. The great surprise was Pétain, the Savior of Verdun and thus a symbol of French determination to resist Germany. Ribbentrop was known to have a perverse sense of humor, and perhaps that explains serving *jambon de Prague* (ham Prague-style: steamed, smoked, and salted—not a bad analogy to the fate of the Czechs). Steel magnate and great patriot François de Wendel pronounced the visit an "utter scandal." [29]

Receiving blows from above is always easier when they can be passed on downward, and the same principle applies to humiliation. Bowing to Germany at Munich meant continuing to bow, as the Ribbentrop visit proved. But Daladier had already discounted the abasement of this utter scandal by goring his domestic enemies a week earlier. At last he was indeed the "bull of Vaucluse," at last regarded as a "strongman."

The lowering of horns and the pawing of feet to charge began with the cabinet's internal debate about how best to jolt rearmament. Marchandeau, the minister of finance, argued for going directly to a war footing with tight exchange controls and measures to encourage autarky. Reynaud, the minister of justice, countered that profit alone could restore French productivity. During the last five years he had been more often right, and ignored, than anyone else about the economy. Now although the two men despised one another over foreign policy, he had the support of Caillaux and of the other Radical senators, who remained vigorous defenders of nineteenth-century "classical liberalism." Daladier's sympathies had always been with the Left on economic matters, but he knew the disposition of his new majority. If by nature he hesitated, he also knew that he was running out of time. As Romier wrote in *Le Figaro*, France did not have six months or a year to recover, and the decree power expired on 15 November. With the vital hour at hand Daladier launched himself irrevocably. On 27 October in Marseille at the Radical Party congress, he read out the Communists from any role in his government, claiming "the violence, the intransigence of this party has paralyzed my action." And that determined his choice on the economy: "The most urgent necessity is the increase in national revenue, thus the increase in productivity and trade, thus the increase in the effort by all the French, bosses and workers alike. . . . We have no intention of abrogating the forty-hour law, although it is not in effect in any other great nation. Yet where required by the true needs of industry and commerce, it must be adjusted without vain formalities, made flexible according to circumstances. . . . As the son of a worker become an artisan, I have the right to speak of these problems not as a theoretician but as a man who has lived them at the family table." Once returned to Paris, Daladier met his cabinet on 31 October and in "Olympian" fashion demanded a transfer of responsibilities, Marchandeau to become minister of justice, Reynaud to take over the ministry of finance.[30]

And what a takeover. In ten days Reynaud devised a program that would truly revitalize France's economy after almost a decade of failing policies. He had assistance from young men of destiny, above all Michel Debré, who twenty years later would be the first prime minister of the Fifth Republic, and Alfred Sauvy, who became France's greatest economic historian. Time was short, and they sometimes worked more than twenty hours a day. Their guiding principle was the conviction that the deflationary policies of the early 1930s could have succeeded if accompanied by an early devaluation of the franc and that the devaluations taken by the Popular Front could have succeeded if not accompanied by the forty-hour week. Thus, the formula for success was imposing new deflationary measures, maintaining the franc at its current level, and extending the workweek.

Reynaud announced his program on 12 November. To inspire confidence—meaning investors—the government adopted a stern fiscal regimen. Through increases to practically all taxes direct and indirect, revenue was to rise nearly 10 billion francs. The largest single amount and almost a third of the total, 3.25 billion, came from changes to the income tax, especially a surtax of 2 percent. Because of exemptions and progressivity, this exaction affected few below the middle class. For the remaining two-thirds everyone felt the impact, from the tax on production (an early version of value-added) to taxes on spirits and sugar and tobacco, to customs duties, to government stamps, to bus and rail fares, to postage. Through the ending of practically all public works, the closing of inefficient rail lines, and the elimination of approximately 1.4 million civil service and government jobs, expenditure was to fall nearly 5 billion francs. To enforce this regimen the government would not issue any short-term bonds for six months. The pledge was made less onerous by an economic sleight of hand by which 30 billion of the 48 billion francs advanced by the Bank of France to the government in 1937 and 1938 were absorbed through a revaluation of the gold reserves. To lure back capital sent abroad, no exchange controls were imposed. To increase productivity, the forty-hour workweek was extended by mandatory overtime. Merely by notifying the ministry of labor, employers gained the right to add fifty additional hours per year—thus a workweek of forty-one hours. Upon the—clearly forthcoming—authorization of the ministry, they could add additional blocks of forty hours until the workweek reached forty-eight. As an encouragement to do so, the supplement for overtime hours was cut to 10 percent for the first 250, 15 percent for the next 150, and 25 percent, the Popular Front standard, only after 400.[31]

Once imposed, Reynaud's program worked exactly as he had confidently predicted. During the next eight months, to July 1939, the level of production rose from 87 to 100, a 14.9 percent increase. Unemployment fell from 367,100 to 343,500, a 6.4 percent decrease. The franc held steady against the pound, from 178.67 to 176.74, up 1.1 percent, and the dollar, from 37.95 to 37.74, up 0.6 percent. History rarely supplies a clearer verdict.[32]

In November 1938 this vindication could only be imagined, and even the implementation was open to question. Through decree laws voted without the support of the Socialists and over the opposition of the Communists, Reynaud was eviscerating the great symbol of the Popular Front. As disdainful as he was able, he fanned resentment with his dramatic radio speech on the night of 12 November. He began well with a candor rarely heard: "You wish to know the truth of our finances.

I shall tell you. The situation is extremely grave. . . . We are in the last rank of industrial production. . . . The country itself is in play. The daily bread for each of you is at risk. . . . We are going blindfolded towards an abyss." And when he had explained the new austerity, he did well to warn: "However hard all that may seem, it is only a beginning. I tell you so without pretense because the issue is saving the country, not punishing it." But he struck the wrong tone when he minimized the cost of new taxes as averaging "only 25 centimes a day" (90 francs a year), when he described public works as a "luxury," and when he declaimed with too-obvious satisfaction, "People abroad are listening to me, and I say that the 'week with two Sundays' has ceased to exist in France." [33]

Although stocks and bonds began a long rally, the middle classes were anxious. *Le Figaro* praised the program but questioned "whether we possess a government strong enough to apply it." *Le Temps* barely managed an endorsement, "In the hope of a better future, each will accept courageously the penance briefly imposed on all and will wish the success of this new experience in rectification." Pensioners worried: Georges Rivollet, leader of the Confédération Nationale des Anciens Combattants et Victimes de la Guerre (National Confederation of Veterans and Victims of the War), declared that Great War soldiers had already sacrificed enough, while his counterpart, Henri Pichot of the Federal Union, called the program a "disappointment and a delusion." The Socialist response was muted, the same helpless attitude the party had taken since Munich. Blum, who seemed incapable of learning anything new, insisted only that a longer workweek "can exercise no real action on the French economy." Bitter hostility began farther leftward. The General Labor Confederation was meeting at Nantes, and its secretary-general, Léon Jouhaux, all but accused Daladier and Reynaud of preparing a French version of fascism: "The government is trying to achieve economic recovery by inspiring banking and industrial capital with confidence. At the same time coercion is being used against the working class—is this the basis on which labor and capital are expected to cooperate? . . . Poor France, what humiliations have you not suffered already? Now an attempt is being made to prepare the worst humiliation of all—to divide you internally and so prepare the conditions for your complete decline. France, once the light and the conscience of humanity, will sink into darkness and will become the servant of the dictatorships."[34]

If Jouhaux meant his words, the unions had to confront these proto-fascists with their ultimate weapon, the general strike. And Jouhaux threatened that he could go that far. Spoiling for a fight and with nothing more to lose in the post-Munich political alignment, the Communists were willing to go even farther. On the northeast outskirts of Paris at Noisy-le-Sec, Thorez ignited a rally by shouting: "Down with the men of Munich! Down with the men of renunciation and capitulation! Down with the decree-laws of destitution!" But if the Left wanted a test of strength, Daladier wanted it at least as much. He was eager to prove that he could impose order and, more important psychologically, impose submission. In a radio speech he referred to the Communists as "adversaries" trying to "compromise the recovery by troubling the country. I denounce their pernicious acts. I mock their schemes. . . . I shall no more be the man of bankruptcy than I have been the man of war." Before a meeting of the Radical Party he growled: "The state must have the final word. You can count on me to be a Jacobin. If they want to overthrow the government, let them try. If they succeed, they will have to find their way through the debris."[35]

Seeking to embarrass the government, the unions and the Communists made trouble just as Chamberlain and Edward Lord Halifax arrived on 23 November for two days of consultations. Demonstrators tried to break up the welcome at the Gare du Nord (North Station) by chanting the expected "Down with Munich!" and the sharper "Long live Eden!"—in honor of the first cabinet minister to resign over appeasement. Sit-down strikes broke out first in approximately forty defense-related factories around Lille and then in the massive Renault automotive plants of the Paris region. With Albert Sarraut in Turkey as France's representative to the funeral of Mustapha Kemal (Atatürk), Daladier took charge at the ministry of the interior. Under the Popular Front Dormoy had never dared clear strikers by force. Daladier hesitated not a second in sending troops with orders to "throw them out." The soldiers used tear gas, cracked heads, and arrested everyone in sight. Judges then took their turn because the charge, "rebellious conduct," was a misdemeanor to avoid the jury trial of a felony case. Almost without exception and almost without evidence, they found the nearly five hundred defendants guilty and sentenced them to a jail term of two to four weeks. Because Daladier demonstrated his intention to play rough, Thorez and Jouhaux had to surrender abjectly or call a general strike—and soon. As one union leader put it: "We are now engaged in a great battle, an unprecedented battle in the history of the French working class. We prefer a fight to capitulation."[36]

Once the strike date was set for 30 November, the cabinet took up two great weapons that ensured its failure, radio and requisition. On successive nights, 26 and 27 November, first Reynaud then Daladier broadcast speeches portraying this conflict as the decisive test of national survival. For Reynaud: "When France is in peril, special interests have no voice. . . . Despite all the obstacles, despite all the pitfalls, we will save the country." For Daladier: "The threats, the occupation of factories . . . are a showdown between the Republican democracy and the dictatorship of a minority among the proletariat. . . . Do not let your hands undermine the dignity and nobility of France by furthering or even tolerating these futile convulsions. Unite for the common good. If, despite my efforts, these threats are realized, I shall fulfill my duty, all my duty, with the certainty of being right, for I have no thought other than to assure respect for law and to protect the interests of our homeland." Beginning on 27 November, the cabinet "requisitioned" public services—schools, railways, gas, electricity, water, mail, telegraph, telephone—meaning that government employees were now required by law to appear for work. Daladier warned that any absence, any interference with the normal routine, would be treated as a "grave offense." Private employers needed no encouragement to tell their workers the same.[37]

As the cabinet anticipated, public opinion turned decisively against a general strike that would damage recovery efforts and appeared to be motivated entirely by political malice. Disillusionment at the failure of the Popular Front and fear of losing their jobs begot caution among many of the working class. Government employees were certain that striking would lead to dismissal. Because the Socialists were no longer needed for his majority, Daladier ignored entirely a resolution by their executive committee condemning his "politics of reaction and systematic provocation toward labor." He also shrugged off an appeal from veterans groups to mediate. Knowing that the strike would fail, he wanted no one to intercede. And fail it did—utterly. The impact on public services and businesses was negligible. Although some postal workers and about a fifth of the taxi drivers in Paris stayed home, trains, buses, subways, utilities, schools, shops, department stores, banks, and restaurants were all open and functioning as usual, meaning nothing beyond typical delays and annoyances. Heavy industry was more affected, absences running about 25 to 30 percent in the metallurgical plants of the Paris region and the coal mines of the northwest. The strike shut down only the building trades and the docks, their workers always militant. Over the next several weeks the bourgeoisie replaced their fear of the Communist Party with scorn, and so many workers deserted the General Labor Confederation that its membership fell by almost a third.[38]

Daladier crowed: "When one speaks the language of France, one is always understood by the French. What triumphed today is the very principle of the Republic, respect for law, respect for work, respect for the homeland. . . . The authority of the state is the guarantee of liberty. The people, not the street, must be sovereign. The whole world now knows that France has just overcome her uncertainties and that she is stronger today than she was yesterday. The government will know how to organize fruitful cooperation between owners and workers in a spirit of mutual understanding and respect for our laws." But first there would be more meting out of justice. Invoking the penalties for violating the requisition order, prosecutors charged 1,731 government workers with dereliction and obtained 806 prison terms. For coming to work late or for making minor nuisances, approximately 3,000 postal workers received sanctions. Private employers took vengeance on so-called ringleaders and especially union delegates, firing more than 10,000 to encourage the "spirit of mutual understanding" among the rest of the workforce.[39]

Thus do the horns of a snail become the horns of a bull. On 8 December, the same day Ribbentrop departed, Daladier called the legislature into session for the first time since the Munich vote more than two months earlier. He was confidently ready to claim approval from the nation's elected representatives for his policies, imposing the decree-laws on the economy, subduing the general strike, and signing the statement of friendship with Germany. The measure of how far he had moved politically since April came when the far Right anti-Semite Xavier Vallat pledged his vote to "a government that had spared France useless carnage and imposed respect for the law." Of course, the debate in the Chamber of Deputies on that day and the next was the moment for his enemies to raise their protests and thus sharpen the line of the new majority. The Socialists were acutely conscious of standing just outside. They had voted for the Munich Agreement and so could not easily disparage the new pact with Germany. But, having abstained on the decree power, they had room to criticize the manner in which it had been applied. Albert Sérol, Augustin Laurent, and finally Blum complained about the "unfairness" of Reynaud's program and about the "repression" used against the general strike, but what upset them most of all was their new exclusion. Not just outside the majority, the Communists were, especially since 30 November, in outer darkness. They had no incentive to temper their words: futility encourages invective. With equal parts gusto and contempt Jacques Duclos denounced the cabinet's "politics of submission to big capital, politics of insolence toward the working class, politics of servitude toward fascism," and demanded a return to "Republican" government. Likewise, Péri labeled "friendship" with Germany a "second-offense" of the Munich crime and "a step toward new and disastrous abdications." For her salvation France "had to break with both the spirit of Munich and the men of Munich."

As sure of his majority as he had been of crushing the strike, Daladier answered with a belligerence proving that triumphalism also encourages invective. Bluntly, he laid claim to being France's new great man: "I am responsible for my own actions and not hostage to any party." Bluntly, he defended crushing the strike: "Democracy has only a single sovereign, the law. If the law is undermined, there is no more democracy! The law must be respected. It has been. And the victory is not that of the government but of the French people." Bluntly, he defended appeasing Germany: "The policy of 'firmness' would have led to war in the worst conditions imaginable and in which one or two million French peasants would have been sacrificed. I was an infantryman, and I know that from 1915 on, peasants made up 90 percent of most companies."

Bluntly, he defended his conception of government: "Respect for the Republican order has been placed above all else. Does one cease to be a Republican for desiring the maintenance of law and order? Does one cease to be a patriot for refusing to lead his country down the path to war? The cabinet has marked out the road to follow." This last line was the invitation for his majority to demonstrate its strength and cohesion and will—as it did: the cabinet received 315 votes in favor (almost all the Right and Center), 241 opposed (the Communists and the Socialists), with 53 abstentions (a few from the far Right and 29 Radicals elected with Communist or Socialist support in 1936).[40]

Political candor is most easily pretended by avoiding explanation. Daladier did not mention the raging conflict in the Far East, where Japan continued its conquest of Chinese territory by taking the cities of Canton and Hankow. He did not mention the deteriorating situation in the British mandate of Palestine, where what amounted to civil war between Arabs and Jews forced the declaration of martial law. He most especially did not mention the work of the international commission established by the Munich Agreement to determine the new frontiers of Czechoslovakia. On 4 October Daladier had told the Chamber of Deputies, "the Czechoslovak Republic can live on as a free country, and we shall do all we can to help." Before German threats and the complete absence of British support, "all we can" turned out to be an empty promise. The final report, signed on 20 November, inflicted "heavy sacrifices" on the Czechs. Ashamed by Munich, President Lebrun made a personal contribution of fifty thousand francs to the fund created by the French Red Cross to assist refugees fleeing from German rule in the Sudeten region.[41]

Above all, Daladier did not mention Italy, because the direction of advantage was not yet clear. Like Bonnet and the many among the Right and the Center, Kérillis included, who kept arguing that France should make up to Mussolini, he could hope that the "Tunisia! Corsica! Nice!" chant on 30 November was simply a bluff. After all, French military leaders had a low regard for Italy's army even as they admitted that its submarines could menace Mediterranean shipping. On 5 December, after François-Poncet reported Ciano's disingenuous assurance that the demonstrations were not "official policy," the Quai d'Orsay declared "the incident closed." Bonnet and the diplomats meant to continue cultivating Mussolini. But French public opinion had had enough: the very idea that *Italy* had territorial ambitions against *France* was qualitatively different than that Germany had territorial ambitions against Czechoslovakia, Poland, Romania, Lithuania, the Ukraine, or anywhere else. Corsicans and Tunisians taught a lesson in nationalism with spontaneous anti-Italian rallies punctuated by the oath, "We swear to die French!" Students in the Paris Latin Quarter taught a lesson in wit with sardonic claims to "Venice and Vesuvius" for their vacations. So, why bother worrying whether Italy was bluffing when more was to be gained by calling that bluff? Recognizing the opportunity, Daladier announced that he would visit Corsica and Tunisia in early January to show French resolve. When the Fascist press exclaimed that his going to "Italian Corsica" would be an "intolerable provocation," they made him all the more a hero.[42]

As a result, Bonnet suddenly found defending appeasement foreign policy more complicated, but he was adroit before the Chamber's foreign affairs committee on 14 December. His antagonists from 6 October, Pezet and Péri, joined by Kérillis and former foreign minister Delbos, bore in on the Franco-German pact. They condemned the "badly chosen moment" of Ribbentrop's visit, coming right after *Kristallnacht* and the harsh treatment of Czechoslovakia by the international commission. They asked whether its unacknowledged price was a free hand for Germany in Eastern Europe. They interpreted Italy's claims as both *chantage* (blackmail) and *marchandage* (haggling) to gain French recognition of the Nationalist victory in Spain. As a lie of omission Bonnet replied coolly, "If Poland, Russia, and Romania defend themselves, why, then we shall go to their aid." He did not reveal Ribbentrop's assertion that Eastern Europe was henceforth a German sphere of influence. But he did maintain that Ribbentrop had told him, "Do you imagine that we are going to attack France not for the sake of Alsace-Lorraine but simply in order to help out Italy?" Some on the committee considered this particular expression of Franco-German friendship remarkably providential for Bonnet's argument.[43]

How long would such dubious reassurances suffice against ambitions personal and strategic? After the debacle of the general strike

Communist leader Thorez sorely needed to take hold of a winning issue, and what better than to imitate the man who had bested him. If Daladier was going to Tunisia and Corsica in January, he could go to Nice in December. There on the day after Bonnet's prevarications he called Italy's claims "a humiliation originating in the national disaster of Munich." Two more days later Mussolini's government delivered a formal but confidential renunciation of the January 1935 agreement Laval had negotiated to resolve colonial disputes. Bonnet now recognized that stiffer language was necessary and before the Chamber of Deputies on 19 December declared that the government would not consider yielding a "single inch of French territory." Briefly, he even managed to work himself up to the only threat of war he made in 1938, "Any attempt to achieve these ambitions can lead only to an armed conflict." But ever the practitioner of omission, he did not reveal the repudiation of the 1935 agreement, hoping that its confidentiality meant the Italians might reconsider. And he concluded by retreating to his previous equivocations, "If France ardently desires friendship with all nations whatever their system of government, it would be wrong to see in this wish for peace a sign of abnegation or weakness." Here was a remarkable reaffirmation of the appeasement policy and its great lie.[44]

Although antiwar by tradition and pacifist at heart, the Socialists showed themselves made of sterner stuff. Meeting over Christmas on the southern edge of Paris at Montrouge, their annual congress took up competing motions on foreign policy. His nerve somewhat restored, Blum asked them to choose courage, to insist that France stand by her alliances in Eastern Europe, especially to the Soviet Union. Paul Faure, the party secretary-general, argued for severing those ties and negotiating whatever arrangements were possible with Italy and Germany—essentially Bonnet's stance. The delegates voted for Blum, 4,322 to 2,837, with 1,014 abstentions, and one of his supporters, Louis Sibué, quickly found an opportunity to live out his vote. On 22 December, probably tipped off by Mandel, *L'Ordre*'s Emile Buré revealed the Italian repudiation and forced an acknowledgment from the Quai d'Orsay. When the Chamber next met a week later, Sibué demanded that Bonnet explain why his remarks on 19 December omitted this further worsening of relations. Scenting blood, Péri took up the cry. Offended by an apparent violation of parliamentary governance, Marin joined in from the Right. A clearly embarrassed Bonnet first denied that he had known of Italy's renouncing the agreement, but, given the chronology, that excuse was scarcely possible. Then he asserted that even had he known, he had an obligation to discuss the issue with his fellow ministers before saying anything publicly. Finally, in frustration he simply refused to answer at all: "I neither deny nor confirm it." Lies and damn lies had caught up with Bonnet. For a second year running the foreign minister of France was having an unpleasant end to December. Even the glacial weather that chilled Delbos was back. But the cabinet as a whole was in no jeopardy. Some in its new majority might well deplore Bonnet's duplicity, but not his conduct of policy. For Daladier, France's strongman, was at that moment preparing to board the battleship *Foch,* which with the mighty escort of a cruiser and three destroyers would leave for Corsica on New Year's Day and then on to Tunisia.[45]

Marcel Carné's second movie of the year, *Hôtel du Nord* (*North Hotel*), opened in Paris two days after Ribbentrop left and seven months after his first, *The Port of Shadows*. Like it, *North Hotel* captured the sensibility of the moment. Compared to May, December was pale and calm, and so the two movies. But just as December conjured memories of May, so also the two movies. Panama's bar becomes a hotel in working-class Paris near the Canal Saint-Martin where everyone gathers to escape from life outside. The suicidal artist, Michel, becomes the suicidal couple, Pierre (played by Jean-Pierre Aumont) and Renée (played by Annabella—Suzanne Georgette Charpentier). The lovers running from their past, Jean, a deserter, and Nelly, a ward, become Edmond, a pimp (played by Louis Jouvet), and Raymonde, a prostitute (played by Arletty—Léonie Bathiat). The denouement of Jean gunned down by his jealous rival, Lucien Legardier, becomes the shooting of Edmond by his former gang members. The ending proclaiming the impossibility of escape becomes the effort to get on with life otherwise. *Le Figaro*'s reviewer, Jean Laury, described the characters as caught in a squirrel cage. They turn round and round, go nowhere, and worry about the future. How like France in December.[46]

Another link between the moment and the movie became apparent only after the debacle of French defeat in 1940 and the widespread collaboration with the German victors which followed. France in December first revealed the relish with which some of the French would submit to Nazi wishes and the indifference to this prostration by almost everyone else. The movie was the screen debut of Arletty, who after the Liberation in 1944 was hounded for "horizontal collaboration." She defended herself famously: "my ass is universal, my heart is French." [47] How like Bonnet's foreign policy.

Conclusion

On 20 December 1938 Dom Néroman, president of the French Astrological College, offered his predictions for 1939: "Bad year, very blurred, very freakish, entirely subject to the deplorable influence of the moon. On 21 March, things worsen, and on 3 May, the day of the moon's total eclipse, the astral configuration which made Munich will reverse itself, with diplomacy, science, industry—all subject to the disposition of Mars. By 23 June, this malevolent planet will be the axis of influence for France. There will be a slight easing in August but a falling apart in September. Authority weakens, demagogy triumphs. With the eclipse of the sun in October, a powerful movement in favor of peace will emanate from Paris and will no doubt have its martyrs. The regime will totter, but it will not die, because it is only to die in 1944."[1] In 1938 woe was a rumor. In 1939 woe arrived.

On 15, not 21, March Adolf Hitler seized the remaining bit of Czechoslovakia left after Munich. He reserved 21 March for the seizure of Memel from Lithuania. By 3 May the French and British were thoroughly disabused of the notions that motivated their Munich diplomacy. They gave their guarantee to Poland on 31 March, and on 23 June France signed a mutual assistance pact with Turkey. For a while in August vain hopes lingered that the Danzig crisis could be resolved. Blitzkrieg on

1 September exploded such dreams, but in October, through elaborate self-delusion, France could believe that Hitler would stay east. So began the "Phony War" and the rise of defeatism which accompanied it. The Third Republic died at Vichy in July 1940, but Dom Néroman may have been seeing the decision of Charles de Gaulle in 1944 not to revive it. Here is a set of predictions far superior to those of anyone else—all in all, an argument that historians should read psychics and intuitives as well as editorialists and politicians.

When accepting the 1970 Nobel Prize for Literature, Aleksandr Solzhenitsyn stared back at a half-century of totalitarianism to offer this moral perspective: "The Spirit of Munich is not a thing of the past, it was more than a short episode. I would even venture to say that the spirit of Munich is predominant in the twentieth century. The entire civilized world trembled as snarling barbarism suddenly reemerged and moved into the attack. It found it had nothing to fight with but smiles and concessions. The spirit of Munich is an illness of the willpower of rich people. It is the everyday state of those who have given in to the desire for well-being at any price, to material prosperity as the main aim of life on this earth. Such people—and there are many of them in the world today—choose to be passive and to retreat, just so their normal lives may last a little bit longer, just so the move into austerity may not happen *today*. And as for tomorrow, it'll be all right, you'll see. . . . (But it won't be all right! The price you have to pay for your cowardice will be all the worse. Courage and victory come to us only when we resign ourselves to making sacrifices.)"[2] When it was not all right, when France got war in 1939 and defeat in 1940, the past was not always prologue in predicting individual paths.

By the late 1930s Marshall Philippe Pétain was less the Savior of Verdun and more the emblem of unquestioned authority, even the stopgap monarch, envisioned by the political Right. He became premier on 16 June 1940 in the midst of military disaster, and, rather than fight on, he agreed to an armistice with Germany which was signed six days later. Three-fifths of France, the northeast, the north, and the Atlantic coast, came under German occupation. Italy got a small section in the southeast. The rest, the south-central region and most of the Mediterranean coast, Hitler left for the French themselves to govern—compliantly. This so-called free zone came to be called "Vichy France" from its capital at the famous spa. Most of the deputies and senators made their way there and heard a proposal by Pierre Laval, who had become the real power behind Pétain, to establish a dictatorship. Sitting together as the National Assembly, the Chamber of Deputies and the Senate would grant "all powers to the Government of the Republic under the authority and the signature of Marshall Pétain to promulgate by one or several acts a new constitution of the French State." The rationale was that an authoritarian France would be better suited to a Nazi-dominated Europe, or, as Laval said bluntly, "It is to gain a peace that will hurt France the least." The touchstone for assigning the elected representatives of the Third Republic to the status of collaboration or resistance is how they voted on the death sentence to their regime during the afternoon of 10 July: 569 in favor, 80 opposed, 17 abstentions.[3]

An overwhelming majority, 85 percent, embraced this desertion of liberal ideals. Not just the far Right of monarchist zealots or anti-Semites such as Xavier Vallat, not just the Catholic conservatives of the Republican Federation, not just the fed-up of Colonel François de La Rocque's French Social Party, not just the moderate conservatives of the Democratic Alliance, but the Radicals, so long the essence of Third Republican government, and even the Socialists handed Pétain more power than anyone had wielded in France since Napoléon. Their reasons ranged from exhilaration at the opportunity to undo the Revolution of 1789 to craven fear at what German victory portended. The Communist Party alone was spared this choice because Daladier outlawed it after Stalin became Hitler's ally in August 1939 and stripped its deputies of their seats. Prominent in support for Pétain were the appeasers: Joseph Caillaux, their symbol for three decades; Pierre-Etienne Flandin, their principal spokesman; Joseph Barthélemy, their legal strategist; Jean Mistler, chairman of the Chamber's foreign affairs committee; Georges Bonnet, Camille Chautemps, Anatole de Monzie, Charles Pomaret, and Guy La Chambre, their leaders in the Edouard Daladier cabinet. They were voting for Pétain to seek France a place at the high table of Hitler's New Order in Europe and thus confirmation that they had been right to oppose war. Some of the appeasers held office under Vichy: Barthélemy as minister of justice, Flandin briefly as foreign minister, and Chautemps as a representative to Washington. Some of them had second thoughts: Caillaux soon withdrew to his home in Mamers (Sarthe), where he lived quietly until his death in 1944, and Bonnet fled to Switzerland in 1943.

Only eighty dared vote against this descent into semi-fascism and did so with varying courage. Cowed by death threats, Léon Blum made clear his absolute opposition but uttered not a single word in public. His foreign minister, Joseph Paul-Boncour, was willing to give Pétain power but not as much as Laval demanded. Other Popular Front ministers, Vincent Auriol, Marx Dormoy, Paul Ramadier, and Yvon Delbos, made up for Blum's silence through their firm denunciations. Joining them were Auguste Champetier de Ribes from Daladier's cabinet, Louis Marin, who made up for his lack of resolution in 1938 but could not convince the rest of his Republican Federation to follow him, and Emmanuel d'Astier, friend of Henri de Kérillis, who shouted at the end of the vote, "Long live the Republic anyway!" For some of them the cost was dear: Champetier de Ribes arrested, Delbos deported, Dormoy murdered. Blum was imprisoned and later tried at Riom in 1942, essentially for having led the Popular Front. By then he knew he had nothing to lose and so regained his fortitude that he turned the proceedings into an indictment of Vichy's collaboration. Handed over to the Germans, he survived both Buchenwald and Dachau. Paul-Boncour spent the same years in retirement writing his memoirs.

The men who did not vote divide into utterly different categories. At Vichy, Albert Lebrun, as president of the Republic, and Jean Jeanneney, as president of the Senate and thus of the National Assembly, had no vote, but they did nothing to stop Laval. Neither did Edouard Herriot, president of the Chamber and the personification of the Radical Party, who abstained. Neither did Paul Reynaud, who simply refused to attend the session of the National Assembly. At least he had the excuse of having been injured a few days earlier by the automobile accident that killed Countess Hélène de Portes. Neither did Henry Bérenger, chairman of the Senate's foreign affairs committee, who was so appalled by the outcome of the appeasement he supported that he took refuge with his sister at Saint-Raphaël (Alps-Maritimes). Two certain votes against Pétain were absent because Kérillis, the epitome of a republican nationalist, and Pierre Cot, the Popular Front minister for the air force and prob-able Soviet agent, were fleeing Vichy arrest warrants and eventually reached the United States. Thirty more votes against Pétain were missing because the twenty-nine deputies and one senator who would have cast them were in Algeria. On 21 June Daladier, César Campinchi, Georges Mandel, Jean Zay, and the rest left Bordeaux, where the French government had taken refuge after Paris was threatened, aboard the liner *Massilia*. Arriving at Casablanca three days later, they intended to carry on the war from France's North African territories, but officials in Morocco had sided with Pétain and accepted the armistice. Denounced from Bordeaux and then Vichy as deserters and traitors, they were transported to Algiers and held until after the vote on 10 July.

With two exquisitely curt sentences Winston Churchill condemned Neville Chamberlain and Munich for all time: "You were given the choice between war and dishonor. You chose dishonor and you will have war." In the French case their leaders chose dishonor, got war anyway, and then chose further dishonor. Again, Churchill had a lapidary summation: "For the French government to leave her faithful ally, Czechoslovakia, to her fate was a melancholy lapse from which flowed terrible consequences. Not only wise and fair policy, but chivalry, honour, and sympathy for a small threatened people made an overwhelming concentration." Of Daladier, who made the critical decisions in September 1938, Pertinax complained, "He's a bull who belonged in the cowshed; . . . he has the stout neck but certainly not the taste for charging at obstacles." Four decades later General Telford Taylor was kinder but no less damning: "Edouard Daladier was an intelligent and incorruptible French patriot with very considerable political ability, but his will could not sustain the reach that his intellect perceived."[4]

What of history in the subjunctive: Daladier and Chamberlain reject dishonor. If Daladier had carried out his threat to fly home from Munich after Hitler's initial diatribe, Chamberlain almost certainly would have had to do so as well. His bluff called, Hitler would likely have proceeded with the German military's plan to invade Czechoslovakia. War would have followed. And then? In the midst of the crisis President Franklin D. Roosevelt predicted to British ambassador Sir Ronald Lindsay that "even if Great Britain and France and Russia were fighting loyally together they would be beaten if they tried to wage war on classic lines of attack." At the dark moment of Dunkirk in May 1940, Chamberlain wrote, "Whatever the outcome, it is clear as daylight that, if we had had to fight in 1938, the result would have been far worse." An assessment by General Taylor combines the perception of both a soldier and a scholar to argue that the fighting in 1938 would have been inconclusive: By the end of the year Germany would defeat Czechoslovakia. France and Great Britain would make cautious offensives in the west to little avail. The Soviet Union would wait to see where advantage lay. Poland would fear attack from both Germany and the Soviet Union. Italy, Spain, and Japan would remain neutral. The future progress of the war would be slow because Germany could not turn west as long as the eastern risk remained. And if so, in a long war the powerful naval resources of France and Great Britain would weigh heavily. The United States might well intervene. War in 1938 would have favored the Western democracies just as war in 1939 favored Germany.[5]

The man to lead such a heroic France was Mandel. He imbibed the distilled essence of Jacobin rigor from his mentor, Georges Clemenceau, during the terrible years of 1917 and 1918. An outsider and a Jew and a man of honor, he understood better than anyone else in French government the meaning of 1938: the Nazi ideals of *Ein Reich, Ein Volk, Ein Führer* were directly challenging the democratic ideals of *Liberté, Egalité, Fraternité.* Like Georges Duhamel, he understood that the Descartes line could be abandoned only at unacceptable cost. The best evidence comes from those bitter days of mid-June 1940, when the Germans were routing French forces everywhere. Paul Reynaud had—finally and too late—taken over as premier from Daladier in March 1940 and made Mandel his minister of the interior. Having retreated to Bordeaux, the Reynaud cabinet was considering whether to desert Great Britain and seek an armistice. Mandel made bold to say that they were cowards and demanded that the government carry on the war from North Africa if France herself were lost.

Late that day, 16 June, his friend of twenty years, General Edward Spears, came to the darkened building that was Mandel's office. Churchill was now prime minister in Great Britain and Spears his personal representative. By the light of a single candle the two men confronted the reality that Reynaud would resign that night, Pétain take his place, and France capitulate. Spears asked—begged—Mandel to fly with him and Charles de Gaulle to Great Britain, promising a seat on the plane for his mistress, Béatrice Bretty, the famous actress from the Comédie Française. He told Mandel that Churchill himself was making the request: "There must be an authorized French voice, not pledged to surrender, to guide the French Empire." After a long pause Mandel said: "You fear for me because I am a Jew. Well, it is just because I am a Jew that I will not go tomorrow; it would look as if I was afraid, as if I was running away." They never saw each other again. At Casablanca French officials arrested Mandel when he attempted to contact the British consul general. Vichy imprisoned him, turned him over to the Germans in November 1942, then took him back in July 1944, only to have its *Milice* (Militia) shoot him dead in cold blood. Throughout this ordeal Bretty was his stalwart and married him. So much in France during these years was vile and pernicious. Look no farther for proof that courage and devotion survived among a few.[6]

Notes

PROLOGUE

1. This interpretation of French foreign policy is elaborated in my book *France and the Après Guerre, 1918–1924: Illusions and Disillusionment* (Baton Rouge, 1999).

2. Yvon Lacaze, *La France et Munich: Etude d'un processus décisionnel en matière des relations internationales* (Berne, 1992), 98–99; Telford Taylor, *Munich: The Price of Peace* (New York, 1979), 482–83.

3. *Le Temps*, 27 November–4 December 1937, quoting Delbos, 4 December; Alexander Werth, *France and Munich, before and after the Surrender* (London, 1939), 21–24; Lacaze, *La France et Munich*, 99.

4. *Le Temps*, 4–7 December 1937, quoting Beck, 5 December; Lacaze, *La France et Munich*, 99–100; Taylor, *Munich*, 483–84; Werth, *France and Munich*, 24–25.

5. *Le Temps*, 8–12 December 1937, quoting Delbos, 11 December; Werth, *France and Munich*, 25–27; Taylor, *Munich*, 484.

6. *Le Temps*, 13–15 December 1937; Werth, *France and Munich*, 27–29, quoting Delbos on the train, 29; Taylor, *Munich*, 484.

7. *Le Temps*, 16–19 December 1937, quoting Delbos, 17 December; Taylor, *Munich*, 484–85; Lacaze, *La France et Munich*, 100; Werth, *France and Munich*, 29–30.

8. *Le Temps*, 20 December 1937, quoting Delbos; Werth, *France and Munich*, 31.

9. *Le Temps*, 21–31 December 1937; Delbos reporting on 22 December.

10. F. Scott Fitzgerald, "The Crack-Up: Pasting It Together," *Esquire* 7 (February 1936): 41.

11. The historiography of the Third Republic is immense. Excellent guides are: Jean-Marie Mayeur and Madeleine Rebérioux, *The Third Republic from Its Origins to the Great War, 1871–1914,* translated by J. R. Foster (New York, 1984); Philippe Bernard and Henri Dubief, *The Decline of the Third Republic, 1914–1938,* translated by Anthony Forster (New York, 1985); Jacques Chastenet, *Histoire de la Troisième République,* 7 vols. (Paris, 1952–63); Georges Bonnefous and Edouard Bonnefous, *Histoire politique de la IIIe République,* 7 vols. (Paris, 1956–67); and Denis William Brogan, *The Development of Modern France* (London, 1940). For my own account of this period in detail, see *Count Albert de Mun: Paladin of the Third Republic* (Chapel Hill, N.C., 1978); and *France and the Après Guerre.* Eugen Weber's work is essential: *Peasants into Frenchmen: The Modernization of Rural France, 1870–1914* (Stanford, 1976); *France: Fin de Siècle* (Cambridge, Mass., 1986); *Action Française: Royalism and Reaction in Twentieth-Century France* (Stanford, 1962); and *The Hollow Years: France in the 1930s* (New York, 1994).

12. Robert de Jouvenel, *La République des camarades* (Paris, 1913).

13. Martin, *France and the Après Guerre,* 16–20.

14. Alfred Sauvy, *Histoire économique de la France entre les deux guerres,* 2 vols. (Paris, 1965–67), 1:444–45, 501.

15. Sauvy, *Histoire économique,* 1:444–45, 501.

16. Sauvy, *Histoire économique,* 1:444–45, 454, 464, 477, 501, 511.

17. Tim Kurt Georg Fuchs, "The Tardieu Moment: André Tardieu's Failure as Prime Minister of France, 1929–1930" (Master's thesis, Louisiana State University, 2002).

18. Sauvy, *Histoire économique,* 2:15–27, 488–89, 506, 528, 554, 562–63.

19. Sauvy, *Histoire économique,* 2:27–76, 506, 554, 577.

20. Sauvy, *Histoire économique,* 2:77–93, 488–89, 506, 528, 554, 562–63.

21. Sauvy, *Histoire économique,* 2:94–180, 506, 528, 554, 562–63.

22. Sauvy, *Histoire économique,* 2:181–240, 488–89, 506, 528, 554, 562–63, 577.

23. Sauvy, *Histoire économique,* 2:241–68, 488–89, 506, 528, 554, 562–63, 577.

CHAPTER 1: WINTER

1. *La Gazette des Tribunaux,* 19–21 January 1938; see also Geo London, *Les Grands procès de l'année 1938* (Paris, 1939), 1–7.

2. *La Gazette des Tribunaux,* 9–13 March 1938; see also London, *Les Grands procès de l'année 1938,* 46–64.

3. Joel Colton, *Léon Blum: Humanist in Politics* (New York, 1966), esp. 55–64, quoting Daudet, 59. See also Gilbert Ziebura, *Léon Blum et le parti socialiste, 1872–1934,* translated by Jean Duplex (Paris, 1967); and Georges Suarez, *Nos seigneurs et nos maîtres* (Paris, 1937).

4. *Le Populaire,* 4 May 1936; *Le Temps,* 6 May 1936.

5. *Le Populaire,* 8 June 1938.

6. *Journal Officiel,* Chambre des Députés, Débats parlementaires (hereafter cited as JOC, Débats), 6 June 1936.

7. See Colton, *Léon Blum*, 245, for "my soul"; *Le Populaire*, 7 September 1936.

8. Charles de Chambrun, *Traditions et souvenirs* (Paris, 1952), 228.

9. See *Le Populaire*, 23 June 1937, for Blum's speech; see John Morton Blum, ed., *From the Morgenthau Diaries: Years of Crisis, 1928–1938* (Boston, 1959), 474, for Bullitt.

10. JOC, Débats, 13–14 January 1938.

11. *Le Petit Parisien, Le Matin, Le Figaro, Le Temps, L'Oeuvre*, 1 January–14 February 1938; for d'Ormesson, see *Le Figaro*, 14, 21 January 1938; for Albert, see Werth, *France and Munich*, 33.

12. Yvon Lacaze, *L'Opinion publique française et la crise de Munich* (Berne, 1991), 103–17.

13. *Le Temps*, 21–24 February 1938; *Guardian* (Manchester), 21–23 February 1938.

14. For the debate and the press coverage, see JOC, Débats, 25–26 February 1938; *Le Petit Parisien, Le Matin, Le Figaro, Le Temps, L'Oeuvre*, 26–27 February 1938.

15. *Le Petit Parisien, Le Matin, Le Figaro, Le Temps, L'Oeuvre*, 30 January–11 March 1938.

16. *Le Figaro*, 12 March 1938; Maurice-Gustave Gamelin, *Servir*, 3 vols. (Paris, 1946–47), 2:315–16; for Kérillis, see *L'Epoque*, 12 March 1938; for Romier, see *Le Figaro*, 11 March 1938; for d'Ormesson, see *Le Figaro*, 12 March 1938; and *Le Temps*, 12 March 1938.

17. *Le Populaire*, 13 March 1938; Colton, *Léon Blum*, 291–96.

18. *Le Petit Parisien*, 12 March 1938; *La Liberté*, 13 March 1938; Caillaux, quoted in *Le Figaro*, 13 March 1938.

19. D'Ormesson, writing in *Le Figaro*, 13–14 March 1938; Daudet, writing in *L'Action Française*, 13, 15 March 1938; Kérillis, writing in *L'Epoque*, 17 March, 4 April 1938.

20. *Le Temps, Le Populaire, Le Figaro*, 14–24 March 1938; for d'Ormesson, see 19 March 1938, "Après le rapt."

21. Taylor, *Munich*, 499–502.

22. Douglas Porch, *The French Secret Services: From the Dreyfus Affair to the Gulf War* (New York, 1995), 115–35; Christopher Andrew and Oleg Gordievsky, *KGB: The Inside Story* (New York, 1990), 215, 445–47; Thierry Wolton, *Le Grand recrutement* (Paris, 1991), 284–85.

23. Porch, *French Secret Services*, 136–40; Ernest R. May, *Strange Victory: Hitler's Conquest of France* (New York, 2000), 133–37.

24. May, *Strange Victory*, 118–19; Judith M. Hughes, *To the Maginot Line: The Politics of French Military Preparation in the 1920s* (Cambridge, Mass., 1971); A. Kemp, *The Maginot Line: Myth and Reality* (New York, 1988); Gen. Paul-Emile Tournoux, *Haut-Commandement: Gouvernement et défense des frontières du Nord et de l'Est, 1919–1939* (Paris, 1960).

25. For the fitness report, see Jean Lacouture, *De Gaulle, the Rebel, 1890–1944*, translated by Patrick O'Brian (London, 1990), 70; for Maurin, see JOC, Débats, 15 March 1935; Porch, *French Secret Services*, 149; Taylor, *Munich*, 494.

26. Eugenia C. Kiesling, *Arming against Hitler: France and the Limits of Military Planning* (Lawrence, Kans., 1996), 12–60; Herrick Chapman, *State Capitalism and Working-Class Radicalism in the French Aircraft Industry* (Berkeley, 1991), 123–54.

27. Kühlenthal is quoted in Martin S. Alexander, *The Republic in Danger: General Maurice Gamelin and the Politics of French Defense, 1933–1940* (Cambridge, 1992), 32; for "silk shirt," see Loustaunau-Lacau, *Mémoires d'un français rebelle* (Paris, 1948), 92; for Gamelin on Daladier, see Paul de Villelume, *Journal d'une défaite, août 1939–juin 1940* (Paris, 1976), 42–43; Porch, *French Secret Services*, 136–50; May, *Strange Victory*, 117–40.

28. Sauvy, *Histoire économique*, 2:305, 307.

29. Sauvy, *Histoire économique*, 2:279–307.

30. Sauvy, *Histoire économique*, 2:274–78; Colton, *Léon Blum*, 300–03; JOC, Débats, 6 April 1938; *Le Petit Parisien, Le Figaro, Le Temps, L'Oeuvre*, 5–7 April 1938.

31. *Journal Officiel*, Sénat, Débats parlementaires (hereafter cited as JOS, Débats), 8 April 1938; *Le Petit Parisien, Le Figaro, Le Temps, L'Oeuvre*, 8–9 April 1938; T. G. Barman, *Times* (London), 6 April 1938.

CHAPTER 2: SPRING

1. *La Gazette des Tribunaux*, 28–30 April, 18 May, and 1 July 1938; see also London, *Les Grands procès de l'année 1938*, 96–111, 151–55; Marcel Montarron, *Tout ce joli monde: Souvenirs* (Paris, 1965), 39.

2. *Le Populaire*, 10 April 1938; *Le Temps, Le Figaro*, and *Le Petit Parisien*, 9–11 April 1938, for the quotations from Wladimir d'Ormesson, 9 April; *Le Petit Journal*, 12–14 April 1938, for the quotation from Jean Ybarnégaray, 14 April; *L'Action Française*, 11 April 1938; JOC, Débats, 12 April 1938; JOS, Débats, 13 April 1938; *L'Epoque*, 13 April 1938.

3. Maj.-Gen. Sir Edward Spears, *Assignment to Catastrophe*, 2 vols. (New York, 1954), 1:41–42; Werth, *France and Munich*, 137–38; Elisabeth du Réau, *Edouard Daladier, 1884–1970* (Paris, 1993), 15–49.

4. *L'Humanité*, 8 February 1934; *La Victoire*, 8 February 1934.

5. Réau, *Edouard Daladier*, 136–212; Taylor, *Munich*, 498–99.

6. Réau, *Edouard Daladier*, 288–89; Spears, *Assignment to Catastrophe*, 1:90–92; Charles Joseph André Géraud [Pertinax], *Les Fossoyeurs: Défaite militaire de la France, armistice, contre-révolution*, 2 vols. (New York, 1943), 1:130–31; André Maurois, *Tragedy in France* (New York, 1940), 67.

7. Pierre Lazareff, *De Munich à Vichy* (New York, 1944), 103–5; Spears, *Assignment to Catastrophe*, 1:90–92; Maurois, *Tragedy in France*, 67–68.

8. Spears, *Assignment to Catastrophe*, 1:60, 2:318; John M. Sherwood, *Georges Mandel and the Third Republic* (Stanford, 1970).

9. Joseph Paul-Boncour, *Entre deux guerres: Souvenirs sur la IIIe République*, 3 vols. (Paris, 1945–46), 3:96–101; Spears, *Assignment to Catastrophe*, 2:30, quoting Mandel; William L. Shirer, *The Collapse of the Third Republic: An Inquiry into the Fall of France in 1940* (New York, 1969), 337, for his own assessment and quoting Gamelin; Werth, *France and Munich*, 135, for the story of the German officer and quoting Nizan.

10. JOC, Débats, 12 April 1938; *La Nation*, 11–12 March 1938; *Le Figaro*, 27 March 1938; *La Liberté*, 27 March 1938.

11. *Le Journal*, 17–28 March 1938; *Le Figaro*, 23 March 1938; *Le Petit Journal*, 23 March, for La Rocque; *L'Epoque*, 12 March and 3 April, 1938, for Kérillis; Jean-Paul Sartre, *Les Chemins de la liberté: Le Sursis* (Paris, 1945), translated by Eric Sutton as *The Reprieve* (New York, 1947), 395–96.

12. *Le Temps*, 12, 17 April 1938; *Gringoire*, 6, 13 May 1938; Lacaze, *La France et Munich*, 121–22.

13. Taylor, *Munich*, 507–10; Lacaze, *La France et Munich*, 122–27; Werth, *France and Munich*, 145–51; *L'Epoque*, 17 April 1938.

14. Lacaze, *La France et Munich*, 451–65; Georges Bonnet, *Dans la tourmente, 1938–1948* (Paris, 1971), 16.

15. Sauvy, *Histoire économique*, 2:308–11, 488–89.

16. Werth, *France and Munich*, 152; Sauvy, *Histoire économique*, 2:555; for fashions and reassurances, see, for example, *Le Figaro*, 10 April–16 May 1938.

17. Sauvy, *Histoire économique*, 2:312–13, 528.

18. *Le Figaro*, 16 May 1938.

19. Taylor, *Munich*, 390–95 (quotation from 392).

20. *Le Journal*, 25 and 29 May 1938; *Le Matin*, 26 May 1938; *L'Ordre*, 22–23 May 1938 (quotation from 22 May); *L'Epoque*, 22–24 May 1938 (quotations from 22 and 24 May); *L'Humanité*, 22–25 May 1938; *Le Populaire*, 22–25 May 1938; *Le Petit Journal*, 23 May 1938; *Le Figaro*, 22–25 May 1938; *L'Europe Nouvelle*, 28 May 1938.

21. Malcolm Gladwell, *The Tipping Point: How Little Things Can Make a Big Difference* (Boston, 2000); *Le Temps*, 23 May 1938; *Le Figaro*, 11 (Austrian lawyers), 24 May 1938; *Le Petit Parisien*, 29 May 1938.

22. Taylor, *Munich*, 517–19.

23. Taylor, *Munich*, 449–50.

24. Lacaze, *La France et Munich*, 132–41 (quotations from 139, 140, 141).

25. *Quai des brumes:* a film by Marcel Carné: producer, Grégor Rabinovitsch; director, Marcel Carné; screenplay, Jacques Prévert, from Pierre Mac Orlan's novel *Le Quai des brumes* (1927); cinematographer, Eugen Schüfftan, assisted by Louis Page, Marc Fossard, Henri Alekan, and Philippe Agostini; set decoration, Alexander Trauner; costumes, Coco Chanel; music, Maurice Jaubert; sound, Antoine Archimbaud; editor, René Le Hénaff; production manager, Simon Schiffrin; filmed at the studios of Pathé-Cinéma in Joinville-le-Pont; recording by RCA; sound copy by Pathé-Cinéma; running time, 91 minutes; premier, 17 May 1938, Marivaux Theater, Paris. Edward Baron Turk, *Child of Paradise: Marcel Carné and the Golden Age of French Cinema* (Cambridge, Mass., 1989), 96–128; Charles Rearick, *The French in Love and War: Popular Culture in the Era of the World Wars* (New Haven, 1997), 298 n. 41; *Le Journal de la Femme*, 27 May 1938; *Le Figaro*, 29 May (Laury), 8 June (Carco) 1938. Dialogue from the film is my translation.

26. Turk, *Child of Paradise*, the most penetrating study of Carné, insists: "Carné's film, however, stands as perhaps the most incisive cinematic expression of the 'psychology' of France in the late 1930s" and "*Le Quai des Brumes* is a very exact expression of prewar France" (98, 126).

27. *Le Temps,* 13 June 1938, Flandin at Vienne; Taylor, *Munich,* 520–21; Lacaze, *La France et Munich,* 140–44.

28. *Le Temps,* 6 June (Daladier at Lyon), 18 June (Flandin before the foreign affairs committee), 1938; *Le Journal,* 10 June 1938; *La République,* 21 June 1938; *La Nation,* 11 June 1938; *L'Epoque,* 7 June 1938; *Le Figaro,* 29–31 May (Davis Cup), 10 June (Maurras), 19 June (Franco) 1938; *L'Oeuvre,* 16 June 1938; Taylor, *Munich,* 520–21, quoting Mistler and Caillaux, 521; Lacaze, *La France et Munich,* 147–50, quoting Ribbentrop, 147, and Benes, 149.

29. Jean-Paul Sartre, *Les Chemins de la liberté: L'Age de raison* (Paris, 1945), translated by Eric Sutton as *The Age of Reason* (New York, 1947); *Les Chemins de la liberté: Le Sursis* (Paris, 1945), translated by Eric Sutton as *The Reprieve* (New York, 1947); *Oeuvres romanesques,* edited by Michel Contat and Michel Rybalka, with Geneviève Idt and George H. Bauer (Paris, 1981).

30. Simone de Beauvoir, *Mémoires d'une jeune fille rangée* (Paris, 1958), 340; Michel Contat and Michel Rybalka, "Chronologie," in Sartre, *Oeuvres romanesques,* xxxv–lxi.

31. Sartre quoted, from 1964, in Michel Contat, "*Le Sursis:* Notice, personnages historiques liés à la conférence de Munich et apparaissant dans *Le Sursis,* bibliographie, note sur le texte, fragments inédits du *Sursis,* notes et variantes," in Sartre, *Oeuvres romanesques,* 1963–2012; Michel Contat, "*L'Age de raison:* Notice, documents, textes complémentaires, dossier de presse, bibliographie, note sur le texte, notes, et variantes," in Sartre, *Oeuvres romanesques,* 1886–1963; Victor Brombert, *The Intellectual Hero: Studies in the French Novel, 1880–1955* (Philadelphia, 1961), 202–3.

32. Sartre, *Age of Reason,* 3–46 (quotations from 12, 17, 46). Sartre insisted that Ivich was pronounced "Ivik."

33. Sartre, *Age of Reason,* 47–64 (quotations from 57, 63, 64).

34. Sartre, *Age of Reason,* 65–83, 90–102 (quotations from 71, 83, 99, 100).

35. Sartre, *Age of Reason,* 84–89, 102–212 (quotations from 138, 161, 205).

36. Sartre, *Age of Reason,* 213–60 (quotations from 221, 224, 236, 237–38, 244–45, 255–56).

37. Sartre, *Age of Reason,* 261–84 (quotations from 269, 271–72, 280).

38. Sartre, *Age of Reason,* 284–341 (quotations from 320, 327, 329, 330, 333, 335, 340–41).

39. Sartre, *Age of Reason,* 342–84 (quotations from 343, 352, 367, 373, 374).

40. Sartre, *Age of Reason,* 384–96 (quotations from 390, 392, 394, 395).

41. Sartre interviewed by Christian Grisoli, *Paru* 13 (December 1945): 5–10, quoted in Contat, "*L'Age de raison,*" 1913; Sartre, *Age of Reason,* 397.

CHAPTER 3: SUMMER

1. *La Gazette des Tribunaux,* 22–23 July 1938; see also London, *Les Grands procès de l'année 1938,* 156–68.

2. Spears, *Assignment to Catastrophe,* 1:207, 262.

3. *Le Petit Parisien, Le Figaro, Le Temps,* 15 July 1938, for Bastille Day.

4. *Le Petit Parisien, Le Figaro, Le Temps, Le Populaire,* 20–23 July 1938.

5. *Paris-Soir, Le Populaire, L'Ordre, L'Epoque,* 19 July; *Le Figaro,* 20 July; *Le Petit Journal,* 21 July 1938.

6. *Le Figaro,* 2–4 July for Lenglen and Wimbledon, 16 July for Martin du Gard, 23–24 July for Davis Cup; *Le Temps,* 11–15 July 1938, for Reims, war rumors, bond procedures, Italian racial theories; Sauvy, *Histoire économique,* 2:315.

7. *Le Temps,* 12 July 1938.

8. Lacaze, *La France et Munich,* 156–58; Werth, *France and Munich,* 203.

9. *Le Figaro,* 26–31 July and 1 August; *Le Temps,* 26–29 July; *Le Petit Parisien,* 29 July 1938.

10. *Le Populaire,* 27 July; *Le Petit Journal,* 26–29 July; *Gringoire,* 29 July; *La Nation,* 6 August; *L'Epoque,* 9 August; *L'Europe Nouvelle,* 30 July, 6 and 13 August 1938.

11. Werth, *France and Munich,* 208.

12. *Le Petit Parisien, Le Figaro, Le Temps,* 29 July–6 August 1938.

13. *Le Petit Parisien, Le Figaro, Le Temps,* 5–16 August 1938.

14. *Le Temps,* 13 August; *Le Figaro,* 17 August; *L'Oeuvre,* 14 August; *Le Populaire,* 17 August; *Le Petit Journal,* 17 August; *L'Epoque,* 21 August; *L'Ordre,* 14 August; *La Nation,* 20 August 1938.

15. *Le Petit Parisien, Le Figaro, Le Temps,* 10–21 August 1938.

16. *Le Petit Parisien, Le Figaro, Le Temps,* 22 August 1938; Sauvy, *Histoire économique,* 2:315–16.

17. *L'Humanité,* 6 July and 23 August; *Le Populaire,* 22–23, 25, 27–28 August 1938.

18. *La Nation,* 27 August; *Le Figaro,* 22 August; *Le Petit Journal,* 23 August; *L'Epoque,* 25 August 1938; for the executive committee, see *Le Temps,* 25 August; for Caillaux, see *Le Figaro,* 29 August 1938.

19. Sauvy, *Histoire économique,* 2:488–89, 528, 555; Réau, *Edouard Daladier,* 240–42; Spears, *Assignment to Catastrophe,* 1:59–60.

20. Lacaze, *La France et Munich,* 164–68; Taylor, *Munich,* 524–25.

21. *New York Times,* 17, 19 August, *Times* (London), 28 August 1938.

22. *Le Figaro,* 23 August, Romier; 24 August, Bérenger and Bonnet; *Le Petit Journal,* 19 August; *L'Epoque,* 19 August; *Le Temps,* 19 August 1938.

23. *Le Temps,* 28 August–2 September; Flandin in *Le Petit Parisien,* 28 August; *Paris-Soir,* 2 September; *Le Figaro,* 29 and 31 August; *L'Europe Nouvelle,* 3 September 1938.

24. *Le Temps, Le Figaro, Le Petit Parisien,* 5 September 1938.

25. *L'Ordre, Le Figaro,* 5 September; *Le Petit Journal,* 7 September; *New York Times,* 10 September 1938.

26. *La République,* 6 September; *Times* (London), 7 September 1938; Taylor, *Munich,* 526–28; Lacaze, *La France et Munich,* 177–79.

27. Christel Peyrefitte, "Les Premiers sondages d'opinion," in *Edouard Daladier, Chef de Gouvernement: Avril 1938–Septembre 1939,* edited by René Rémond and Janine Bourdin (Paris, 1977), 271; *Le Petit Parisien,* 7 September; *Le Figaro,* 8 September 1938.

28. *Le Populaire*, 7–9 September; *L'Humanité*, *Le Petit Journal*, 8 September; *L'Europe Nouvelle*, 10 September; *L'Epoque*, 9 September 1938.

29. Geneviève Tabouis, *Ils m'ont appellé Cassandre* (New York, 1941), 342; Taylor, *Munich*, 528; Lacaze, *La France et Munich*, 180–81; *Times* (London), 12 September 1938.

30. Lacaze, *La France et Munich*, 182–83; *Le Petit Parisien*, *Le Figaro*, *Le Temps*, 12 September 1938; Taylor, *Munich*, 527; Werth, *France and Munich*, 248–49.

31. *L'Humanité*, *Le Figaro*, *Le Petit Parisien*, *Le Populaire*, 13 September; *L'Epoque*, *Le Temps*, *Le Petit Journal*, 14 September 1938.

32. Taylor, *Munich*, 529–30; Lacaze, *La France et Munich*, 190; Werth, *France and Munich*, 251–55; *Le Figaro*, 9 September 1938.

33. Taylor, *Munich*, 530–33; Lacaze, *La France et Munich*, 190–92.

34. Taylor, *Munich*, 533; *La République*, *Le Journal*, *Le Populaire*, 15 September; *Evening Standard* (London), *Paris-Soir*, *Le Temps*, *L'Humanité*, *L'Epoque*, 16 September 1938.

35. Taylor, *Munich*, 533–34; Lacaze, *La France et Munich*, 193, 633.

36. Guy de Girard de Charbonnières, *La Plus évitable de toutes les guerres: Un Témoin reconte* (Paris, 1985), 159–60.

37. Jean Zay, *Carnets secrets* (Paris, 1942), 4–6; Réau, *Edouard Daladier*, 259–60.

38. Werth, *France and Munich*, 263–66; *L'Humanité*, *Le Populaire*, *L'Epoque*, *Le Temps*, *Le Figaro*, *La République*, *Le Petit Parisien*, *Paris-Soir*, *La Liberté*, *L'Action Française*, 20 September; *Le Petit Journal*, 22 September 1938.

39. Lacaze, *La France et Munich*, 140–49; Taylor, *Munich*, 784–94; Winston Churchill, *The Second World War: The Gathering Storm* (Boston, 1948), 302–3; Werth, *France and Munich*, 266–69; *Le Temps*, *Le Figaro*, 22 September 1938.

40. Taylor, *Munich*, 795–819.

41. Réau, *Edouard Daladier*, 265; *Le Temps*, *Le Figaro*, *Le Petit Parisien*, 23–25 September 1938.

42. Werth, *France and Munich*, 275–78; Taylor, *Munich*, 839–40; Anthony Adamthwaite, *France and the Coming of the Second World War, 1936–1939* (London: 1977), 220; Lacaze, *La France et Munich*, 225; *L'Action Française*, *Le Matin*, *La Nation*, 24 September 1938.

43. Taylor, *Munich*, 819–30; see 830 for the Czech response.

44. Anatole de Monzie, *Ci-devant* (Paris, 1941), 37; Zay, *Carnets secrets*, 8–9; Girard de Charbonnières, *La Plus évitable de toutes les guerres*, 166; Taylor, *Munich*, 855–57; Lacaze, *La France et Munich*, 229–30.

45. Taylor, *Munich*, 857–61; Lacaze, *La France et Munich*, 230–32.

46. Orville H. Bullitt, *For the President, Personal and Secret: Correspondence between Franklin D. Roosevelt and William C. Bullitt* (London, 1973), 290–91; *Le Figaro*, 27 September 1938; Lacaze, *La France et Munich*, 233.

47. Shirer, *Collapse of the Third Republic*, 381; Lacaze, *La France et Munich*, 234–38; *Guardian* (Manchester), *L'Humanité*, *L'Epoque*, *Le Temps*, 27 September; *Le Figaro*, 27–28 September; *L'Action Française*, *La Liberté*, 28 September 1938.

48. Zay, *Carnets secrets,* 18–21; Lacaze, *La France et Munich,* 238–40.

49. *Le Populaire, L'Action Française,* 27–28 September; *Le Figaro,* 28 September 1938, for Daladier's remarks; Werth, *France and Munich,* 298–302; Taylor, *Munich,* 878–81; Lacaze, *La France et Munich,* 240.

50. Taylor, *Munich,* 874–75, 881–82; *Times* (London), 28 September 1938.

51. Taylor, *Munich,* 882–97; Lacaze, *La France et Munich,* 240–49; Werth, *France and Munich,* 308–9; *Paris-Soir,* 28 September; *Le Temps, Le Figaro, Le Petit Parisien,* 29 September 1938.

52. Sartre, *Reprieve,* quotations from 14–15, 209, 24–25, 346.

53. Sartre, *Reprieve,* quotations from 207, 66, 273, 115–16, 108, 103.

54. Sartre, *Reprieve,* quotations from 350–51, 362–63, 375, 388.

55. Sartre, *Reprieve,* quotations from 360–61, 381, 401–2.

56. Sartre, *Reprieve,* quotation from 421; *Le Populaire, L'Epoque, Le Temps, Le Petit Journal, L'Humanité, Le Figaro,* 29 September 1938.

57. Lacaze, *La France et Munich,* 250–51; Etienne de Crouy Chanel, *Alexis Léger, l'autre visage de Saint-John Perse* (Paris, 1989), 231–32.

58. Taylor, *Munich,* 17–18, quoting Daladier "Everything depends," 18; Réau, *Edouard Daladier,* 274–77, quoting Daladier "trap," 277.

59. Taylor, *Munich,* 24–34; Lacaze, *La France et Munich,* 255, quoting Daladier "crime"; Réau, *Edouard Daladier,* 277–79, quoting Daladier "return to France," 278.

60. Taylor, *Munich,* 34–46, quoting Daladier "ease the position," 40, "unacceptable," 43, Munich beer, 44; Réau, *Edouard Daladier,* 279–80; Lacaze, *La France et Munich,* 256, quoting Daladier "warmongers."

61. Taylor, *Munich,* 47–57, quoting Daladier as "miserable," 47, quoting François-Poncet 48, quoting Bonnet "Everybody will be happy," 54; Lacaze, *La France et Munich,* 255–58, quoting the Bonnet-Krofta exchange, 258; André François-Poncet, *Au palais Farnèse: Souvenirs d'une ambassade 1938–1940* (Paris, 1961), 329–34; Réau, *Edouard Daladier,* 273–80; Georges Bonnet, *De Munich à la guerre: Défense de la paix* (Paris, 1961), 197–200; Paul Stehlin, *Témoinage pour l'histoire* (Paris, 1964), 106.

62. *Le Figaro, Le Temps, Le Petit Parisien, Paris-Soir,* 30 September 1938; Réau, *Edouard Daladier,* 283–84; Lacaze, *La France et Munich,* 259–60; Taylor, *Munich,* 59–64.

63. Crouy Chanel, *Alexis Léger,* 235; Werth, *France and Munich,* 318–20; Taylor, *Munich,* 58–59; Sartre, *Reprieve,* quotations from 444–45.

CHAPTER 4: FALL

1. Robert Coulondre, *De Staline à Hitler: Souvenirs de deux ambassades, 1936–1939* (Paris, 1950), 181; Sartre, *Reprieve,* quotation from 444.

2. *La Gazette des Tribunaux,* 5–15 December 1938; see also London, *Les Grands procès de l'année 1938,* 208–60.

3. *Le Figaro,* 1–2 October; *L'Epoque,* 2 October; *L'Humanité,* 1–2 October 1938; Sartre, *Reprieve,* 439; "Advice to Aggressors," *New Statesman* 16, 24 September 1938, 450; Piers Brendon, *The Dark Valley: A Panorama of the 1930s* (New York, 2000), 626.

4. *Le Petit Parisien,* 3–4 October 1938.

5. Réau, *Edouard Daladier,* 288, 290.

6. JOC, Débats, 4 October 1938; JOS, Débats, 5 October 1938.

7. Lacaze, *La France et Munich,* 259; *Le Petit Parisien,* 9 October 1938.

8. Lacaze, *L'Opinion publique française,* 526–29; *Le Figaro, Le Temps,* 7 October 1938.

9. Lacaze, *L'Opinion publique française,* 529–31.

10. *L'Action Française,* 29 September; *Le Temps, Le Figaro, Le Petit Parisien, Le Petit Journal,* 14–20 October 1938.

11. *Le Temps,* 4 October; *Le Journal,* 30 September; *L'Epoque,* 2 October; *Le Figaro,* 1 October 1938.

12. *L'Epoque,* 2 October; *L'Europe Nouvelle,* 8 October; *Le Figaro,* 12 October, for Pichot; *Le Temps,* 17 October; *La Victoire,* 14 October; *L'Action Française,* 14 October 1938.

13. *L'Action Française* and *L'Europe Nouvelle,* 8 October; *L'Epoque,* 13 October; *L'Humanité,* 14–15 October 1938.

14. *L'Humanité,* 8, 9, and 15–20 October 1938.

15. *Le Populaire,* 28 October, 1, 3, and 6 November 1938 (quotation from 6 November).

16. *Le Figaro,* 5, 6, 9, 10, 12, 16, 18, 20, and 27 October (fashion), 10–15, 17, 19, and 21 October (auto show), 11, 14, and 16 October 1938 (Romier).

17. *Le Figaro,* 3, 5, 7, 9, 12, 15, 18, and 22 November 1938 (quotations from 3, 5, 7, and 12 November).

18. *Le Petit Parisien, Le Temps, Le Figaro,* 27–31 October 1938.

19. *Le Petit Parisien,* 8–16 October 1938.

20. *Le Petit Parisien, Le Temps, L'Oeuvre, Le Figaro,* 8–14 October 1938 (d'Ormesson in 14 October).

21. *Le Petit Parisien, Le Temps, Le Figaro,* 12–17 October 1938.

22. Lacaze, *La France et Munich,* 260–64 (quotations from 260, 264); Coulondre, *De Staline à Hitler,* 165–71 (quotation from 169).

23. François-Poncet, *Au palais Farnèse,* 333; Réau, *Edouard Daladier,* 305–6; Lacaze, *La France et Munich,* 265.

24. Réau, *Edouard Daladier,* 307; *Le Temps,* 13–14 October 1918.

25. *Le Temps* and *Le Figaro,* 8, 20 November, 1–2 December 1938 (Ciano quoted 2 November).

26. *L'Humanité, Le Populaire, L'Oeuvre, Le Figaro, L'Epoque, L'Action Française,* 1–5 December; *Le Temps,* 9 November 1938.

27. Zay, *Carnets secrets,* 36–37; Lacaze, *La France et Munich,* 265; Réau, *Edouard Daladier,* 307.

28. *Le Figaro, Le Temps, Le Petit Parisien, Le Populaire,* 7 December 1938; Monzie, *Ci-devant,* 66; Réau, *Edouard Daladier,* 307–09; Lacaze, *La France et Munich,* 265–66; Werth, *France and Munich,* 383–88.

29. *Le Figaro, Le Temps, Le Petit Parisien,* 8 December 1938; Jean-Noël Jeanneney, *François de Wendel en république: L'Argent et le pouvoir, 1914–1940* (Paris, 1976), 590; Werth, *France and Munich,* 388–89.

30. *Le Figaro,* 19 and 29 October–2 November; *Le Temps, Le Petit Parisien,* 28 October–2 November 1938; Monzie, *Ci-devant,* 50–51, for "Olympian"; Réau, *Edouard Daladier,* 290–93.

31. Sauvy, *Histoire économique,* 2:324–30, 479–81.

32. Sauvy, *Histoire économique,* 2:488–89, 528, 555.

33. *Le Temps, Le Figaro, Le Petit Parisien,* 13 November 1938.

34. *Le Figaro,* 15 (editorial), 16 (Rivollet), and 17 (Pichot) November; *Le Temps,* 14 November; *Le Populaire,* 11 November; *Le Petit Parisien,* 17 November 1938 (Jouhaux).

35. For Thorez, see *L'Humanité,* 22 November; for Daladier, see *Le Figaro* and *Le Petit Parisien,* 18 and 19 November 1938.

36. For the initial skirmishes, see *Le Petit Parisien, Le Temps, Le Figaro,* 23–25 November; for union leader Henaff, see *L'Humanité,* 28 November 1938.

37. *Le Petit Parisien, Le Temps, Le Figaro,* 26–29 November 1938.

38. *Le Petit Parisien, Le Temps, Le Figaro,* 30 November–1 December 1938. Before the general strike the General Labor Confederation claimed approximately 3.5 million members; afterward, roughly 2.5 million.

39. For Daladier's speech, see *Le Petit Parisien, Le Temps, Le Figaro,* 1 December 1938; for the purge of strikers, see JOC, Débats, 3 February 1939.

40. JOC, Débats, 8–9 December 1938.

41. For the international commission, see Lacaze, *La France et Munich,* 268–70 (quotation from 268); for Lebrun, see *Le Figaro,* 15 October 1938.

42. Crouy Chanel, *Alexis Léger,* 179; Réau, *Edouard Daladier,* 309–10; *Le Petit Parisien, Le Temps, Le Figaro,* 5–12 December 1938.

43. See the accounts in Lacaze, *L'Opinion publique française,* 533; and Werth, *France and Munich,* 390–92.

44. *L'Humanité,* 16 December 1938; JOC, Débats, 19 December 1938.

45. For the Socialist congress, see *Le Petit Parisien* and *Le Populaire,* 24–27 December; for Buré, see *L'Ordre,* 22 December; for the cold and Daladier's trip, see *Le Figaro,* 19–31 December 1938; JOC, Débats, 29 December 1938.

46. *Hôtel du Nord:* a film by Marcel Carné; producer, Jacques Lucachevitch; director, Marcel Carné; screenplay, Jean Aurenche and Henri Jeanson, with dialogue by Henri Jeanson, from Eugène Dabit's novel *L'Hôtel du Nord* (1929); assistant directors, Claude Walter and Pierre Blondy; cinematographer, Armand Thirard, assisted by Louis Née; set decoration, Alexander Trauner; costumes, Lou Tchimoukoff; music, Maurice Jaubert;

editor, Marthe Gottie; running time, 110 minutes; premier, 10 December 1938, Marivaux Theater, Paris. Turk, *Child of Paradise,* 129–51; Rearick, *French in Love and War,* 230–32; *Le Figaro,* 22 December 1938.

47. Julian Jackson, *France: The Dark Years, 1940–1944* (Oxford, 2001), 335.

CONCLUSION

1. *Le Figaro,* 20 December 1938.

2. *New York Times,* 11 December 1970.

3. See the detailed account in Shirer, *Collapse of the Third Republic,* 919–46; quoting the proposal, 939; and quoting Laval, 938.

4. Géraud, *Les Fossoyeurs,* 1:113, on Daladier; Taylor, *Munich,* 534, on Daladier; quoting Churchill on Chamberlain, 978; Churchill, *Gathering Storm,* 321, on the consequences of Munich.

5. Taylor, *Munich,* quoting Roosevelt, 846–47; quoting Chamberlain, 985; hypothesizing about the war, 993–95.

6. Brogan, *Development of Modern France,* 728–29; Spears, *Assignment to Catastrophe,* 2:315–18.

Bibliography

PARLIAMENTARY PAPERS

Journal Officiel, Chambre des Députés, Débats parlementaires, 1938, 1939.
Journal Officiel, Chambre des Députés, Documents parlementaires, 1938.
Journal Officiel, Sénat, Débats parlementaires, 1938.
Journal Officiel, Sénat, Documents parlementaires, 1938.

NEWSPAPERS

L'Action Française (Paris), 1938
L'Epoque (Paris), 1938
L'Europe Nouvelle (Paris), 1938
Evening Standard (London), 1938
Le Figaro (Paris), 1938
La Gazette des Tribunaux (Paris), 1938
Gringoire (Paris), 1938
Guardian (Manchester), 1938
New York Times, 1938, 1970
L'Humanité (Paris), 1934, 1938
Le Journal (Paris), 1938
Le Journal de la Femme (Paris), 1938
La Liberté (Paris), 1938

Le Matin (Paris), 1938
La Nation (Paris), 1938
L'Oeuvre (Paris), 1938
L'Ordre (Paris), 1938
Paris-Soir, 1938
Le Petit Journal (Paris), 1938
Le Petit Parisien, (Paris), 1938
Le Populaire (Paris), 1936–38
La République (Paris), 1938
Le Temps (Paris), 1936–38
Times (London), 1938
La Victoire (Paris), 1934, 1938

BOOKS, ARTICLES, DISSERTATIONS, AND THESES

Adamthwaite, Anthony. *France and the Coming of the Second World War, 1936–1939.* London, 1977.
Alexander, Martin S. *The Republic in Danger: General Maurice Gamelin and the Politics of French Defence, 1933–1940.* Cambridge, 1992.
Allard, Paul. *Quai d'Orsay.* Paris, 1938.
———. *Les Responsables du désastre.* Paris, 1941.
Andrew, Christopher, and Oleg Gordievsky. *KGB: The Inside Story.* New York, 1990.
Andrew, Dudley. *Mists of Regret: Culture and Sensibility in Classic French Film.* Princeton, 1995.
Angot, Eugène, and René de Lavergne. *Le Général Vuillemin.* Paris, 1965.
Azéma, Jean-Pierre. *1940, l'année terrible.* Paris, 1990.
Bailby, Léon. *Souvenirs.* Paris, 1951.
Bankwitz, Philip Charles Farwell. *Maxime Weygand and Civil-Military Relations in Modern France.* Cambridge, Mass., 1967.
Baudouï, Remi. *Raoul Dautry: 1880–1951, le technocrate de la république.* Paris, 1992.
Beauvoir, Simone de. *La Force de l'âge.* Paris, 1960. Translated by Peter Green as *The Prime of Life.* Cleveland, 1962.
———. *Mémoires d'une jeune fille rangée.* Paris, 1958.
Béguin. Albert. *Bernanos par lui-même.* Paris, 1954.
Bernard, Philippe, and Henri Dubief. *The Decline of the Third Republic, 1914–1938.* Translated by Anthony Forster. New York, 1985.
Bernstein, Serge. *Edouard Herriot, ou La République en personne.* Paris, 1985.

————. *La France des années 30.* Paris, 1988.

————. *Histoire du parti radical.* 2 vols. Paris, 1980–82.

————. *Le 6 février 1934.* Paris, 1975.

Bilis, Michel. *Socialistes et pacifistes: L'Intenable dilemme des socialistes français (1933–1939).* Paris, 1979.

Birnbaum, Pierre. *Le Moment antisémite: Un Tour de la France en 1898.* Paris, 1998.

Bloch, Marc Léopold Benjamin. *Etrange défaite, témoinage écrit en 1940.* Paris, 1946. Translated by Gerard Hopkins as *Strange Defeat: A Statement of Evidence Written in 1940.* New York, 1949.

Blum, John Morton, ed. *From the Morgenthau Diaries: Years of Crisis, 1928–1938.* New York, 1959.

Boak, Denis. *Roger Martin du Gard.* Oxford, 1963.

Bonnefous, Georges, and Edouard Bonnefous. *Histoire politique de la IIIe République.* 7 vols. Paris, 1956–67.

Bonnet, Georges. *Dans la tourmente, 1938–1948.* Paris, 1971.

————. *Défense de la paix.* 2 vols. Geneva, 1948.

————. *De Munich à la guerre: Défense de la paix.* Paris, 1961.

Bourdé, Guy. *La Défaite du Front Populaire.* Paris, 1977.

Boussard, Dominique. *Un Problème de défense nationale: L'Aéronautique militaire au Parlement, 1928–1940.* Vincennes, 1983.

Borgal, Clément. *Saint-Exupéry: Mystique sans la foi.* Paris, 1964.

Braddick, Henderson B. *Germany, Czechoslovakia, and the "Grand Alliance" in the May Crisis, 1938.* Denver, 1969.

Brasillach, Robert. *Une Génération dans l'orage: Mémoires, notre avant-guerre; journal d'un homme occupé.* Paris, 1941.

Brendon, Piers. *The Dark Valley: A Panorama of the 1930s.* New York, 2000.

Brogan, Denis William. *The Development of Modern France.* London, 1940.

Brombert, Victor. *The Intellectual Hero: Studies in the French Novel, 1880–1955.* Philadelphia, 1961.

Bruge, Robert. *Histoire de la Ligne Maginot.* 4 vols. Paris, 1973–80.

Bullitt, Orville H. *For the President, Personal and Secret: Correspondence between Franklin D. Roosevelt and William C. Bullitt.* London, 1973.

Burrin, Philippe. *La Dérive fasciste: Doriot, Déat, Bergery, 1933–1945.* Paris, 1986.

Caute, David. *Communism and the French Intellectuals, 1914–1960.* New York, 1964.

Chambrun, Charles de. *Traditions et souvenirs.* Paris, 1952.

Chapman, Herrick. *State Capitalism and Working-Class Radicalism in the French Aircraft Industry.* Berkeley, 1991.

Chastenet, Jacques. *Histoire de la Troisième République.* 7 vols. Paris, 1952–63.

Chavardès, Maurice. *Le 6 février: La République en danger.* Paris, 1966.

Churchill, Winston. *The Second World War: The Gathering Storm.* Boston, 1948.

Cointet, Jean-Paul. *Pierre Laval.* Paris, 1993.

Colton, Joel. *Léon Blum: Humanist in Politics.* New York, 1966.

Contat, Michel. "*L'Age de raison:* Notice, documents, textes complémentaires, dossier de presse, bibliographie, note sur le texte, notes et variantes." In Jean-Paul Sartre, *Oeuvres romanesques,* edited by Michel Contat and Michel Rybalka, with Geneviève Idt and George H. Bauer, 1886–1963. Paris, 1981.

———. "*Les Chemins de la liberté:* Notice, chronologie des événements." In Jean-Paul Sartre, *Oeuvres romanesques,* edited by Michel Contat and Michel Rybalka with Geneviève Idt and George H. Bauer, 1859–85. Paris, 1981.

———. "*Le Sursis:* Notice, personnages historiques liés à la conférence de Munich et apparaissant dans *Le Sursis,* bibliographie, note sur le texte, fragments inédits du *Sursis,* notes et variantes." In Jean-Paul Sartre, *Oeuvres romanesques,* edited by Michel Contat and Michel Rybalka, with Geneviève Idt and George H. Bauer, 1963–2012. Paris, 1981.

Contat, Michel, and Michel Rybalka. "Chronologie." In Jean-Paul Sartre, *Oeuvres romanesques,* edited by Michel Contat and Michel Rybalka, with Geneviève Idt and George H. Bauer, xxxv–civ. Paris, 1981.

———. "Note sur la présente édition." In Jean-Paul Sartre, *Oeuvres romanesques,* edited by Michel Contat and Michel Rybalka, with Geneviève Idt and George H. Bauer, cv–cxii. Paris, 1981.

Contat, Michel, and Geneviève Idt. "Préface." In Jean-Paul Sartre, *Oeuvres romanesques,* edited by Michel Contat and Michel Rybalka, with Geneviève Idt and George H. Bauer, ix–xxxiii. Paris, 1981.

Cot, Pierre. *La Procès de la République.* 2 vols. New York, 1944.

Coulondre, Robert. *De Staline à Hitler: Souvenirs de deux ambassades: 1936–1939.* Paris, 1950.

Crémieux-Brilhac, Jean-Louis. *Les Français de l'an 40.* 2 vols. Paris, 1990.

Crouy Chanel, Etienne de. *Alexis Léger, l'autre visage de Saint-John Perse.* Paris, 1989.

Deacon, Richard. *The French Secret Service.* London, 1990.

Demey, Evelyne. *Paul Reynaud, mon père*. Paris, 1980.

Degranges, Jean-Marie. *Journal d'un prêtre député (1936–1940)*. Paris, 1960.

Desan, Wilfred. *The Tragic Finale: An Essay on the Philosophy of Jean-Paul Sartre*. New York, 1960.

Destremau, Bernard. *Weygand*. Paris, 1989.

De Tarr, Francis. *Henri Queuille en son temps (1884–1970): Biographie*. Paris, 1995.

Doughty, Robert Allan. *The Seeds of Disaster: The Development of French Army Doctrine, 1919–1939*. Hamden, Conn., 1985.

Douglas, Roy. *In the Year of Munich*. London, 1977.

Duroselle, Jean-Baptiste. *L'Abîme: 1939–1945*. Paris, 1982.

———. *La Décadence, 1932–1939*. Paris, 1979.

Durtel, Jean. *Les Coulisses de la politique: Une Femme témoigne, 1932–1942*. Paris, 1966.

Dutailly, Henry. *Les Problèmes de l'armée de terre française (1935–1939)*. Paris, 1980.

Emmerson, James T. *The Rhineland Crisis, 7 March 1936: A Study in Multicultural Diplomacy*. Ames, Iowa, 1977.

Fabre-Luce, Alfred. *Journal*. Paris, 1941.

Favreau, Bertrand. *Georges Mandel, ou la passion de la République*. Paris, 1996.

Fitzgerald, F. Scott. "The Crack-Up: Pasting It Together." *Esquire 7* (February 1936): 41–46.

Flandin, Pierre-Etienne. *Politique française, 1919–1940*. Paris, 1947.

François-Poncet, André. *Au palais Farnèse: Souvenirs d'une ambassade, 1938–1940*. Paris, 1961.

———. *Souvenirs d'une ambassade à Berlin, septembre 1931–octobre 1938*. Paris, 1946.

Frank, Robert. *La Hantise du déclin. La France, 1920–1960: Finances, défense et identité*. Paris, 1994.

———. *Le Prix du réarmement français (1936–1939)*. Paris, 1982.

Fridenson, Patrick. *La France et la Grand Bretagne face aux problèmes aériens 1935–mai 1940*. Vincennes, 1976.

Frohock, W. M. *André Malraux and the Tragic Imagination*. Stanford, 1952.

Fuchs, Tim Kurt Georg. "The Tardieu Moment: André Tardieu's Failure as Prime Minister of France, 1929–1930." Master's thesis, Louisiana State University, 2002.

Gamelin, Maurice-Gustave. *Servir*. 3 vols. Paris, 1946–47.

Garçon, François. *De Blum à Pétain: Cinéma et société française (1936–1944)*. Paris, 1984.

Garder, Michel. *La Guerre secrète des services spéciaux français (1935–1945).* Paris, 1967.

Gates, Eleanor M. *End of the Affair: The Collapse of the Anglo-French Alliance.* Berkeley, 1981.

Gauché, Maurice-Henri. *Le Deuxième Bureau au travail (1935–1940).* Paris, 1953.

Genébrier, Roger. *La France entre en guerre: Le Témoinage du chef de cabinet de Daladier.* Paris, 1982.

George, François. *Deux études sur Sartre.* Paris, 1976.

Géraud, Charles Joseph André [Pertinax]. *Les Fossoyeurs: Défaite militaire de la France, armistice, contre-révolution.* 2 vols. New York, 1943.

Gilbert, Martin, and Richard Gott. *The Appeasers.* Boston, 1963.

Girard de Charbonnières, Guy de. *La Plus évitable de toutes les guerres: Un Témoin reconte.* Paris, 1985.

Gladwell, Malcolm. *The Tipping Point: How Little Things Can Make a Big Difference.* Boston, 2000.

Gombin, Richard. *Les Socialistes et la guerre: La S.F.I.O. et la politique étrangère française entre les deux guerres mondiales.* Paris, 1970.

Greene, Nathaniel. *Crisis and Decline: The French Socialist Party in the Popular Front Era.* Ithaca, 1969.

Guillaume-Grimaud, Geneviève. *La Cinéma du Front Populaire.* Paris, 1986.

Gunsberg, Jeffery A. *Divided and Conquered: The French High Command and the Defeat in the West, 1940.* Westport, Conn., 1979.

Hebblethwaite, Peter. *Bernanos: An Introduction.* London, 1965.

Herriot, Edouard. *Etudes et témoinages.* Paris, 1975.

Hoff, Pierre. *Les Programmes d'armement de 1919 à 1939.* Paris, 1982.

Hoffman, Joseph. *L'Humanisme de Malraux.* Paris, 1963.

Horn, Martin. *Britain, France, and the Financing of the First World War.* Montreal, 2002.

Horne, Alistair. *The French Army and Politics, 1870–1970.* London, 1984.

———. *To Lose a Battle, France 1940.* New York, 1969.

Hughes, Henry Stuart. *The Obstructed Path: French Social Thought in the Years of Desperation, 1930–1960.* New York, 1966.

Hughes, Judith M. *To the Maginot Line: The Politics of French Military Preparation in the 1920s.* Cambridge, Mass., 1971.

Imlay, Talbot C. *Facing the Second World War: Strategy, Politics, and Economics in Britain and France, 1938–1940.* Oxford, 2003.

———. "Paul Reynaud and France's Response to Nazi Germany, 1938–1940." *French Historical Studies* 26 (Summer 2003): 497–538.

Ingram, Norman. *The Politics of Dissent: Pacifism in France, 1919–1939*. New York, 1991.

Irvine, William D. *French Conservatism in Crisis: The Republican Federation of France in the 1930s*. Baton Rouge, 1979.

Jacomet, Claude. *L'Armement de la France, 1936–1939*. Paris, 1945.

Jackson, Julian. *France: The Dark Years, 1940–1944*. Oxford, 2001.

———. *The Politics of Depression in France, 1932–1936*. Cambridge, 1985.

———. *The Popular Front in France: Defending Democracy, 1934–1938*. Cambridge, 1988.

Jackson, Peter. *France and the German Menace: French Intelligence and Policy, 1933–1939*. Oxford, 2000.

Jankowski, Paul F. *Stavisky: A Confidence Man in the Republic of Virtue*. Ithaca, N.Y., 2002.

Jeanneney, Jean-Noël. *L'Argent caché: Milieux d'affaires et pouvoirs politiques dans la France du 20e siècle*. Paris, 1981.

———. *François de Wendel en république: L'Argent et le pouvoir, 1914–1940*. Paris, 1976.

Jeanson, Francis. *Sartre par lui-même*. Paris, 1955.

Jordan, Nicole. *The Popular Front and Central Europe: The Dilemmas of French Impotence, 1918–1940*. Cambridge, 1992.

Joubert, Ingrid. *Aliénation et liberté dans "Les Chemins de la liberté."* Paris, 1973.

Jouvenel, Robert de. *La République des camarades*. Paris, 1913.

Kemp, A. *The Maginot Line: Myth and Reality*. New York, 1988.

Kérillis, Henri de. *Français, voici la vérité!* New York, 1942.

Kier, Elizabeth. *Imagining War: French and British Military Doctrine between the Wars*. Princeton, 1997.

Kiesling, Eugenia C. *Arming against Hitler: France and the Limits of Military Planning*. Lawrence, Kans., 1996.

Krakovitch, Raymond. *Paul Reynaud dans la tragédie de l'histoire*. Paris, 1998.

Kupferman, Fred. *Laval*. Paris, 1987.

Laborie, Pierre. *L'Opinion française sous Vichy: Les Français et la crise d'identité nationale, 1936–1944*. Paris, 2001.

Lacaze, Yvon. *France and Munich: A Study of Decision Making in International Affairs*. Boulder, Colo., 1995.

———. *France et Munich: Etude d'un processus décisionnel en matière de relations internationales*. Berne, 1992.

———. *L'Opinion publique française et la crise de Munich*. Berne, 1991.

Lacouture, Jean. *De Gaulle, the Rebel, 1890–1944.* Translated by Patrick O'Brian. London, 1990.

Lapaquellerie, Yvon. *Edouard Daladier.* Paris, 1940.

Larmour, Peter J. *The French Radical Party in the 1930s.* Stanford, 1964.

Lazareff, Pierre. *De Munich à Vichy.* New York, 1944.

————. *Dernière édition: Histoire d'une époque.* New York, 1942.

Lebrun, Albert. *Témoinage.* Paris, 1945.

Lefranc, Georges. *Le Front Populaire, 1934–1938.* Paris, 1978.

————. *Histoire du Front Populaire, 1934–1938.* Paris, 1974.

————. *Le Mouvement socialiste sous la Troisième République: De 1920 à 1940.* Paris, 1977.

Lémery, Henry. *D'une république à l'autre: Souvenirs de la mêlée politique, 1894–1944.* Paris, 1964.

London, Geo. *Les Grands procès de l'année 1938.* Paris, 1939.

Loustaunau-Lacau, *Mémoires d'un français rebelle.* Paris, 1948.

Low, Alfred D. *The Anschluss Movement, 1931–1938, and the Great Powers.* New York, 1985.

Martin, Benjamin F. *Count Albert de Mun: Paladin of the Third Republic.* Chapel Hill, N.C., 1978.

————. *France and the Après Guerre, 1918–1924: Illusions and Disillusionment.* Baton Rouge, 1999.

Martin, John. *The Golden Age of French Cinema, 1929–1939.* Boston, 1983.

Matthews, H. J. "Sartre: Roads to Freedom." In *The Hard Journey: The Myth of Man's Rebirth.* London, 1968.

Maurin, Gen. Jean Louis. *L'Armée moderne.* Paris, 1938.

Maurois, André. *Tragedy in France.* New York, 1940.

May, Ernest R. *Strange Victory: Hitler's Conquest of France.* New York, 2000.

Mayeur, Jean-Marie, and Madeleine Rebérioux. *The Third Republic from Its Origins to the Great War, 1871–1914.* Translated by J. R. Foster. New York, 1984.

Mellow, James R. *Hemingway: A Life without Consequences.* Boston, 1992.

Micaud, Charles A. *The French Right and Nazi Germany, 1933–1939: A Study in Public Opinion.* New York, 1964.

Miller, Michael B. *Shanghai on the Métro: Spies, Intrigue, and the French between the Wars.* Berkeley, 1994.

Minart, Jacques. *Le Drame du désarmement français (ses aspects politiques et techniques), 1918–1939.* Paris, 1959.

Monnet, François. *Refaire la république: André Tardieu, une dérive réaction-naire (1876–1945)*. Paris, 1993.

Montarron, Marcel. *Tout ce joli monde: Souvenirs*. Paris, 1965.

Montigny, Jean. *Le Complot contre la paix (1935–1939)*. Paris, 1966.

Monzie, Anatole de. *Ci-devant*. Paris, 1941.

Mouré, Kenneth. *Managing the Franc Poincaré: Economic Understanding and Political Constraint in French Monetary Policy, 1928–1936*. Cambridge, 1991.

Mouré, Kenneth, and Martin S. Alexander, eds. *Crisis and Renewal in France, 1918–1962*. New York, 2002.

Moutet, Aimée. *Les Logiques de l'entreprise: La Rationalisation dans l'industrie française de l'entre-deux-guerres*. Paris, 1997.

Mysyrowicz, Ladislas. *Autopsie d'une défaite: Origines de l'effondrement militaire française de 1940*. Lausanne, 1973.

Navarre, Henri, et al. *Le Service de reseignements, 1871–1944*. Paris, 1978.

Nizan, Paul. *Chronique de septembre*. Paris, 1978.

Noël, Léon. *Une Ambassade à Varsovie, 1935–1939: L'Aggression allemande contre la Pologne*. Paris, 1946.

Nordman, Jean-Thomas. *Histoire des Radicaux, 1820–1973*. Paris, 1974.

Nordmann, Léon-Maurice. *Journal, 1938–1941*. Paris, 1993.

Paillole, Paul. *Services spéciaux, 1935–1945*. Paris, 1975.

Paoli, Col. François-André. *L'Armée française de 1919 à 1939*. 2 vols. Paris, n.d.

Paul-Boncour, Joseph. *Entre deux guerres: Souvenirs sur la IIIe République*. 3 vols. Paris, 1945–46.

Peyre, Henri. *The Contemporary French Novel*. New York, 1955.

Peyrefitte, Christel. "Les Premiers sondages d'opinion." In *Edouard Daladier, Chef de Gouvernement: Avril 1938–Septembre 1939*, edited by René Rémond and Janine Bourdin. Paris, 1977.

Planté, Louis. *Un Grand seigneur de la politique: Anatole de Monzie*. Paris, 1955.

Porch, Douglas. *The French Secret Services: From the Dreyfus Affair to the Gulf War*. New York, 1995.

Posen, Barry. *The Sources of Military Doctrine: France, Britain, and Germany between the World Wars*. Ithaca, N.Y., 1984.

Prince, Gerald Joseph. *Métaphysique et technique dans l'oeuvre romanesque de Sartre*. Geneva, 1968.

Rearick, Charles. *The French in Love and War: Popular Culture in the Era of the World Wars*. New Haven, Conn., 1997.

Réau, Elisabeth du. *Edouard Daladier, 1884–1970.* Paris, 1993.

Rémond, René, and Janine Bourdin, eds. *Edouard Daladier, chef de gouvernement, avril 1938– septembre 1939.* Paris, 1977.

———, eds. *La France et les français en 1938–1939.* Paris, 1978.

Reynaud, Paul. *Au coeur de la mêlée, 1930–1945.* Paris, 1951.

———. *La France a sauvé l'Europe.* 2 vols. Paris, 1947.

Robidoux, Réjean. *Roger Martin du Gard et la religion.* Paris, 1964.

Sachar, Howard M. *Dreamland: Europeans and Jews in the Aftermath of the Great War.* New York, 2002.

"Sagittarius" (pseud.). "Advice to Aggressors." *New Statesman* 16, 24 September 1938, 450.

Sartre, Jean-Paul. *The Age of Reason.* Translated by Eric Sutton. New York, 1947.

———. *Les Chemins de la liberté: L'Age de raison.* Paris, 1945.

———. *Les Chemins de la liberté: La Mort dans l'âme.* Paris, 1949.

———. *Les Chemins de la liberté: Le Sursis.* Paris, 1945.

———. *L'Existentialisme est un humanisme.* Paris, 1946. Translated by Bernard Frechtman as *Existentialism* (New York, 1947).

———. *Oeuvres romanesques.* Edited by Michel Contat and Michel Rybalka, with Geneviève Idt and George H. Bauer. Paris, 1981.

———. *The Reprieve.* Translated by Eric Sutton. New York, 1947.

———. *Troubled Sleep.* Translated by Gerard Hopkins. New York, 1951.

Sauvy, Alfred. *Histoire économique de la France entre les deux guerres.* 2 vols. Paris, 1965–67.

Schalk, David L. *Roger Martin du Gard: The Novelist and History.* Ithaca, N.Y., 1967.

Sesonske, Alexander. *Jean Renoir: The French Films, 1924–1939.* Cambridge, Mass., 1980.

Sherwood, John M. *Georges Mandel and the Third Republic.* Stanford, 1970.

Shirer, William L. *The Collapse of the Third Republic: An Inquiry into the Fall of France in 1940.* New York, 1969.

Simon, Pierre-Henri. *L'Homme en procès: Malraux—Sartre—Camus—Saint-Exupéry.* 3d ed. Neuchâtel, 1950.

Skidmore, Ellen Towne. *Pierre Cot: Apostle of Collective Security, 1919–1939.* Knoxville, Tenn., 1980.

Soucy, Robert. *French Fascism: The Second Wave, 1933–1939.* New Haven, 1995.

Soulié, Michel. *La Vie politique d'Edouard Herriot.* Paris, 1962.

Spears, Maj.-Gen. Sir Edward. *Assignment to Catastrophe*. 2 vols. New York, 1954.

Stehlin, Paul. *Témoinage pour l'histoire*. Paris, 1964.

Suarez, Georges. *Nos seigneurs et nos maîtres*. Paris, 1937.

Tabouis, Geneviève. *Ils m'ont appellé Cassandre*. New York, 1941.

————. *Vingt ans de "suspense" diplomatique*. Paris, 1958.

Taylor, Telford. *Munich: The Price of Peace*. New York, 1979.

Thomas, Martin. *Britain, France and Appeasement: Anglo-French Relations in the Popular Front Era*. Oxford, 1996.

Tournoux, Gen. Paul-Emile. *Haut-Commandement: Gouvernement et défense des frontières du Nord et de l'Est, 1919–1939*. Paris, 1960.

Turk, Edward Baron. *Child of Paradise: Marcel Carné and the Golden Age of French Cinema*. Cambridge, Mass., 1989.

Vallette, Geneviève, and Jacques Bouillon. *Munich 1938*. Paris, 1964.

Villelume, Paul de. *Journal d'une défaite, août 1939–juin 1940*. Paris, 1976.

Watt, Donald Cameron. *How War Came: The Immediate Origins of the Second World War, 1938–1939*. New York, 1989.

————. *Too Serious a Business: European Armed Forces and the Approach to the Second World War*. London, 1975.

Weber, Eugen. *Action Française: Royalism and Reaction in Twentieth-Century France*. Stanford, 1962.

————. *France: Fin de Siècle*. Cambridge, Mass., 1986.

————. *The Hollow Years: France in the 1930s*. New York, 1994.

————. *Peasants into Frenchmen: The Modernization of Rural France, 1870–1914*. Stanford, 1976.

Werth, Alexander. *France and Munich, before and after the Surrender*. London, 1939.

Wheeler-Bennett, John W. *Munich, Prologue to Tragedy*. New York, 1964.

Wileman, Donald G. "P. E. Flandin and the Alliance Démocratique, 1929–1939." *French History* 4 (1990): 139–73.

Williams, Alan. *Republic of Images: A History of French Filmmaking*. Cambridge, Mass., 1992.

Wiser, William. *The Twilight Years: Paris in the 1930s*. New York, 2000.

Wolton, Thierry. *Le Grand recrutement*. Paris, 1991.

Wormser, Georges. *Georges Mandel, l'homme politique*. Paris, 1967.

Young, Robert J. *France and the Origins of the Second World War*. New York, 1966.

————. *In Command of France: French Foreign Policy and Military Planning, 1933–1940.* Cambridge, Mass., 1978.

Zay, Jean. *Carnets secrets.* Paris, 1942.

————. *Souvenirs et solitudes.* Paris, 1946.

Ziebura, Gilbert. *Léon Blum et le Parti Socialiste, 1872–1934.* Translated by Jean Duplex. Paris, 1967.

Zimmer, Lucien. *Un Septennat policier: Dessous et secrets de la police républicaine.* Paris, 1967.

Index